THE
HAPPY
HERETIC

THE HAPPY HERETIC

JUDITH HAYES

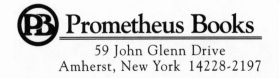

Prometheus Books
59 John Glenn Drive
Amherst, New York 14228-2197

Published 2000 by Prometheus Books

Inquiries should be addressed to
Prometheus Books
59 John Glenn Drive
Amherst, New York 14228–2197
VOICE: 716–691–0133, ext. 207
FAX: 716–564–2711
WWW.PROMETHEUSBOOKS.COM

04 03 02 01 00   5 4 3 2 1

Library of Congress Cataloging-in-Publication Data

Hayes, Judith., 1945–
    The happy heretic / Judith Hayes.
        p. cm.
    Includes bibliographical references and index.
    ISBN 1–57392–802–X (alk. paper)
    1. Secularism. 2. Humanism. I. Title.

BL2747.8 .H39 2000
211'.6—dc21   99–045210
                                                                      CIP

Printed in the United States of America on acid-free paper

*To Pat, my husband,
who makes this world a more fun place to be.*

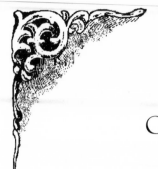

CONTENTS

ACKNOWLEDGMENTS

I OWE GRATITUDE TO MORE people than I can begin to name, for encouragement and support since I went online with *The Happy Heretic*. People from all over the world have graciously taken the time to contact me and offer their appreciative comments. Such messages are cheering indeed.

I also want to offer my heartfelt thanks to Elaine Morgan, who has graced the BBC-TV airwaves with her eloquent prose for decades, and more recently has startled the paleoanthropological community out of its lengthy slumber with her incisive, persuasive books. She's a writer's writer, and as her biggest fan in the United States—a title, by the way, that I am willing to fight to defend—I truly appreciate her kind words of encouragement.

My thanks to Joyce on the west coast and Don on the east coast, who voluntarily, cheerfully, and skillfully became a first-rate clipping service. My thanks also to Sir Colin of the North; Matt, who orders whole, anatomically intact sea bass in San Francisco restaurants; Jim, my 3F friend in Texas; and Margaret, of penguin fame, for their unwavering support. And, of course, I thank the ever-popular "God," without whose nonexistence I would have nothing to write about.

I am grateful for everyone at Prometheus books who went out of their way to accommodate a maverick like me, especially Meg French.

And finally, though foremost, my loving thanks to Pat, my husband, who serenely accepted the fact that a book in progress disrupts a household like a moderate hurricane. Not only that, but he enthusiastically jumped in and proofread the entire book. Twice! Honey, thank you.

INTRODUCTION

I cannot see how a man of any large degree of humorous perception can ever be religious—except he purposely shut the eyes of his mind & keep them shut by force.
—Mark Twain, *Mark Twain's Notebooks and Journals*

ONE DAY I GOT MAD, sat down at my word processor, and started banging away on the keys. That was almost ten years ago, and things have only gotten worse since then.

The decade of the 1990s saw a vigorous, startling surge in Christian fundamentalist crusading. The comforting wall of separation of church and state was repeatedly assaulted and battered, and the resulting fissures are clearly visible. State after state pushed for school voucher plans whereby taxpayer money goes to private, often religious schools—a major crack in the wall. And the furor over posting the so-called Ten Commandments on public property reached a fever pitch when the governor of Alabama threatened to call out the National Guard and the state troopers to prevent the removal of such a plaque from a courtroom wall. It was a decade of religious agitation and turmoil that challenged one of our most precious freedoms—the freedom of *and from* religion.

It was against this backdrop that I decided to take up the gauntlet

11

and plunge into the field of secular humanist writing. I wanted to add my voice to the chorus of denunciations over these incessant attacks on our beleaguered First Amendment. But early on I realized that although there were many excellent periodicals and books out there condemning the erosion of the wall of separation, by and large they tended to be scholarly. This is not to say that scholarly works are not needed; quite the contrary, they are *essential*.

However, there is also a need for books and articles that challenge religious incursions but are written in a less formal, more straightforward style. These I found to be in short supply. Even in the vast reaches of the Internet, there seems to be a dearth of writing that finds a happy medium between erudition and crude, heavy-handed sarcasm. The vast majority of us do not have the time and/or the inclination to delve into the intricacies of various theologies or the complexities of constitutional law, with the unhappy result that most of us don't recognize serious separation issues even as they arise. One of my goals is to help make these issues more understandable and recognizable for the average reader.

In spite of, or rather because of, the many wonderful, far-reaching freedoms we enjoy in this country, we tend to take them for granted. Our religious freedom, unheard of throughout most of history, is something we rarely notice, let alone appreciate. Because of that, when certain groups make it their business to impose their religious beliefs on the rest of us, we don't pay much attention. But it's time we started paying attention.

It is also astonishing to discover how much misinformation is floating around in the world of True Believers. For example, many Catholics believe that the Immaculate Conception refers to the conception of Jesus, and that the history of the papacy is a history of holiness; most Christians believe our nation was founded by Christians; and almost *no one* understands that there is no such thing as the "Ten Commandments" anywhere in the Bible. So another of my goals is to help eliminate some of those misunderstandings.

I have also launched a (rather lonely!) crusade to rehabilitate the word *atheist*. That poor, maligned little word has been thrashed within an inch of its life, loaded down with so many totally inaccurate definitions that it may be beyond resurrection. But I intend to keep trying.

However, when people ask me why I write what I write, I usually answer, "To nudge people." This is literally the truth. I try to nudge people into thinking about things to which they might otherwise never give a passing thought. I try to make it easier for them by using satire, vivid imagery, and a sprinkling of merry nonsense. Judging by the letters I have received in response to my first book, *In God We Trust: But Which One?* as well as my Internet column, *The Happy Heretic*, and other articles for various publications, people do appreciate what I am trying to do. A few samples of those messages are included in this book. And it always brings a smile to my face when I read, "You know, I never really *thought* about that before!" For me, that's a bull's-eye.

There would be no need for books like this, which criticize religion and promote humanism, if it were not for the fact that the Religious Right is seemingly determined to turn the United States into a theocracy—and achieving *far* too many successes in their skirmishes. Until and unless they cease and desist—and we should all live so long—we must fight back. This book is part of my attempt to help in that fight.

This, then, is my attempt to offer a new perspective, perhaps a sharper focus, on the troubling aspects of religious beliefs, and the dangerous ground we tread when those beliefs are commingled with government. It is my hope that it will complement the scholarly works already in print. And equally importantly, I hope it will occasionally make you smile.

1

FAITH IS A WISH YOUR HEART MAKES

It was the schoolboy who said, "Faith is believing what you know ain't so."

—Mark Twain, *Following the Equator*

RELIGIOUS BELIEFS CAN BE VERY comforting. The idea of an eternal paradise of some sort is as comforting as it gets. No one wants to stay dead. And the buildings associated with religions, especially the cathedrals and mosques, can be exquisitely beautiful and inspiring all by themselves. The rituals can provide a soothing sense of security. There is often music—melodic, emotional, uplifting music. And of course there's the pleasure of meeting with like-minded fellow believers, providing a powerful sense of community. It can be beguiling and gratifying: an all around good time.

Of course, religion is not all sweetness and light. The number of things people have done in the name of religion is quite frightening. We all know about the carnage of the Crusades and the outright murder and theft known as the Inquisition. The remnants are still with us in the Middle East and Northern Ireland. And the so-called ethnic cleaning obscenity in the Balkans was not ethnic at all. It was religious—Muslims against Christians. We read about these things so often that after a while we become a bit callous and hardened.

Oh, another pipe bomb killed a busload of children? Too bad. What a shame.

But when we personalize it, it seems so much worse. It isn't, of course, but it *seems* so. It is too repugnant to imagine one adorable four-year-old with big brown eyes, dying of starvation. It offends our sensibilities. Thinking about the world's cruel inequities is extremely distasteful—so mostly we don't. Instead we preen and pride ourselves on our own good fortune at having a God who takes such excellent care of us. But then—we deserve it, don't we?

O GIVE THANKS

Every Thanksgiving, all across the country, families sit down to give thanks to God for the many blessings they have received during the year. Lengthy, obsequious prayers are offered before everyone plunges into the fabulous feast laid before them. Adults as well as children seem to have racing stripes on their forks. The checkered flag signaling the end of this feeding frenzy is the pumpkin pie.

Soon thereafter, the tinkling sounds of china being washed by hand will mingle with the voice of an announcer reporting a football game. Children will run off their carbohydrates as seniors begin to doze. All around, belts will be surreptitiously loosened one notch. Life is good.

O give thanks.

In Bombay, a twelve-year-old girl is pushed into a three-by-six-foot cage on the infamous Falkland Road. Properly bedecked in costume jewelry and brightly colored sari, she is now on display with hundreds of other sex slaves. Through bars on her window facing the street, the girl can look out at the men as they look in at her, sizing her up as a possible rental. She is illuminated with bright lights so that the shoppers can see exactly what they're getting. This particular girl lost her value as a virgin several weeks ago, just before her twelfth birthday. But she is still youthful enough to fetch a handsome fee, all of which will be applied to her "rent" and food. She will never be out of debt. Like fifty percent of her fellow sex slaves, she will succumb to AIDS in a few years.[1]

O give thanks unto the Lord.

In an upper-middle-class suburb of San Francisco, a group of energetic nine- to eleven-year-olds tussle for control of a soccer ball. Their Little League uniforms are pretty well stained by now, as small lungs gasp for air in this fierce competition. It is for the division championship. The score is tied with only minutes to go. There is much at stake. The shrill blast of a whistle announces a foul. One side of the field emits a loud groan in unison, immediately followed by angry protests directed at the referee. The free kick could mean the championship. Coiffured heads quiver with rage as inch-long, lacquered nails stab the air to emphasize pleas to reconsider the unjust call. Nearby males, in expensively casual sportswear with $150 sunglasses dangling from shirt fronts, add their bass voices to the rumble of complaints.

On the other side of the field, equally coiffured heads tilt sideways, lazily, as huge smiles greet the announced foul. These manicured nails delicately encircle bottles of imported mineral water. Dainty sips are taken. An occasional male belly laugh is heard in response to the truly impressive invective echoing from across the field.

Later the winners, with their children in tow (the actual players who won the game for these ecstatic adults), celebrate the victory at a pizza palace. Someone calls for silence, proposing a prayer of thanksgiving. Impatient children scowl as they bow their heads, eyes firmly fixed on the pieces of pizza that they will lunge for as soon as the interminable prayer is over.

O give thanks unto the Lord; for he is good.

In India, a three-year-old girl squats in a shanty. Her tiny fingers are stitching together the six-sided pieces of leather that will ultimately become a soccer ball. She earns six cents an hour for her work. Her hands are too small to manipulate scissors, so her older sister does the cutting for her. At the end of her labors, approximately sixty cents and ten hours later, the shiny new soccer ball will be ready to be shipped to the United States. There, with a major name brand proudly emblazoned on its skin, it will command a price of $30 to $50.

In Pakistan alone, an estimated eleven million children work for similar wages, in equally squalid conditions. The median age of children entering this dead-end workforce is seven. Stitching sheds dot the countryside, filled with child workers who have been sold by poverty-stricken parents for as little as $15 each.[2]

O give thanks unto the Lord; for he is good;
for his mercy endureth.

In a luxury apartment overlooking Central Park, an enraged matron screams at her maid for spilling coffee on the hall carpet. Tiffany jewelry jangling with her furious movements, the outraged employer asks the terrified employee if she knows how much that imported carpet cost. The maid stares at the floor, silently shaking her head to indicate no. At the end of the tirade, the maid is directed to fetch cold water and towels, with the full understanding that her employment ends at the precise moment that the coffee stain is deemed permanent.

Sputtering with impatience, the matron flips open her cell phone and calls the caterer. Just how many calls, she is wondering, will it take to arrange for a simple ice sculpture and food and drink for two hundred people? Her daughter's wedding is only two weeks away, and *none* of the plans has been finalized yet. The florist caused her most recent ulcer flare-up. Why should she suffer just because there was a killer frost in some godforsaken backwater? She wanted the orchids and roses to be an exact shade of pink, and she knew that's why hothouses were invented. So what was the problem?

Now she slams her phone closed while the caterer is still trying to explain about some sort of *warm* spell in Minnesota that made the orange caviar unavailable this season. Warm, cold, this wedding was going to be the death of her. She takes two Valium and begins to calm down.

The calm is short-lived, however, as she watches the maid's futile attempts on the hall carpet. She paid $2,000 for that damn rug! Too late to buy another one before the wedding. She has her firing speech all prepared, but decides to postpone it. She needs the maid for the wedding. Afterward, she will fire her, deducting carpet cleaning charges from the severance pay. There will be no references, of course.

At last, though, the glorious wedding day arrives, sunny and beautiful. As she watches her lovely daughter affirming her marriage vows, she closes her tear-glistened eyes briefly and offers a silent prayer of thanks. Her twenty-year-old daughter has her whole life in front of her, with her handsome, pre-law bridegroom. A flicker of a smile crosses her face as she adds an addendum to her short prayer. She thanks God that the stain had been removed from her precious carpet after all—and for only $250. There is no doubt in her mind at all. God has truly blessed her.

Halfway around the world, in a gloomy, airless room, a ten-year-old boy squats in front of a carpet loom, tying knots. He will stay in this position for twelve to thirteen hours daily, six days a week. He will earn about two dollars for a week's work, the results of which will be an exquisite carpet that will sell for $2,000 in the United States. He is coughing and hacking as his lungs fill up with carpet lint. His spine is becoming deformed from his perpetual squat. Like many of the boys around him, he will not live to see his twentieth birthday.[3]

> *O give thanks unto the Lord; for he is good;*
> *for his mercy endureth for ever.*
> 1 Chronicles 16:34

This verse in 1 Chronicles is one of the most widely quoted from the Bible. People believe it. Never mind the death, starvation, and misery all around us; God's mercy endureth forever. I have yet to see evidence of that mercy, though I once believed it myself. That's because we usually believe what we're taught in our youth. I believed in the Tooth Fairy, Santa Claus, and . . . Hell.* Boy, did I believe in Hell. It terrified me. I no longer worry about it, but plenty of other people do. The biggest, baddest Bogeyman of them all still commands respect among otherwise intelligent adults. They do indeed believe in Hell.

On Sunday, April 21, 1996, the Lakeland, Florida, *Ledger* ran a feature in its "Life" section (read: irony) titled "Visions of Hell." It ran exactly two weeks after Easter, which may or may not have been a snide reminder of what awaits those of us who foolishly fail to heed God's warnings.

The only problem is that no one can agree on exactly what Hell is. There are many detailed descriptions available, of course, but they are all contradictory and therefore mutually exclusive. This poses the usual problem, which by now has become my battle cry. All right. Let's say that there is a Hell. Fine. *But which one?*

According to the seven religious leaders quoted in the *Ledger* piece, Hell can be a place where you are simply separated from God, a supposedly horrible fate, or it can be a place of unbelievable agony. For example, it is said to be a place where your skin will be boiled off, only to grow back so that it can be boiled off again. This goes on for all eternity. Or it is a place where you will have a hot metal stake pierced through your tongue. Or you will freeze to death (aren't you *already* dead?) then thaw, then freeze again, over and over. Or Hell is just a place of darkness, flames, and screaming—your basic, no-frills Hell. Or Hell is merely symbolic, not an actual place. Or, finally, Hell doesn't exist at all.

The Muslim Hell (boiling, freezing, tongue piercing) seems most unappealing, a very nasty place all the way around. And apparently the Prophet Muhammad's vision of Hell included more women than men. Why? Because the women had been ungrateful to their husbands. This makes sense since Islamic women have been notoriously ungrateful for having their genitalia sliced off and/or

---

*I am choosing to use the upper case for "Hell," just as you would for any other proper name for a place. Like Washington, D.C.

sewn shut, for being bartered like beads in a bazaar, and for being forced into harems. They pretty much define ingratitude, so Hell seems like their just deserts.

The Catholic Hell sounds more generic, with general torment meted out more or less evenly in the form of darkness, flames, and screaming. While it doesn't sound like a day at the beach, it seems that the Catholic Church has toned down its Hell in recent decades. I distinctly recall, as a young child, "borrowing" parts of Hell from my Catholic friends to complement my own Lutheran one. We put our heads together in the earnest endeavor of youth, fully convinced that Hell existed, and determined to unravel every one of its mysteries. As young children are prone to do, my Catholic friends cheerfully and explicitly provided me with many horrifying details, and they did so with ghoulish glee. I know I was impressed. These details included boiling tar (like on roofs) and a devil constantly piercing your flesh with a pitchfork so as to let in the boiling pitch. To this day I can see those pitchforks and smell that tar.*

O give thanks?!

The Unitarian Hell is symbolic, although a spokesperson for the Unitarian position played a linguistic shell game. While claiming that the language of religion is mythology, he nevertheless insisted, in the same breath, that religion is *not* fantasy or fiction. Perhaps being unfamiliar with dictionaries, he wanted it both ways.

Some Jewish sects and all Baptists teach Hell. For Jews it is a punishment for violating Jewish Law, and for Baptists Hell is for anyone rejecting Jesus Christ. (Doesn't that include the Jews?)

Finally, Hell doesn't exist at all for traditional Creek Indians. Your reward for a good life is—a good life.

The subtitle for "Visions of Hell" was "Religions vary on their views about the afterlife." I think that is a whopping understatement. "Vary" doesn't get the job done. "Positively contradict each other" is more like it. But what does it all mean? The lesson would seem to be that we should all be Creek Indians. However, the real

---

*When I asked my mother to verify these details, she just scoffed at the idea, but warned me never to do anything that would enable me to find out for myself. I promised I wouldn't, and the nightmares began.

lesson here is that while some claim that religion brings out the best in people (a most questionable proposition) it definitely brings out the worst in us. Nothing could demonstrate that more clearly than our conceptions of Hell.

You have to wonder who sat down, quill pen in hand, and dreamed up these ugly, venomous torments. Whoever they were, were they drooling with salacious pleasure as they did so? It seems likely, since descriptions of Hell are unambiguous examples of pure sadism. Those of us who wish this kind of pain on others are sadistic, plain and simple. Such descriptions also validate my theory that Christians (and Muslims, for that matter) aren't merely excited at the prospect of spending eternity with God; they are thrilled at the prospect of their enemies, real or imagined, spending eternity in Hell. Judging by some of the unabashedly violent sermons preached about Hell, this appears to be the case. It reflects an ugly aspect of human nature.

The word *Hell* itself is identified with the Hebrew *Sheol* and the Greek *Hades*, both referring to an underworld, the abode of the dead. It is also related to a real place south of Jerusalem that was a pit where garbage was burned in the first century. Perhaps we can see mythology in the making here. There, for all to see, was a real pit of fire, one that was foul, odious, and generally disgusting. It would be quite an allegory in trying to frighten your children (or your congregation) into behaving. "Do you want to spend all of eternity in Hell, you fool?" The fool might ask, "But what is Hell?" The answer might be, "Well, it would be like living in, uh, that burning pit there. Forever!" It *would* be an attention getter, especially if it came from a voice of authority.

Is this what we want to be preaching today? How can we still believe in such obvious myths? And if we do believe in Hell, why aren't we demanding that our religious leaders get together with all other religious leaders, in some sort of worldwide conference, and hammer out a definitive agreement as to the exact nature of Hell and who is in danger of ending up there? Until such a unanimous pronouncement is made, the prudent seeker of spiritual truth is in a hell of a predicament. Do we get to choose which Hell we believe in, like a multiple-choice question? May we *shop* for Hell? Or is it a matter of having the luck to be born into the right family? If so, that certainly isn't fair. It means that Hell awaits the unlucky.

The religious denomination known as Religious Science teaches that we all create our own good and bad. People create their own Hell, they tell us, when they get themselves into bad situations and frames of mind. So, then, the RN who is beaten and raped as she heads for her car after her evening shift is putting herself into a bad situation. With several broken ribs and internal hemorrhaging, she becomes addicted to the needed pain medication, and ends up an unemployed addict, hating all men and fearing all people. She certainly has put herself into a very bad frame of mind as well. Hell *should* await anyone witless enough to fall into such a predicament, right?

Islam teaches that in addition to Hell, there is also a fair amount of suffering that takes place in the grave prior to Judgment Day. A demon will continuously crush the head of the sinner with a sledgehammer until the day of resurrection. Moreover, the sinner's body will be slowly crushed by the narrowing of the grave. (I am not making this up.) Aside from the obvious biochemical factors overlooked here—decomposition, the omission of which reflects a childlike, primitive worldview—there is also a childish nature to the type of punishment being described. *Sledgehammers?* Any creative 9-year-old could come up with something more imaginative than that.

Of course the torments of Hell are not all that True Believers believe in. There are also miracles, guardian angels helping us find things like our car keys, apparitions, ecstatic visions, and all manner of supernatural phenomena. We especially like the apparitions.

VICTUAL VIRGINS

FRESNO, August 14—An image of the Virgin Mary appeared on the face of a waffle, to the astonishment of diners at the International House of Pancakes just off of Highway 99 in Fresno, California. On a Tuesday morning at 8:30 A.M., a miracle was served up with the maple syrup, according to Louise Crowder of Bakersfield.

"I was reaching for the butter, because I like a lot of melted butter on my waffles, you know, instead of just drowning them in syrup, like most people do," explained Crowder, "when I saw the face of the Blessed Virgin right there, on my waffle! Just imagine! She was on *my* waffle."

Crowder's cry of surprise brought many diners as well as IHOP employees to her table. People crowded around and gazed in awe at the image of the Virgin Mary, which was marred only slightly by a crease in her forehead caused by a butter knife. Alan Snyder, manager of the IHOP, gasped, "It *is* the Blessed Virgin!" as several people fell to their knees, knocking over a cart that held raspberry syrup and marmalade. "Damn!" muttered an onlooker as she tried to wipe the raspberry syrup from the knees of her white slacks. "Well, who cares about syrup anyway?" she cried. "This is the *Virgin Mary*!" Everyone murmured reverent agreement as all eyes were momentarily drawn to the bright purple knees.

"No doubt about it," said Dean Fowler, a truck driver who had been enjoying a short stack and a side of hash browns, "it was the Virgin Mary. I'd know her anywhere." Fowler had only stopped at this particular IHOP because he had to wait while a flat tire was being repaired. He considers the flat to be a miracle itself. "If I hadn't had that flat," he mused solemnly, "I never would have come into this place and I never would have seen the Virgin on the waffle. Also, my tire was fixed in record time, and they only charged me half of what it usually costs. Coincidence?" he asked knowingly. "I don't think so."

When asked what he thought of the appearance, Patrick O'Donnell, bishop of the local diocese, answered, "It is a once-in-a-lifetime event. Truly a miracle. How often do you see Waffle Virgins?"

So far, at this IHOP, in the two weeks since the appearance, there have been reports of a dozen healings, brought about just by ordering the waffles; four confirmed gastrointestinal cures ("strawberry waffles don't give me gas any more!"); and hundreds of reports of flat tires that healed themselves by not happening in the first place. Since the appearance, business has been booming for this previously near-bankrupt IHOP, and owner Snyder feels he was truly blessed. He summed it up by saying, "This is the real miracle—the Virgin Mary helping a flapjack flipper find his way back to solvency."

PINK HILL, N.C., September 14—Way down yonder and far to the south, in a town called Pink Hill, North Carolina, a sawmill worker noticed the Virgin Mary in his plate of grits. "She was just *there*," Albert Grimes explained emotionally, his eyes brimming with tears. "The Virgin Mary was in my *grits*." Family members confirmed the sighting.

Grimes's aunt, Thelma Mae, elaborated. "We was all just sitting around the table, passing the black-eyed peas and the red-eye gravy, when all of a sudden Mary Belle—she's my half-sister, Albert's mother, but that still makes me his aunt, even though Mary Belle and I have different fathers—well, actually all seven of us have different fathers, but none of us puts up with no trash talk about Mama, and don't you forget it. So anyway, Mary Belle just plopped a mess of grits on Albert's plate and there she was! The Virgin Mary! Then two of them black-eyed peas slid right into place and Bingo! The Virgin had eyes! It was the damnedest thing you ever did see. Mind you, I don't really think that the Blessed Virgin was cross-eyed, but that ain't no never mind. Thing is, it was the actual Virgin herself, plain as day, surrounded by a halo of red-eye gravy." Thelma Mae paused to spit a wad of tobacco juice across the room, missing the spittoon by mere inches, which prompted an encouraging, "Gettin' closer, Grandma!" from one of the many Grimes cousins. "And just think," she concluded humbly, wiping her chin with the back of her hand, "the Virgin chose our own little bitty cabin for her visitation."

The cabin isn't quite so humble any more after the donations from the hundreds of visitors to the Grits Shrine. And those donations have been put to good use. The outhouse is long gone, replaced by indoor plumbing that includes one of those shiny, pearly colored toilet seats, making the Grimes's dwelling a neighborhood showplace. But the family makes it clear that money is not the issue.

"If we turn a deal on a pickup out of this, ain't no harm," offered Elmo Grimes, Albert's father, "but that ain't what this is all about. It's about the look of rapture on the sweet faces of them visitors when they view the grits for the first time—we had the grits freeze-dried so's everything would stay in place—and everyone leaves here with true peace in their hearts. Well, 'ceptin for some of the young'uns who giggle at a cross-eyed Virgin Mary—and they oughta be whupped if you ask me. But everyone else finds that inner peace." Elmo repeated the phrase as he emptied the donation box for the third time that day, "Yessir, inner peace."

ROCK RIDGE, N.D., October 5—"You coulda knocked me over with a feather," were the words of Edna Muldoon from Rock Ridge, North Dakota, as she explained seeing the Virgin Mary clearly outlined on her kitchen floor in Carter's Little Liver Pills. "I spilled the whole darn bottle on the linoleum," she explained, "and it made such a godawful clatter it set my teeth on edge. Of course they ain't my own teeth any more!" she added with a slap of her thigh and a huge cackle that revealed no teeth at all in the Muldoon mouth at the moment. "But there's no doubt about it—those liver pills spread out and formed an image of the Virgin, and here's the pitchers to prove it!"

As the reporters gathered around the photographs they saw the liver pills, in the shape of the Virgin Mary, strewn across Muldoon's kitchen floor. One reporter whispered, "Jesus! It looks like the chalk outlines the cops do after a murder!" "Hey, knock it off!" someone growled. "Don't be sacrilegious!" The reporter was silenced and dutifully studied the Virgin/liver pill photos.

As Muldoon passed around the photos, she explained why they didn't look exactly like the outline that was currently on her floor. "Damn cat ate a couple of those pills just before you got here." Another raucous cackle and then, "Say, fellas, any of you ever play sail-cat? That's one tabby won't be back for a while!"

Invited into the house where the kitchen had been roped off for several days with some clothesline, one reporter noticed that all of the pills were oriented, lengthwise, in a north-south direction. When he asked Muldoon how so many pills could have scattered randomly yet ended up aligned so precisely, she snapped, "Who are you to question how God works his miracles? What do you think happened here, anyway? You think I got down on my hands and knees, throwing out my back again, and arranged the pills so's they'd look like the Virgin? And then called ol' Jake down at the *Dispatch* and asked him to come take a look? Only Jake was at the bar again, as usual, so I had to leave a message with that no-count Delbert? And while I was waiting I straightened out all the pills so's they'd be just so? Is that what you think happened, Smarty Britches?!"

At that the reporters rolled their eyes and began drifting away. They were nearly trampled by the first busload of pilgrims who had just arrived to view the Liver Pill Virgin.

There may be a lesson in this for all of us. We would all do well to look carefully before rolling up that next tortilla, or plunging a fork into that piece of lemon meringue pie, or tearing into that pizza. Examine those victuals closely. You might be just a Pop-Tart away from a Victual Virgin Visitation.

© *The Heretical News*

TWO DOWN AND FOUR TO GO

Some things you just can't laugh at, however. Some things are just heartbreaking. It is difficult to be tolerant of religious "freedom" when that freedom inflicts suffering on children.

An AP story that ran on April 22, 1996, featured the photo of a very happy woman in Beirut. She was overcome with joy as she flashed a huge smile and a thumbs-up sign. You see, she was attending the funeral of her twenty-three-year-old son, and there was simply no containing her excitement. She was obviously glorying in the moment. This was the second son she had buried this way, so she was truly doubly blessed. Allah be praised.

Her ecstasy is easy enough to understand, of course, when you consider *how* her son died. Like his brother before him, he died killing Jews. Can there be a more noble death? What Muslim mother could ask for more? "I'm happy," she beamed. "My sons will enter paradise because they're fighting the Zionist enemy. I have four more [sons] and they, too, are ready to join in the fight." Well, I guess it's two down and four to go.

So pack them some sandwiches, lady, and send them on their way. With any luck they'll all be dead by next Tuesday. Kind of brings a lump to a mother's throat, doesn't it? A pile of dead sons. Like cord wood. Surely this is cause for maternal rejoicing.

Whenever religionists or humanists bristle at my antireligious statements (such as the above) calling them negative and counter-productive, I direct their attention to insane obscenities (such as the above). Religious killing has been big business since religions began, and it is sickening.

Every Sunday nice little Christians sit in their nice little pews and listen to nice little sermons about being nice little Christians. At first glance, bloodletting and ruthless murder would seem to have no possible connection to this peaceful, pastoral, postcardlike image. Yet at the very core of the Christian religion is, first of all, a bloody, gruesome death by crucifixion. This was followed shortly by the bloody deaths of Christian "martyrs" who died because of religion. Then, as soon as Christians achieved dominance, they promptly began to persecute other religions. They killed back-sliders, heretics, and "witches." They killed each other when they felt that their fellow Christians (Lutherans, Anabaptists, Catholics, Calvinists, take your pick) were worshipping incorrectly. And, of course, Jews were always fair game.

The Roman Catholic Inquisition, which was inaugurated to ferret out backsliders, added torture to the rather mundane business of just killing people. The Catholics came up with some truly impressive forms of torture that would have been the envy of any jackbooted Nazi storm trooper.

When it was time for the Crusades to begin, in those earliest double-digit centuries, Christians became less fussy about who they killed. When the pope launched the Crusades, Christian soldiers just hopped on the ships headed for the Holy Land, and killed anyone "wearing a sheet." Often these were fellow Christians who were simply dressing sensibly for the climate. However, since the prevailing Christian wisdom of the times was that the only good turban wearer was a dead one, the killing continued.

The Crusades were an unmitigated disaster for Christians, but there was never a shortage of volunteers to try to pry the Holy Land out of the hands of the Muslim "Infidels." Why? Because those Christians believed that if they died killing Muslims, they would go straight to heaven. No waiting period. No Purgatory, no possibility of Hell, no detours of any kind. It made no difference how many women and children they raped and tortured and killed during their forays. No act was too heinous to preclude heaven. And, as an added bonus, they didn't even have to offer confession or receive absolution before they died. As long as they were in the process of killing Muslims when they died, they would go straight to heaven. The pope had so decreed. God be praised.

As the Crusades fizzled, European Christians had to content themselves with killing each other. The Thirty Years' War, the Massacre of the Huguenots, and so on, which pitted Protestants against Catholics, had to satisfy the religious bloodlust. If that didn't pan out, of course, you could always kill some Jews. Pogroms at least gave Christians a chance to kill *someone* in the name of God. The Jews were, according to Christians, "Christ killers," so they really did deserve to be killed. It made perfect Christian sense.

There must be something deeply soul-satisfying about killing people in the name of God, since history is so filled with it. It has been said that religion is divisive. That is a colossal understatement. From the Aztecs to the assassination of Yitzhak Rabin to the fanatically religious terrorists that still plague us, religion has been deadly.

Why dredge all this up? you may ask. It's all ancient history anyway, right? Well, let's see. The Catholic/Protestant clashes are still echoing in the bomb blasts of Northern Ireland. During the Persian Gulf War in 1991, the Muslims, the Israelis, and our own General Schwarzkopf all expressed a humble gratitude that God was on their side. (My constant battle cry, so to speak: *Which* God are they talking about? They couldn't all be thanking the same God, now, could they?) The Serbs (read: Orthodox Eastern Church) and the Croatians (read: Roman Catholic) and the Bosnians (read: Muslim) all killing each other is a fairly recent phenomenon. And remember Jonestown in Guyana, the World Trade Center bombing, and David Koresh in Waco, Texas? Hardly ancient history.

The Muslim mother in the newspaper photo, ecstatically burying her son, is no fluky aberration. Muslims have been known to rush headlong into a certain death joyously crying, "Tonight in Paradise!" Apparently Allah, like the Christian God of the Crusades, offers the same kind of "no waiting period" paradise for soldiers who die while killing their religious foes. A Muslim mother envisions her son in paradise with Allah. The Christian mother envisions her son in heaven with Jesus. I wonder who's right.

Such enthusiasm for death would be equally appropriate for Christians, but strangely it is not. However, if Christians really believe what they say they believe, then ear-to-ear grins should be all that you ever see at Christian funerals. A Christian's death should be cause for celebration. What could be more wonderful than to know that your loved one is now in heaven with Jesus? Your own piddling little loneliness pales into absolute insignificance when compared to the rapturous joys of heaven. So why do any Christians *ever* cry over a death? It's a very interesting question.

It would be different if a Christian worried that someone was going to hell. That would indeed be worth some tears. But heaven? Isn't there some hypocrisy, or at least some real uncertainty, being exposed when Christians cry at funerals? Is there some genuine fear, lurking just beneath the surface, that death is really the end for all of us? If not, bereaved Christian tears are inexplicable.

Moreover, if you carry the theory of salvation and heaven to its logical end, the most wonderful act any Christian could perform would be to take every newborn baby, baptize it, and then kill it. Christians will argue that killing is against God's law (with scores of exceptions, but that's another story) and so killing babies would be wrong. Well, okay, let's say it's wrong. It still would be a wonderful thing to do, since you would be safeguarding all of those souls from any possibility of missing out on heaven and ending up in hell. What could be more noble? If the Christian doing the killing should end up being damned, can you think of a more glorious way to sacrifice yourself—for the everlasting salvation of thousands and thousands of souls? And anyway, why would God be angry with you for simply furthering his own plans? Supposedly, God wants all of his "children" to end up in heaven with him, and this certainly seems like the foolproof solution.

All this talk of death and funerals and killing is, of course, to make a special point: Most religions are obsessed with death and dying. They seize on it, preach about it, sing hymns about it, and frighten the wits out of their children about it. It's almost like sharks in a feeding frenzy, or a dog with a bone. They just can't leave it alone.

Instead of enjoying our five minutes in the sun, we allow our religions to hobble us with fears and shame and pangs of guilt. Guilt for what? For being human. Religions put a sick spin on the human experience, making death the primary focus of life. Most religions are nothing more than continuous reminders of the Grim Reaper. Imagine the impact this has on young children. Having been there myself, I can tell you the death thing is powerful, consuming, and frightening. Such beliefs do not frighten the death out of children. It frightens death into them. Death becomes an obsession.

But there should be joy in *life*—not in waiting to die. We should be savoring the fragrance of the roses, not planning how we want them arranged on our coffins. "They are not long, the days of wine and roses. . . ." We must treasure them *and our children*, while we may.

JEHOVAH'S JUVENILE WITNESS

On a personal level, I know a woman who sacrificed her son—but in a different way. Someone I'll call "Barbara" loved her three children. She worked two jobs to support them, since her ex-husband could never seem to manage to come up with the child support. So it was nothing less than a shock when we all heard that this very ex-husband was suing for custody of their oldest child, a thirteen-year-old boy. Shock turned to disbelief when we learned that the boy, "Eric," who loved his two little sisters unreservedly, wanted to go live with his father. Why? Well, it was all about God.

Child custody battles are invariably ugly, and emotions run high, but the children invariably come out the losers. In this case Barbara was a friend of mine. I knew she was a Jehovah's Witness, she knew I was an atheist, so needless to say we didn't discuss religion. She did make one plucky attempt to introduce me to Jehovah's benevolence. I calmly responded by directing her attention to the results of that benevolence—wars, starvation, the Holocaust—and she let it go. But I never dreamed that her stalwart faith would be the reason she lost her son—legally and emotionally.

Eric was around nine years old when his parents divorced, and it was perhaps no coincidence that shortly thereafter his mother was converted from a vague, nominal Protestant to a passionately enthusiastic Jehovah's Witness. Those doorbell ringers found an ardently receptive recruit in Barbara. It was like a duck to water. At the time, her daughters, "Jamie" and "Denise," were only three and one, respectively, and didn't know God from the Tooth Fairy. But Eric, though he initially accepted the new God, soon decided he wanted no part of this stern, demanding Jehovah. He became a nine-year-old backslider.

With the fervor found only in new converts, Barbara kept after the poor child, relentless in her efforts to "get some Jehovah" into him. The more she pushed, the more he resisted—a fairly predictable outcome. So her spiritual leaders concluded, unbelievably, that since Eric had initially been receptive (at age nine) but was now "renouncing," he was a sinner. And sinners had to be punished. Accordingly, when Barbara and her bewildered little girls ("Why isn't Eric coming with us, Mommy?") went to their twice-weekly Jehovah's Witness meetings, Eric was taken along, against his will, but left in the car alone. At night. For two hours or more. Twice a week.

This went on for almost two years until Eric finally complained to his father about it. I had no idea it was going on. However, I was most unhappily aware of other aspects of Barbara's religious activities. Once, stopping at my house after work, she called her home to tell the sitter she'd be a bit late. Jamie, around six now, was excited to get on the phone and tell Mommy how she had been "strong for Jehovah." Jamie had refused to participate in her kindergarten class project of making Christmas decorations—snowmen and snowflakes. Not a hint of religion. But since Jehovah's Witnesses do not believe in observing Christmas, cutting out snowmen was somehow sinful. So here we have a sweet little six-year-old girl, self-ostracized over some glitter and glue decorations, and a mother beaming joyously because her daughter had been "strong for Jehovah." It was poignant and depressing. Little Jamie was carrying a burden far too large for such small shoulders.

When I finally heard about Eric's car-imprisonment evenings, I was appalled. The image of that little boy, almost thirteen now, all alone, shivering in his parka jacket while locked in a parked car, was sickening. I didn't hear about these little adventures until the custody suit was well under way. I can understand Barbara's reluctance to talk about it, but I could not understand her actions. I asked her how she could possibly treat a child that way. Defensively, she offered the Jehovah/sinner thing, and abruptly ended the conversation. She also abruptly ended our friendship, assuming, I can only suppose, that I was in league with the devil.

The tragic part of all of this is that Barbara truly loved her children. I can't imagine the conflicts she experienced in treating her son that way. She was heartbroken when the court took Eric away from her, but I don't see how she could have expected anything else.

Is there a lesson to be learned from this dreadful narrative? Well, aside from never answering your doorbell, perhaps there is. For all the bickering that goes on between us freethinkers/humanists/atheists/et ceteras, we can all agree on one thing: None of our groups would ever demand that a parent leave a young child unattended in a car at night! Humanism's goal is ambitious but worthy—the best life possible for everyone on earth. And that could never include a shivering, frightened little boy being forsaken because he would not bow down correctly to the right God.

EXPLAINING THE UNEXPLAINABLE

In the years I have been writing about religion, I've asked many unambiguous, straightforward questions. Many True Believers have written or e-mailed me claiming to have the answers. But all they have done is preach their brand of religion, describing the glory and truth to be found there. They simply tiptoed around my questions. They would dodge, weave, and avoid like crazy.

An excellent example of that would be Wayne Jackson, editor of the Christian publications *Christian Courier* and *Reason & Revelation* (oxymoron?). He was apparently rattled by my book, *In God We Trust: But Which One?* Had he not been, he would not have devoted, to me alone, one full page of the three-and-a-half-page issue of the March 1997 *CC* and almost half of an essay in *R&R*. I obviously touched a nerve.

Wayne and I had previously exchanged a few letters wherein he proposed public debates. I had to decline, since public speaking is no more a part of my repertoire than are rodeo riding, skydiving, or marine biology. I would approach them all with about the same amount of confidence. Repeatedly, I have been urged to speak at various functions, while being reassured that public speaking can be learned. Well, so can marine biology. I am a writer. I write. But when I suggested to Jackson, also a writer, that we enter a written debate, he flatly refused. Now I know why.

In my book I challenged the concept of God in general and Christian fundamentalism in particular. I posed the age-old questions: Does the One True God speak though the pope? If God wanted perfect people, why didn't he create them? Who created evil? I also posed some original questions (well, at least I hadn't heard them before) such as: Why would Jesus have prayed to be released from his imminent, sacrificial death, which literally defined his only reason for existence? And why would Jesus' disciples all have scoffered, abandoning him just before the crucial moment of his supreme sacrifice, if they really believed in his mission?

There are scores of other challenges like this throughout my book. Yet Wayne Jackson, Christian apologist, chose to focus his entire critique of my book on my brief assertion that Jesus' historicity may be in doubt. It is almost an aside, since my main concern was the whole "create sinners/curse the sinners/demand a bloody sacrifice because they *are* sinners" scenario. But Jackson ferociously, tediously, and disingenuously defends Jesus' historicity as if it were the whole point of my book. Far from it, it doesn't matter one way or the other if a Jesus ever existed. It is the entire barbaric, sadistic, sin/hell/blood-atonement concept that concerned me. And it is this that I unmasked for the primitive impossibility that it is. These salient points are scrupulously avoided by Jackson as he drones on about the historicity of Jesus.

This, of course, is a favorite tactic of Christian apologists. Since they cannot defend the crucifixion and resurrection story, riddled as it is with contradictions and cruelty on a cosmic scale, they will instead pounce on side issues. However, once Jackson had decided to defend Jesus as a real person, he could at least have avoided the overworked, specious arguments that (1) Jesus' resurrection *must* have been real because martyrs would never have sacrificed their lives for a myth, and (2) the scarcity of early documents referring to Jesus does not point to his nonexistence, since there is a scarcity of documents about almost everything in those early centuries.

(1) Muhammad *must* have been inspired by God himself because Muslim martyrs would never sacrifice their lives for a myth. Would Christians agree with this statement? Why can't they see that this "martyrdom for a myth" argument can be applied to any belief system ever known? David Koresh *must* have been Jesus because his martyrs would never. . . . Jim Jones *must* have been. . . . It's almost too easy to destroy this argument. Humans have been dying for (and murdering for) countless gods throughout recorded history. This may speak to the overall cruelty and foolishness of humans, but certainly does not argue for the actual existence of any gods. This embarrassing argument should be abandoned.

(2) The scarcity of early documents about other topics means

nothing when discussing the life of Jesus. There are events and then there are *events*. If there had been a windy rain shower on some spring afternoon in the year 30, for example, which pelted pedestrians of Jerusalem with mud splatters, I would not expect to find a mound of scrolls documenting that event. Mud, after all, is just mud. However, if a virgin had given birth to a miracle worker, whose birth was announced by angels; and who later went on to perform true miracles throughout the area such as healing the hopelessly ill and *raising people from the dead*; and whose sacrificial death caused darkness at noon, an earthquake, and graves to open up allowing the dead to rejoin the living; and who capped an already dazzling career by raising *himself* from the dead and then ascending into Heaven in front of witnesses; I would indeed expect to find a mound of scrolls describing this spectacular being named Jesus.

Moreover, I would certainly expect that the many people chronicling these wonders would have done so the moment they happened, not sixty or seventy years later as if it were no big deal. You would only expect such nonchalance, such a glaring time delay, if the time were needed to allow an embryonic, wistful hope for life after death (so ubiquitous throughout history) to evolve and ripen into a full-fledged resurrection myth. Eager embellishments by word of mouth would ensure just that, and would explain the otherwise inexplicable, curious, lengthy delay in documenting such marvels as were later attributed to Jesus.

In *Reason & Revelation*, Jackson misstated my reason for becoming an atheist. He claimed I became an atheist because I could not tolerate the idea of a friend of my youth, Susan, a Buddhist, going to hell. The trouble is he left something out. My worry over Susan did prompt me to plunge earnestly into a thorough, cover-to-cover reading of the Bible—to assuage my fears. But it was *that reading*, not my worry over Susan, that destroyed my faith. The Bible itself, upon close scrutiny, proved so barbaric, primitive, and contradictory, that my naive faith was extinguished. My faith had been based on ignorance of the Bible's real words (an ignorance possessed by most Christians), and it was a careful examination of those words that ended my faith. Jackson's failure to mention that all-important point is—once again—disingenuous.

Still, the only others Jackson mentioned in this same essay were Isaac Asimov, William Henley, and Aldous Huxley, with me receiving more space than the other three combined. I consider this high praise indeed, and am honored to be in such company.

In this same issue of *R&R*, Jackson took on the late Carl Sagan, a huge mistake if ever there was one. He criticized Sagan for not "researching" the "historical evidence" for Jesus' resurrection. Which evidence is that, you ask? Why, it's the resurrection itself, which you can read about in the Bible. Circular arguments, anyone?

Carl Sagan, of all people, was in no need of guidance on adequate research techniques. Jackson's presumptuousness is breathtaking—and wholly ineffective. Jackson would do well to confine himself to much smaller game—like me. But even at that, he should try to learn the art of criticizing without peppering his works with ad hominem attacks. They are very distracting, appeal only to the most limited of intellects, and just generally make you weary. In less than a thousand words, Jackson managed to work in: obnoxious atheists; vicious bitterness; ignorant venom and crudeness; reckless, lame logic; and bungling incompetence. Well, I'm impressed. What eloquence.

Jackson actually asked me, in print, about my book's publication date, 1996. "Nineteen hundred and ninety-six years *from what*, Judith?" That's easy, Wayne. It's from an arbitrary date decreed by Pope Gregory XIII in 1582, and I assume the question means that Jackson recognizes papal authority, although he's a Protestant fundamentalist. Well, the year of Jackson's publications was the Chinese Lunar Year 4695, the Year of the Ox. Four thousand six hundred ninety-five years *from what*, Wayne? Or do you not recognize the Chinese as part of our human family?

But fundamentalists somehow come equipped with blinders. They see what they want to see, evidence to the contrary notwithstanding. And when it comes to deciphering the book of Revelation in the Bible, the most convoluted and confusing book in the whole Bible—or perhaps anywhere—you really *can* see anything you want to see. Kingdoms being established, the end of the world, the beginning of a new world, the new millennium, the Dow-Jones average—you name it and somebody will find it in Revelation. The whole book is a guessing game. It's similar to the supposedly prophetic verses of Nostradamus. Given enough latitude, you can find whatever you want in either. That makes it easy to "explain" the "unexplainable."

Of all the strange beliefs held so dearly by staunch believers, perhaps the most strange and most difficult to explain is the belief that doesn't exist. That is, why can no one tell us where we were before we were born? Almost every human culture yet discovered has found it necessary to believe in an afterlife of some sort, but not a "before-life." Why? Why are there so many versions of heaven, paradise, and the Great Beyond, but almost none about the Great Before?

The human mind has been almost inexhaustible in its creative descriptions of life beyond the grave and how to go about arriving at the correct destination. Historically, humans have maintained a fiercely stubborn insistence on the existence of an afterworld and a baffling lack of curiosity about their whereabouts before they were born. Why should this be?

In looking at the world around us, we are fixed in time and space. We are *here* and it is *today*. The possibility of time travel fires our imaginations, which is why it is the subject of so much popular science fiction. But even in those scenarios, as we travel backward or forward, we are still *us*, and the moment (whatever the year) is still *now*. The I-am-here-and-it-is-today perception of the world is so universal we rarely think about it. Except for perhaps Albert Einstein and a handful of similar geniuses, we have no other options in thinking about the world. We are limited by our usually nongenius intelligence and our ultimate sense of self.

Babies display the unwavering conviction that the universe revolves around them, and growing up is really just a nonstop exercise in being disabused of this notion. Religion could therefore be described as a means of holding on to that infantile conviction. It is simply an extension of our egos. It reassures us that we are very important indeed.

And our egos make no bones about it. They speak quite clearly on the subject. "Now that *I'm* here," we tell ourselves, "the world is an important place. And not only that, but I can see no possible way for the universe to continue without *me* in it. So, though I am smart enough to understand that I must die someday, that doesn't necessarily mean that I must *end*. I'm too important to just *end*." And the rest, as they say, is religious history.

Once we're here, we immediately recognize our importance and proceed to figure out ways to ensure that some part of us will always be here, or at least somewhere. But we don't seem to care much, one way or another, where we were *before* we were here. Who cares what was going on before *I* existed? Certainly not I! And in a way, it makes a sort of self-centered sense.

Although this view of existence may explain how some of our religious myths came into being, it is still a mystery why so many religions, particularly Christianity, devote so little thought to the question of "pre-existence." At least the theory of reincarnation attempts to answer this where-were-you question. Recycling, so to speak, answers the question by suggesting that you were always *somebody*, even if not exactly yourself. (Discussions of religions make us say some strange things. What do I mean, "not exactly yourself?!") But Christianity acts like it isn't even a problem, this concern over where we were before we existed. However, it is a major problem if you postulate, as Christians do, an "eternal" soul. If eternal, those souls had to be *somewhere*, doing *something*, before joining their new human bodies. And they had to have been doing whatever it was they were doing for a never-ending period of time, regressing inexorably and forever *backward* in time. It's hard to imagine, then (for me anyway), how they could ever get to "today."

Christianity is based on the Bible, which tells concrete stories about concrete events in real time. On the fourth day, God did thus. During the reign of King Somebody, these battles took place, and so on. Time is measured in years and days, as we have come to know them; but the *eternal* nature of God's plans for us is a constantly woven thread throughout that same Bible. Therefore, this biblical timeline must be able to be traced backward into eternity, accounting for everything that has ever happened, including events that preceded our existence. If Christian theologians cannot do this, their failure means that they don't understand existence or time any more than I do, which is to say not at all.

I cannot begin to understand the concept of eternity. I just can't get a handle on it. So it is not surprising that I can't begin to understand any sort of eternal paradise, the hypothetical resting place for that intangible essence of humanity—the "soul." Even if I *could* understand eternity, though, I think the concept of a "soul" would still elude me.

The "soul," which cannot be seen, heard, touched, smelled, or detected in any way by the human senses, is also invisible to X-rays, CAT scans, MRIs, and blood tests. It is said to have no physical properties, meaning it has no mass. This pretty well defines nonexistence. While it's true that thoughts, for example, can be said to "exist" without possessing mass, the neurons required to create those thoughts most certainly have mass. So I'm afraid the human "soul," totally detached from any physical body, literally hasn't a leg to stand on.

But Christians steadfastly claim certain knowledge of a very real place called heaven, where these ephemeral souls will reside for all of eternity, and where time runs in only one direction—forward. The childlike assertion that on Day One God created the universe explains nothing. To maintain credibility, Christians must explain eternity, which means explaining what happened the day *before* Day One.

When I was a young child I asked my mother what God was doing before he created the world. I was told he was making switches for people who asked such questions. Thanks for the enlightenment, Mom. But as far as I know, no Christian theologian has answered that question any better.

I've heard the quaint little story about how we were all angels before we were born, at which point we came "down" to Earth to take on our mortal cloaks. Aside from the undeniably fairy-tale-ish nature of this explanation, which hasn't a thread of theology to support it (even though there is theology aplenty to support some truly outlandish claims) this scenario has real practical problems.

If a preexisting angel or spirit of some sort descends to join a human body, does that event take place mere minutes after sexual intercourse, at the precise moment that sperm joins ovum? Does ensoulment take place while a woman is, say, showering? Or on the bidet? Or snoring? If a zygote is a fully human being, as many anti-choice fundamentalists claim, then these are indeed the times at which the soul enters the body. But isn't there something very wrong with these images? Doesn't the word *unseemly* apply?

If ensoulment takes place later, then when? At thirty or forty days after conception, as the Catholic Church once taught? At birth? Does anybody know? Shouldn't it be important to know?

Christians carry on about heaven, offering details about it and the rapture involved. They can provide equally detailed accounts of the agonies that await sinners in hell. But if you ask where they were before they were born, they just shrug. There seems to be a yawning void in their "certain" knowledge of things eternal. But they may not shrug this off. If they are going to ring our doorbells and preach to us about the intricacies of salvation and damnation, then they must also be able to explain the equally important issue of where we were before we . . . were.

The burden of proof is not on me in this discussion. I threw up my hands long ago and cheerfully conceded that I haven't a clue as to what "forever" means. I cannot, and need not, try to explain it. Christians, though, are making authoritative, proprietary (and loud) pronouncements about the subject, and bandy about the word "eternal" with reckless abandon. All right then, Christians, explain eternity. But please explain *both* directions of it. Please explain the "other end" of eternity—the back end, if you will. Explaining time in one direction only (forward) is like explaining the life cycle of a chicken without mentioning the egg. Eternal paradise and eternal souls are pure wishful thinking unless this problem is addressed and solved.

So, I challenge all believers in an afterlife to explain precisely where they were and what they doing *before* they were. If I had to guess what *I* was doing before I existed, I would hazard that I was probably writing an essay about what it was like to be nonexistent.

THE POWER OF PENGUINS

Another mystery, a most bewildering aspect of religious fundamentalism, is the miracle. People swear by them. It is the most obvious, prominent symptom of blind faith. Blind faith can be dangerous (David Koresh) or goofy (Jim and Tammy Bakker) or tragically desperate, as it was with my friend "Jenny." Her story is heart wrenching and almost unbelievable. But it really happened.

Jenny's firstborn son, Timothy, was long awaited and loved beyond measure. I have never seen such love for a child, before or since. She worshiped that boy. So when Timothy developed a malignant brain tumor shortly after his eighth birthday, you can imagine the terror in Jenny's heart. For Jenny, the world ceased to exist except for her son.

Not just Jenny and her family, but an entire one-thousand-member Presbyterian congregation began praying for Timothy. They held special church services just to pray for him. There were easily fifty thousand prayers offered to God for the recovery of this one sweet little boy. God was asked to bring about the success of the chemotherapy, and to ensure improvement in the successive CAT scans. Finally, God was asked to make the high-risk brain surgery a success. But Timothy never reached his ninth birthday. He died in Jenny's arms.

Jenny's grief was immeasurable. She was inconsolable. As if her anguish were not enough, the doctors immediately announced that they wanted to perform an autopsy. Why? The official reason was that any time an unexplained death occurs, the law requires an autopsy. *Unexplained?* Well, anyway, this pushed Jenny over the edge. She could not bear the thought of her precious Timothy being autopsied, and she would not sign the consent forms. She was then informed that they could legally perform an autopsy anyway, and they intended to do so. Jenny cried and begged them not to do this thing, to no avail.

So Jenny positioned herself in the doorway of Timothy's hospital room, blocking the way, and announced that she would not let them take his body until they agreed not to perform an autopsy. Arms stretched across the doorway, Jenny began praying. She prayed for God not to allow the autopsy. And she stayed in her position, crying and praying, until someone finally came and granted her request. There would be no autopsy.

Jenny and I lost touch some years ago, being separated by the miles. When last I spoke with her, she said that the only reason she didn't kill herself (and thereby join her precious son in heaven) was because she had another child. She feared that, because of that child, her suicide would be frowned upon by God and she would not be allowed in heaven with her Timothy. Other than that, her husband and living child didn't matter to her. Last I heard she was spending most of her time in the cemetery talking to her dead son.

The point of this awful story is not to minimize, in any way, the agony that poor woman went through. The point is that, when it was all over, Jenny cried triumphant tears of joy as she told me how grateful she was that God had answered her prayers. The cancellation of the autopsy was unequivocal proof that God answers prayers, and she would not let go of the subject until I agreed with her. I agreed with her. But even if I had been callous enough to disagree, I would not have known what to say. I was too dumbfounded.

Jenny was positively exultant in her "proof" that God answers prayers. It never occurred to her that the hospital staff was seeking to end an ugly scene and thwart a possible lawsuit. No, in Jenny's mind, God had intervened. It had been a miracle. Faith like that is frightening to behold in its irrational fierceness.

Jenny's wonderful God, who had answered her heartbreaking

prayers about the autopsy, had, for some reason, not thought it preferable to answer her (or anyone else's) heartbreaking prayers about the chemotherapy. Or the surgery itself. Or, for that matter, her daily prayers to keep her beloved son healthy and happy before his illness ever occurred. Not seeing this glaringly obvious point is what blind faith is all about.

Jenny was displaying an extreme form of the sort of rationalization that is necessary to reconcile a benevolent God with a cruel world. Even knowing that thousands of the world's children die of starvation every day, True Believers see nothing wrong with $3-million-per-year football players asking for, and receiving, God's intervention to influence the outcome of a game. Likewise, in offering a silent prayer during a lengthy search for, say, a wallet, a believer has no doubt that his prayer has been answered when he finally finds it. It never occurs to him how absurd and inappropriate such a use of godly power would be.

True Believers will chuckle with disdain and condescension, and ask how our ancestors could have believed in volcano worship, for instance. They don't realize that we rationalists are asking that very thing about True Believers. Mystical, magical thinking is always the same no matter which century or which country it occurs in.

Believers cannot tolerate the certainty and serenity of those of us who acknowledge no god and no spirit world, just as Jenny could not tolerate mine. A few years ago, an essay of mine was published in a local newspaper. In a responding letter to the editor, a Christian pointed out that I had a belief system because I believed in not believing. I am not making this up. Irrational as it is, it demonstrates the threat believers feel when confronting nonbelievers. The very serenity of nonbelievers is what unnerves believers, because it effectively challenges their supernatural, always-difficult-to-explain beliefs.

One of the best ways for True Believers to defend their indefensible claims is to have the state give those beliefs some sort of stamp of approval. This is what we're witnessing whenever the Religious Right pushes for public-school prayer, the public posting of the Ten Commandments, and so on. Insecure fundamentalists challenge the separation of church and state *because* of their insecurity.

Perhaps life *would* be easier if there were a god—one single, easy-to-recognize, worldwide god. It would certainly end all of this UFO, numerology, reincarnation, and astrology stuff. And it might make life a more soothing experience all the way around. But then, come to think of it, I guess that's why we invented gods in the first place, isn't it?

There are doubtless thousands of stories similar to the one about my friend Jenny. You probably have to pause for only a moment to think of one—not necessarily as tragic, but equally illogical in assigning cause to effect. Even if you are a believer, you must admit that when you have prayed for the really big things—an end to a metastasizing cancer, or peace in the Middle East—your success rate is almost nil, yet you never blame God. But when you pray for the smaller things—passing a test in school, a safe airplane landing—and they happen, you immediately credit God for them. This is not only illogical, but opens the door for experiments that can "prove" the power of almost anything. I conducted just such an experiment.

The parameters were simple. When I wished for something to happen which, in my Christian years, would have prompted a prayer, I decided instead to rub the tummy of a stuffed animal, in this case a penguin. This was no ordinary stuffed animal, mind you. This was given to me by a very special person for a very special reason. I would close my eyes, think intently about the problem, and rub the penguin's belly. It was a most interesting exercise. It brought back memories of praying, and I realized that at this point in my life the two activities seem equally sane and equally silly.

Anyway, I kept this up for about three weeks, and here are the results: My penguin failed to bring peace to the Middle East or Northern Ireland; world hunger was not eliminated; inner-city drug dealing did not disappear; and a beloved, ill, elderly dog died in spite of my actions.

However, on the positive side, my Grand Penguin lowered the crime rate in a major city; ended a UPS strike; reunited a married couple on the brink of divorce; cleared up a friend's sinus infection; and helped another friend find much-needed employment. I'd certainly call that remarkable. So then, what's to be learned from my efforts? Well, if you're allowed to count only the "hits" while ignoring the "misses," as do all the people who extol the power of prayer, then it turns out that my fuzzy little penguin is one hell of a miracle worker.

Try as they might, True Believers have left so much unexplained that it is an impossible task to look at all the world's religions and try to separate the wheat from the chaff. I'm afraid it's all chaff.

SALT LAKE CITY, June 9—The Southern Baptist Convention (SBC) released its official interpretation of the New Testament admonishment instructing wives to submit to their husbands. The formal announcement stated, "Wives must *graciously* submit themselves to their husband in *all things*. This includes who controls the thermostat, who has charge of the remote control, and who has to refold the map so it will fit back in the glove box. It also includes cleaning up pet poop."

"The key to understanding the directive," explained a Baptist representative, "is the qualifier *all things*. For example, if a husband wants his wife to mud wrestle, naked, with a llama, she is bound by heavenly mandate to oblige him. Likewise, if he wants her to fetch Frisbees on the front lawn, she is equally obligated." The proclamation goes on to emphasize that the directive is in no way intended to be demeaning to women.

As to the exact definition of "graciously," there has been widespread controversy within the Convention. Some insist it means obeying each male whim with a sincere smile frozen on one's face, while others claim that only the actions themselves are important. If the latter is true, then under-the-breath muttering through gritted teeth would technically not be a violation of the "graciously" part of the mandate. Further debate is expected. The terms "genuflect,"

"Lord and Master," and "ass kissing" were edited out of the first draft, over much protest.

In a related story, Southern Baptists are waging an "evangelical Blitz" in Salt Lake City to "convert those damn Mormons." And James Wibley has been hired by the Southern Baptists to "convert those damn Jews." Wibley maintains that both the Mormons and the Jews have been "led astray." Said Wibley, "It's not that we view the Mormons and the Jews as our enemies. It's just that everything they believe is a bunch of bullshit and it is our job to set them straight." Wibley cited the modern idea of "Dual-Covenant Theology." "Both Christians and Jews have an equal and valid pact with God," explained Wibley. "It's just that the Jews are wrong."

Leonard Simon, spokesman for the Anti-Defamation League of B'nai B'rith, expressed outrage over the SBC statements. "Our Jewish heritage is ancient and has stood the test of time," he growled. "We were observing Passover before Baptists were even a gleam in their great-grandfathers' eyes! So to speak."

When asked what his position was on Catholics, Muslims, Hindus and Buddhists, SBC's Wibley groaned, "Jesus! Gimme a break, will you?! One errant, muddle-headed, blasphemous religion at a time!"

On the Mormon front, at a joint press conference in Salt Lake City, Wayne Higgins of the SBC and Orville Tweed of the Church of Jesus Christ of Latter-day Saints squared off in a war of words. "What can we say other than Mormons have their heads up their wazoos," said Higgins. An irate Tweed replied, "Oh, yeah? Well, all Baptists are dickheads!" At that, Higgins made a lunge for Tweed but was restrained by colleagues.

After more heated words were exchanged, the two finally opted for pistols at dawn, one week from Tuesday, in Temple Square. Tickets for the event are now on sale at Ticketron, and include a complimentary beverage. Kids under eighteen must be accompanied by an adult.

© *The Heretical News*

In June 1998 the Southern Baptist Convention really *did* issue the "submit graciously to your husbands" edict, and most of the world laughed out loud.[4] Such blatant misogyny, which abounds in the Bible, is awkward enough to deal with, but to blare it out through a bullhorn is just plain stupid. Of course I'm personally tickled that they did it. They only validated their harshest critics. Like me.

In addition, the Southern Baptists really *did* launch an "evangelical blitz" to convert Mormons, and James Sibley's title within the SBC actually was "coordinator of Jewish Ministries for the North American Mission Board's interfaith evangelism team."[5] The SBC, in an unabashed display of arrogant condescension, produced a videotape, "The Mormon Puzzle," that attacks Mormon theology as non-Christian. And an article in one of their magazines asks, "How can a false religion be so successful?"[6]

Such doctrinal wrangling only gives credence to the question, "Are *all* religions false?" Because if the Mormons are right, the Jews and the Baptists are wrong. If the Jews are right, then the Mormons and Baptists are wrong. And so on. You could follow through with this line of reasoning, making sure to include *all* the world's religions, *past and present*, and, like a nuclear chain reaction, you'd soon reach critical mass and the whole concept of religious "truth" would melt down into a murky puddle of myths. Enter the Internet.

The Internet is having an amazing impact on religion, and religions are not happy about it. They are having a much more difficult time hiding their dirty laundry. Child-molesting priests are being ferreted out like earwigs under a wet rock. The "submit graciously" thing swept around the world in a flash and was met with worldwide derision. News travels *fast* on the Internet. And it is this very speed of communication that may soon spell big trouble for religions. Why?

Consider how religions began and how they spread. Mainly they traveled no faster that humans could walk, or at most a horse's canter. Human migrations were at a snail's pace. For most of human history, in most parts of the world, villagers were born and lived and died without ever traveling more than ten or twenty miles from home—most not even that far. Oceans, mountain ranges, and mere miles kept people apart, and that very isolation reinforced local religious beliefs. No one was exposed to anything different, everyone believed what everyone else believed, and this went on for centuries. When cultures finally did collide the result was usually war. History is a depressing, dreary litany of wars. Humans are basically conservative and don't like sudden, extreme change. We fight back when we meet something alien.

But now think about how quickly all that is changing. In just one decade home computers have spread like wildfire. In just the last few years the Internet has changed human communication in an almost incomprehensible way. When I started my own domain, *The Happy Heretic*, in 1997, my husband bet me that in that first year I would hear from ten different countries outside the United States. I laughed at him, I really did. And he *was* wrong. It was forty. I have been in touch with people from all over the world—people that I otherwise never would have heard from. It would not have been simply unlikely; it would have been impossible.

Now if you apply this breathtaking speed and ease of communication to religion, it gets a bit dicey for religious leaders to keep their flocks controlled. It's much harder now to claim that you have sole access to the ear of the One True God. There are just too many One True Gods out there, and they're all bumping into each other on the Internet. *And our children are watching the collisions.* This, I believe, may spell the beginning of the end of many religions. It is also, in my opinion, the reason for the pope's tenacious insistence on archaic doctrine, the Southern Baptists' asinine submission thing, Baptists trying to convert Mormons and Jews, and the rather desperate attempt by Roman Catholics and Lutherans to show a "united" front.[7] They're circling the wagons.

Religions can no longer ignore each other, but at the same time they don't know how to act when they're thrown together in a way they've never been thrown together before. Ever. The Internet spotlight is glaring and illuminating, and young Net surfers will not so easily settle for a pat on the head and, "Don't you worry about what

Jimmy says. Just listen to Mommy and Daddy." Well, Mom and Dad now have to explain far more than "what Jimmy says." It's sort of like free trade—except that it's religious beliefs that are now easily available for careful scrutiny by any and all. Religious leaders are now going to have to crack the whip a little harder to keep their flocks intact. The natives are getting restless.

Wishing is sometimes fun. But wishing has never accomplished anything. In order to make this a better world, we need to *do* something about it, not just wish for things to change. And when you close your eyes, fold your hands, and offer silent prayers to an invisible, unknowable God, it is simply wishful thinking. If prayer really worked, there wouldn't be a war or a starving child or a terminally ill human being anywhere on earth. Sadly, we know that none of that is true.

However, working together, I believe we *can* make the world a better place. If we redirect all the energy, compassion, and *money* that is currently being expended on religious practices, and instead devote it all to the betterment of humankind, just imagine what we could accomplish! Hunger, overpopulation (closely related problems), war, and disease may never disappear altogether; but by taking our heads out of the clouds and pitting our considerable talents against such obstacles, we could, without a doubt, improve the lives of millions for the foreseeable future.

Children make wishes before blowing out the candles on their birthday cakes. But in trying to improve the human condition, surely we can do better than that!

NOTES

1. "India's Shame," *Nation*, April 8, 1996, p. 11.
2. "Six Cents an Hour," *Life*, June 1996, p. 38.
3. Ibid.

4. Caryle Murphy, "A Gathering Full of Purpose: Baptists Put Mormons, Marriage on Agenda," *Washington Post*, June 6, 1998, p. B9.

5. "Jim Sibley," *Baptist Press* [online], www.sbc.net/ [April 9, 1999].

6. Murphy, "A Gathering Full of Purpose."

7. "Religion: Catholics, Lutherans Reach Fundamental Accord," Microsoft® Encarta® Encyclopedia, June 1999.

2

THE REAL
ROMAN EMPIRE

*There was never a century nor a country that was short of experts
who knew the Deity's mind and were willing to reveal it.*
—Mark Twain, "As Concerns Interpreting the Deity"

THE WEARING O' THE GREEN

THE GOD OF MY YOUTH was a Lutheran God,
A Triune; a proper three-seater;
And unlike the Catholics (mere Pagans in drag)
We *knew* not to worship St. Peter!

Of course they had Mary, a *virgin* no less,
With halo, and angels to greet her;
She'd decorate pageants, parades, and revues—
At Christmas you just couldn't beat her.

St. Patrick was also their private domain,
With Shamrocks and booze by the liter;
I'd wear my orange ribbon (my envy pure green)—
Drab Luther was *not* a compete-er!

53

Though saint-less and pope-less, we knew we were right,
And this made our Fridays much sweeter;
While they choked on fish bones (filleted their own souls),
I gloated, a true hot-dog eater!

The Church reigned supreme, though, for hundreds of years,
Though Protestants tried to unseat Her;
The torrents of blood that were spilled in the quest
Were still not enough to defeat Her.

So few now remember the Orange and the Green—
The Church's dark stains that precede Her;
Instead mugs are hoisted on St. Patty's Day,
As celebrants totter and teeter.

But kindness and tolerance must win the day!
Avoid every bigotry breeder!
Beliefs can be challenged, but folks are still folks—
Though most still play Follow-the-Leader.

So let's lighten up on this St. Patty's Eve—
Consider my thoughts in this meter;
I'll raise my own glass in a toast to us all—
I hope you'll do likewise, dear reader!

Well, I was certainly in a good mood when I wrote that. It's an odd mixture of lampooning and pathos. There's room in this world for both, of course. But history is generally a grim little teacher. And the history of the papacy is no exception.

The pope is perhaps the most respected man in the world. Whether or not he deserves such respect is a matter of opinion. He wields enormous power, both spiritual and worldly. When he talks, people listen. By extension, the papacy is considered to be one of the most respectable of institutions, worthy of veneration. This is not a matter of opinion. It is simply false.

According to the Roman Catholic Church, for example, Pope

John Paul II is the 263rd pontiff. But that number is meaningless. It is no more than a rough estimate. The papal claim of twenty centuries of precise successions, the papal scepter passing from one hand to another, like runners handing off a baton in a relay race, is wholly misleading. On no less than twenty different occasions, from the third century right on through the fifteenth, there were concurrent, rival claimants to that most holy high office. More than once there were three different "popes" all claiming, simultaneously, to be the real McCoy, the genuine article. In the twelfth century there were five of them battling it out at the same time, each with his own staunch supporters. So it can be stated with certainty that today's papal authority can legitimately be traced to . . . no one.

A thorough study of the history of the papacy is an astonishing, mind-boggling assortment of murder, thievery, adultery, ruthless power struggles, licentiousness, and just about every form of immorality imaginable. There are some nice men and good deeds here and there that help to remind you that you are reading about *popes*. Overall, though, the track record of the papacy is very unsavory.

In the year 930, Pope Steven VIII had his ears and nose cut off by his furious followers. In 964, Benedict V raped a young girl and then ran away—with the entire treasury of St. Peter's in tow. He was eventually killed by a jealous husband. Steven VII (896–897) dug up the corpse of one of his papal predecessors and proceeded to charge the corpse with becoming pope under false pretenses. The corpse had been buried for nine months. Steven nevertheless dressed it in full pontifical regalia and carried out a formal trial on the dreadful remains. The remains were found guilty and thrown in the Tiber River. Steven was later strangled.

Pope Boniface VIII took office in 1294. At one point he included among his mistresses a married woman and her own daughter. Most popes in the early centuries had mistresses and some had wives. It was no secret. Clement VI (1342) was known for his amorous adventures, but at least he *did* finally legitimize all his children. In 1501, with his son, Cesare, and daughter, Lucrezia, Pope Alexander VI (a Borgia) attended a festival called "The Joust of the Whores." Fifty of Rome's finest prostitutes danced naked while His Holinesss and His Holiness's children threw them chestnuts.[1] Sounds like a wholesome family outing.

There is so much more, but the point has been made. The hands that passed the Holy Scepter were dirty indeed.

Even today popes and bishops can say and do things so utterly out of step with the times, so incomprehensible, that you wonder what could possibly be motivating their actions. Nineteen ninety-eight produced two notable stories that seemed to come right out of a previous century.

POPE SHOOTS SELF IN FOOT; BISHOP REALLY SHOOTS HIMSELF

VATICAN CITY, July 1—Using a .22 Ruger, Pope John Paul II scored a bull's-eye with a through-and-through wound at the base of the middle toe of his left foot. In a stunningly medieval, unenlightened Apostolic Letter titled "In Order to Defend the Faith," the pontiff carved into stone via Canon Law the bans on birth control, women priests, voluntary euthanasia, and teaching mynah birds to talk. Asked about the birds, John Paul replied, "The power of speech is God's precious gift to man alone. The mynah is just a dumb bird." But when asked if the ban then also applied to parrots, the pontiff snapped, "Of course not! Those birds are incredible! They talk better than most people!"

Chastened by the papal outburst, no one dared ask about parakeets. But an inside source at the Vatican said that budgies would be exempt from the ban because, "In the first place, they aren't mynahs, are they?! And in the second place, those crummy little birds are so hard to understand nobody cares." The penance for mynah bird training will be fifteen Hail Marys and the ritual sacrifice by fire of the offending feathered vocalist.

Catholic bird lovers were shocked by the news. "I love my little Pee-Wee!" lamented one bird owner. "And he already knows how to talk! So why should I have to kill him now? It isn't fair!" Others were more resigned to their fate. "If it's God's will," sighed Charles Sangretti, "then so be it. I am a good Catholic. But I have over a dozen mynahs. It's gonna be one hell of a bonfire."

ISLAMABAD, May 7—A Roman Catholic bishop and prominent animal rights defender fatally shot himself to protest the death sentence on talking mynah birds. Bishop Sans Sensé, chairman of an animal rights commission established by the Catholic Bishop Conference of Pakistan, shot himself in the head Wednesday with a pistol while holding a mynah bird in the other hand. Unfortunately, the bird was squashed to death in the process.

Hundreds of Christians gathered outside the courthouse in Islamabad, while hundreds of others held a candlelight vigil outside the local Society for the Prevention of Cruelty to Animals. They chanted, "Words for birds! Words for birds!" Many mynahs also participated in the chanting.

Sensé had previously gone on a hunger strike as part of an American protest against forcing salmon to climb fish ladders. "If I won't speak out for the salmon, who will?" he is quoted as saying. When his actions proved successful and salmon were no longer forced to climb the ladders, Sensé ended his hunger strike with a dinner that featured a tossed green salad, a twice-baked potato, and salmon amandine.

© *The Heretical News*

Catholic Bishop John Joseph really *did* commit suicide in Pakistan to protest a death sentence pronounced on a fellow Christian, and it is not a funny thing.[2] But what prods people to do such ghastly things in the name of religion? I mean no disrespect toward Bishop Joseph or his memory, but I have nothing but furious contempt for religions that push people to such tragic extremes. Joseph killed himself to protest the death sentence against a Christian for blaspheming Islam. The irony is overwhelming. But it all boils down to oppressive, restrictive religious doctrines—both Islamic and Catholic. Will they never go away? We must crawl out of the Middle Ages where death and religion were so gruesomely intertwined.

Likewise, Pope John Paul II really *did* change Canon Law the way I described it.[3] Except for the mynah birds. The policies aren't new, but they had not been enshrined in Canon Law. Now they are. Canon Law has been changed only a few times in recent centuries. So John Paul decided to go down in history by changing it like this. Some legacy. The church treats married women like breeding machines. It seems it has an absolute vendetta against progress. Since the earth is already groaning under the weight of its overflowing human cargo, the enshrinement of the birth control ban is nothing short of criminal and is unforgivably irresponsible.

This stiffening of already inflexible policies only increases dissension, especially among liberal theologians. And for once I'm pulling for dissension. I hope this affirmation of medieval bigotry causes irreparable rifts in this behemoth known as the Catholic Church, this archaic shrine to intolerance.

Still, now and again the Roman Catholic hierarchy does something that is just plain silly.

In 1997, the National Conference of Catholic Bishops Pro-Life Committee proposed reinstating meatless Fridays as a means of improving the "penitence" of the faithful among their flock.[4] The reason American Catholics are supposed to do Friday penance in the first place stems from their belief that Jesus was murdered in Palestine on a Friday afternoon around two thousand years ago. They believe that Jesus died for their sins, and in response they have sardine sandwiches for lunch on Friday. Makes perfect sense to me.

But I am having trouble understanding the nature of this kind of atonement. I don't understand how you can be considered a proper penitent if you have Campbell's clam chowder for lunch, but a sinful backslider if you have the chicken noodle. (Actually, I think the clam chowder is much better.)

Nevertheless, according to the Catholic powers that be, the following Friday menu plan could theoretically represent that of a sincere, penitent, observant Catholic:

> *Breakfast*: fresh-squeezed orange juice, lox, bagel and cream cheese, and half of a honeydew melon filled with strawberries.
> *Midmorning snack*: cinnamon roll or jelly doughnut.
> *Lunch*: Trout Amandine, rice pilaf, stuffed artichoke salad, and whole wheat rolls.
> *Dessert*: raspberry sorbet or lemon meringue pie.
> *Hors d'oeuvres*: imported Norwegian pickled herring on rye crackers; or oysters on the half shell; or cashews and smoked almonds; or all of it, if the trout has worn off.
> *Dinner*: shrimp cocktail, Caesar salad, Lobster Thermidor, stuffed mushrooms, and twice-baked potatoes.
> *Dessert*: Baked Alaska, Boston Cream Pie, or Napoleon Pastry.

Some people would not call this fasting.

I remember when I was a young, pious Missouri Synod Lutheran, some of my young, pious Catholic friends would eat meals almost as sumptuous as the above, and preen shamelessly about their piety in doing so. My scorn knew no bounds. Of course, I was privileged to belong to the One True Religion, so I naturally had the right to view the whole thing with condescending disdain. Now, as I look back, I have to ask myself if others looked on me as a smug, self-righteous pain in the ass. I somehow think the answer to that is yes.

Anyway, the bishops said that if Catholics would have meatless Fridays, it would give them a way to "publicly display their penitence." Agreed. Nothing can make you feel more penitential than eating oysters on the half shell—especially in the wrong month. Of course, if you ate these Friday penitential meals on a regular basis you'd rightly be called a glutton and the numbers on your bathroom scale would soon soar into the stratosphere. I think there's a paradox in there somewhere. "Abstaining" and obesity somehow don't go together.

Cardinal Bernard Law of Boston (do you suppose he liked the cream pie?) expressed regret that Catholics may be losing sight of the importance of being penitential "since the obligation of abstinence on Friday was removed." Say, could we please define this "abstinence?" The first definition in my dictionary says that it is a noun meaning "The act or practice of refraining from indulging an appetite, as for food." Look again at the above menu. It would be allowable under the proposed meatless Friday rules, but it positively *defines* indulging.

Cardinal Adam Maida of Detroit proudly referred to his childhood, when his Friday staples were potato soup and potato pancakes. Whoa! This is starvation on a masochistic scale! Those pancakes really leave your tummy grumbling, don't they? And Monsignor Lorenzo Albacete of New York "pointed to his portly shape" and admitted he should probably be eating more fish. No, Lorenzo. You should be pushing your portly shape away from the table sooner, and donating the (undoubtedly generous portions of) uneaten food to the poor.

Supposedly the Friday meat ban is intended to help Catholics express their opposition to, among other things, "war, violence, and drugs." Works for me. Stuff yourself with fish-and-chips and you're promoting peace and nonviolence. Where do they *get* this stuff?

On the rare occasions when the Catholic Church changes its rules, it really confuses things. When hell awaits, you at least want to be playing by the right set of rules. The Friday meat ban was cancelled back in the 1960s, but as the irrepressible George Carlin observed in the 1970s, (and I'm paraphrasing), "There are still people in hell doing time on a meat rap. Can you imagine going to hell for a hot dog?" Likewise, the Catholic "limbo," the supposedly eternal resting place of unbaptized babies, was "cancelled," though it's difficult to imagine how one goes about canceling an eternal resting place. Limbo was apparently somewhere between heaven and hell. Referring to this cancellation, Carlin wryly commented, "I sure hope everyone got promoted."

Jerry Pokorsky, a priest from Virginia, said that reinstating meatless Fridays would be "a beautiful expression of our solidarity with the unborn." *Solidarity with the unborn?* I think he's got this one all wrong. If you want to express your solidarity with the unborn, you go for the caviar. Now fish eggs make sense. Tiny, salty, unborn fish eggs would at least be symbolically correct. And what could possibly be a more self-sacrificing, more humble act of self-deprivation than to indulge in imported Russian caviar?

The sad thing about all this foolishness is that instead of worrying about whether to have filet mignon or broiled lobster for dinner, we should all be worrying about the millions of the world's children who go to bed at night after having had nothing at all for dinner. Starvation is a very real issue. Inexcusably, forty thousand of the world's children under the age of five die *every day* from starvation, easily preventable diseases, and neglect.[5] And what are the portly priests doing about it? They are threatening Catholic parents with eternal damnation if they try to limit their children to a number they can feed and care for. The Catholic position on this is unshakable, unyielding, and utterly cruel: If the babies starve, they starve; so be it. It's no skin off those portly, priestly, Catholic bellies.

As a humanist, I find this reprehensible. But what do we do about it? Many in the humanist movement complain that we spend too much time criticizing religion instead of promoting humanism. The problem with that complaint is that it's almost impossible to do the latter without also doing the former. When an institution as powerful as the Roman Catholic Church *causes* so much avoidable human misery, how can we humanists not criticize that? Overpopulation is one of the world's biggest problems, but Catholicism refuses to budge on birth control. This is inexcusable, and the suffering will never end until their monstrous, archaic policies are abolished. And that's never going to happen until the harsh spotlight of reason and compassion illuminates their cruel practices. But someone's got to focus that spotlight. And, of course, that focusing is known as religious criticism.

A SCIENTIST AND A SAINT

Nineteen ninety-six and 1997 witnessed the deaths of Carl Sagan and Mother Teresa. Sagan was given a respectful and dignified farewell by the media. His admirers all over the world were heartsick at his loss. I was one of those. Agnes Gonxha Bojaxhiu (aka Mother Teresa) commanded worldwide front pages for ten straight days, with extensive coverage by almost every syndicated columnist in addition to those front pages. Television news was no less tenacious in filling our screens with images of Mother Teresa's face. A good rough estimate would be that Teresa's death received about ten times more publicity than did Sagan's. Society needs to reevaluate its priorities.

If ever there have been giants among us, Carl Sagan was one of them. Almost single-handedly, and with considerable resistance from his own peers, he changed the face of science. He rescued the wonders of science from their obscure, arcane, fiercely defended citadels, and presented them to the whole world, for us to examine and admire. He gave us back the magic.

More than anyone in recent memory, Sagan fired our imaginations in a way that made space exploration, and our general contemplation of our place in the cosmos, an understandable, exciting undertaking. We looked upward at the stars and thought, really *thought*, about them—many of us for the first time ever. The possibility of life elsewhere in the universe was no longer the exclusive domain of science fiction. We were all treated to a wondrously new, breathtaking view of the universe, finally shaken free of its musty cobwebs and incomprehensible jargon. Sagan dusted off the universe and lovingly placed it in our hands.

Comparing Carl Sagan to Mother Teresa is perhaps unfair, and perhaps a case of apples and oranges. But I do so only to emphasize our persistent, and dangerous, reliance on things ancient and utterly useless in today's world. Sagan looked ahead with a brilliance and wisdom that few of us will ever achieve. Teresa looked only backward, to a time when witches were deemed real and exorcisms eminently sensible. We can no longer afford to look backward.

I do wonder what superstitious, demon-fearing, cemetery-avoiding True Believer coined the saying, "Never speak ill of the dead." Why shouldn't we? If you're going to speak ill of anyone, wouldn't it be better to target someone dead rather than someone alive who might be hurt by it? I am informed that the reasoning is that the dead aren't here to defend themselves. Does this mean we should not speak ill of Hitler, Stalin, Ivan the Terrible, Ted Bundy, and so on because they're not here to "defend themselves?" No, that argument is a transparent attempt to conceal the real reason for the old adage—the fear that the ghost of the maligned deceased will come back to haunt you. That is the true origin of that bit of super-stition. However, since I have no fears about being stalked by Mother Teresa's supposedly ethereal, eternal essence, I shall speak my mind.

The spectacle of the obsequious, worldwide eulogizing of Mother Teresa was a humanist's nightmare. Reporters fell all over themselves as they raced for microphones and searched for superla-tives to describe this bland, head-in-the-clouds Macedonian with a ninth-century mentality. While mourners gushed sentimentally, cheered by the expectation of sainthood, the whole thing gave me, like many others I'm sure, a monumental headache. What mis-placed, ardent idolization!

We love our heroes, and there's probably nothing wrong with that. But how we go about nominating people for "hero-dom" is very important. Few would nominate Charles Manson, for example, and that's nice to know. But Mother Teresa, while certainly no Manson, most certainly was responsible for far more deaths than he ever was, to the tune of thousands more. The little bit of good she did was overwhelmingly dwarfed by the incalculable harm she did.

Our population figures are not yet hopeless, but if we continue at our insane growth rate, they soon may be. The earth's resources are finite, notwithstanding the Catholic Church's ostrich position, and we must look ahead, using every scientific tool at our disposal, to avert the looming catastrophe. That includes the fairly easily employed practice of birth control. The amount of suffering that could be prevented by this one practice alone is immeasurable. So we can not and must not look back, bowing our heads in futile prayers, while our children die.

Our future, if we are to have one at all, depends on our recognition of the undeniable threats now facing civilization. Our population crisis, one of the most dire of those threats, is very real, very pressing, and in need of global attention *now*. It is not simply a theoretical possibility that our continued growth rate will doom millions to horrible deaths. It is a certainty. If we do not halt our exponential growth, nature will do it for us, and starvation will be the means used.

Mother Teresa's trite cliché about how "God will provide" is an insult to thinking people. If there is a God who is able to provide for humanity, he has certainly proved that he's not willing to do so. Every day more little ones die . . .

Teresa also said, "I think it is very beautiful for the poor to accept their lot . . . the world is being much helped by the suffering of the poor people."[6] I find this obscene. So much for compassion. When asked to agree that there were too many children in India, she answered, "I do not agree because God always provides."[7] Really? Regarding world peace she said, "Today, abortion is the worst evil, and the greatest enemy of peace."[8] This is simply inane. If anyone can explain how voluntary abortion is a threat to world peace, I'm ready to listen.

Teresa's dogged, single-focused vocation as a Roman Catholic missionary directed her every move. She trained her workers to ask dying patients if they would like a "ticket to heaven" and a positive response prompted a speedy baptism into Roman Catholicism.[9] She preached relentlessly against birth control even though surrounded by starving children.[10]

Compare that outlook to Dr. Sagan's: "If the world is to escape the direst consequences of global population growth . . . we must invent safe but more efficient means of growing food. . . . It will also take widely available and acceptable contraception, significant steps toward political equality of women, and improvements in the standards of living of the poorest people."[11]

While Teresa prattled on about a providing God, 423 million

people in "her" India were living in absolute poverty, 73.1 million children under five were malnourished,[12] and the number of illiterates was 350 million.[13] Said Sagan: "The gears of poverty, ignorance, hopelessness, and low self-esteem mesh to create a kind of perpetual failure machine that grinds down dreams from generation to generation. We all bear the cost of keeping it running. Illiteracy is its linchpin."[14]

Eschewing strong painkillers (why?!) Mother Teresa told a dying patient in the agonizing last stages of cancer, "You are suffering like Christ on the cross. So Jesus must be kissing you." To which the patient reportedly replied, "Then please tell him to stop kissing me."[15] Said Sagan: "The world is so exquisite, with so much love and moral depth, that there is no reason to deceive ourselves with pretty stories for which there's little good evidence."[16]

When people were speculating about sainthood for Teresa, there was much discussion about proof of miracles, a requirement for sainthood. But I say there is *definite* proof of at least one miracle. And that is that she managed to convince millions of people that she was a good thing for humanity. Her medieval practices were packaged and sold as a boon to humankind, instead of the hindering, progress-impeding things that they were.

While her "patients" were given little or no care, she herself, when ill, checked into some of the costliest hospitals in the world.[17] Hypocrisy, anyone? And of course her incessant parroting of the Catholic position that birth control is "unnatural" makes you want to pound your own forehead. *Of course it's unnatural.* So is operating on a ruptured appendix. Or having a pacemaker implanted in your heart, as Mother Teresa did in 1989.[18] And having surgery to clear a blocked blood vessel is likewise unnatural, though Teresa had that unnatural thing done to her in 1993.[19] *Unambiguous* hypocrisy, anyone?

Sainthood means nothing at all to humanists. Mythical blue ribbons on your chest in a mythical afterlife sounds a bit like a glorified Girl Scout troop handing out merit badges. But I, personally, can find nothing about Mother Teresa's life or memory to revere, in light of the suffering she helped to create for untold millions.

In stark contrast, the solid contributions to knowledge in general and science specifically that Carl Sagan offered were of unarguable benefit to untold millions. It is probably impossible to estimate the number of people who were inspired and encouraged by Sagan's infectious enthusiasm for the wonders of science. Like some sort of Pied Piper, he led us joyously along the pathway to knowledge about the natural world. And we followed happily in droves!

There really are billions *and billions* (too many billions!) of people on earth. But there was only one Carl Sagan. And when we speak of him, we are talking about *greatness*. We moved ahead leaps and bounds just because of this one genius. I fear we will have to wait a very long time indeed before we again see the likes of Carl Sagan. The world is a sadder, more impoverished place without him, while at the same time being enriched for his existence. His memory is deserving of the utmost reverence and respect. Of course he will never be made a "saint," nor would he have wanted it.

However, if the word "saint" may be allowed its secular, compassionate meaning as a true benefactor of humankind; someone who gave to the world so very much more than he took from it— then Carl Sagan, patron and purveyor of knowledge, reason, and kindness, is the walk-away winner in this two-horse race.

DEFENDING MOTHER TERESA

They say that imitation is the most sincere form of flattery. But when it comes to writing anything controversial, your success can probably be judged by the caliber of your critics. So I'm flattered.

Clark Morphew, syndicated columnist for Knight-Ridder, took aim at the winter 1998 issue of *Free Inquiry* magazine because of two articles it contained that were highly critical of the late Mother Teresa.[20] One was written by Susan Shields, a former Missionaries of Charity sister who worked with Teresa. Shields revealed that part of her job was to help keep track of the millions of dollars donated to Teresa's "charity" work. Unfortunately, most of that money sat unused in various bank accounts while the sisters literally had to beg for food from local merchants, since "poverty" is supposedly a virtue. If the locals couldn't help out, the soup kitchens did without. This is charity? With millions sitting idle and Teresa constantly asking for more donations, it makes no sense at all. Apparently Shields thought so too.

The other article was written by me. Morphew was obviously upset with the articles, but his defense of Teresa was surprisingly halfhearted and ambivalent. In his opening paragraph Morphew predicted that criticism of Teresa will continue until "some serious reform comes about." But if Teresa's generously financed clinics were running smoothly, honestly, and compassionately, why would any reform be needed at all? Likewise, after describing Shields's knowledgeable charges about the idle millions of dollars that helped no one, Morphew suggested that since Sister Nirmala had taken over the reigns as Teresa's successor, "grand changes could happen." Again, why should they, unless something was wrong to begin with?

Seeming to want it both ways, Morphew presented Teresa as "one of the most obvious candidates for sainthood," but then conceded that among Teresa's beliefs were the ideas that suffering is *good* and that despite staggering overpopulation, birth control is always wrong. He also noted that wiping out poverty and illiteracy was not Teresa's focus. If all of that is true, it places Teresa somewhere between sadistic and stupid. (Which, interestingly, is where "saint" appears in the dictionary.) I have never heard of a compassionate person who thought that human suffering was ever a *good* thing, and you'd think compassion would be the bare minimum to expect in anyone being considered for "sainthood."

Morphew also pointed out that Teresa "never pretended to be a doctor who could wipe out or even soften the pain of death." This I challenge fervently. So too would the *Columbia University Press Encyclopedia* in which it is written about Teresa: "In 1948 she left the convent and founded the Missionaries of Charity, which now operates schools, hospitals, orphanages, and food centers in more than 25 countries."[21] How would Morphew define "hospital?"

There is no ambiguity whatsoever about the activities Teresa presented to the world as hers. The problem is that what she said she was doing was not what she was doing.

If Teresa was offering spiritual comfort *only*, and not trying to "soften the pain of death," (and why on earth not?!) there should have been no drugs dispensed and no drug paraphernalia of any kind on hand at her "clinics." But there were. Her employees and volunteers used and reused unsterilized syringes to administer ineffective drugs and mild antibiotics to terminally ill people, who suffered the resulting agonies. This is called practicing medicine, and why such malpractice was allowed to go on so long, with no legal challenges, highlights the power—and abuse of power—that is vouchsafed to organized religions. Especially the big ones with a lot of money.

But if, as Morphew asserted, Mother Teresa never intended to offer medical care to the ill, feed the poor, or educate the illiterate, but rather planned only to offer spiritual solace to dying people, then at the very least she was a fraud. Those millions of dollars were donated by caring people to offer medical care to the ill, feed the poor, and educate the illiterate—not to sit in bank accounts earning interest for the Roman Catholic Church, which has been a multibillion-dollar enterprise for decades now. And there are laws about raising charitable contributions for one thing and then using the money for another—as Teresa did. Apparently her goal was to hoard the money, like Midas and his gold. To what end, though, is anybody's guess.

There is a disquieting possibility, however, that presents itself in hindsight. Teresa collected her millions of dollars "in the name of God" and then promptly hid them away like a squirrel readying for winter. She also converted souls "in the name of God," many just before they expired. Was she keeping a rough tally of those souls? I wonder if, in her simplistic view of things, anything she did for God would earn her big-time brownie points in the afterlife. For her, perhaps, this world had no meaning whatsoever, and was just some sort of challenging religious maze, designed by God to determine who gets the best bits of paradise. If so, it might explain, since *nothing else can*, how she could be so callous as to sit on those millions of dollars while children, even in her own part of India, were dying of starvation. This defies rational explanation, and I challenge anyone, from Morphew to the pope himself, to explain it.

A friend of mine tried to excuse Teresa's actions, explaining why they were not all that bad. She said that since people *thought* their money was being used for altruistic purposes, then Teresa was doing a good thing in encouraging those actions. What Teresa *appeared* to be was more important than what she actually was. She represented good, and therefore *was* good.

This seems disingenuous. You could say the same about the televangelists Jim and Tammy Bakker. Until the scandal broke and people heard about their expensive cars and air-conditioned doghouses, people *thought* their donations were going to help spread the Word as well as provide food for hungry people. That's what people were told when they were asked for money. Were Jim and Tammy's *appearances* more important than their true actions? Well, I for one don't think so. Neither did the judge who sentenced Jim Bakker to a lengthy stay in prison for his misrepresentations in asking for money.[22]

It is surprising that no one came forward sooner to talk about Teresa's questionable practices. But then that's what everyone said about priests raping little boys, isn't it—what took so long for the stories to come out? Of course the answer is simple. The Roman Catholic Church has awesome, intimidating powers. Until the publication of Christopher Hitchens's eye-opening 1995 book, *The Missionary Position*, I had no idea what was going on in Teresa's "clinics." Like everyone else, I thought she was literally a saint. I was wrong.

Whatever the motives of the woman from Calcutta, I have seen enough human suffering in loved ones to recoil in horror at the thought of terminal, tormented people being told that their suffering is a *good* thing. Suffering is never a good thing. Especially today, when we have the ability to alleviate so much pain, the mental image of those unfortunates who ended up in a Teresa "clinic" is saddening and angering.

SUFFER THE LITTLE CHILDREN

In 1997, in Dallas, Texas, Monsignor Robert Rehkemper voiced an almost unbelievable opinion. He said that parents were not accepting enough responsibility when their children were raped by Catholic priests.[23] How could anyone say something like that?! It is outrageously arrogant and utterly contemptible. His words were a betrayal of every unfortunate victim of a pedophile's sick perversion of power over the young.

Responding to a whopping $120-million judgment against him for failing to stop a priest from sexually molesting boys, the former monsignor of the Dallas Catholic Diocese said, "They [the victims] knew what was right and what was wrong. Anybody who reaches the age of reason shares responsibility for what they do. So that makes all of us responsible after we reach the age of six or seven." *Six or seven?!* This is outrageous. Such words bear the inescapable stench that attaches itself to all attempts to blame the victim when crimes are committed.

Using Rehkemper's logic, a six-year-old boy being raped by a fifty-year-old representative of God on earth should really shoulder some of the blame for the abomination taking place. But then, on second thought, maybe it makes some sense after all. I haven't met a six-year-old yet who wasn't in full control of his environment and the adults around him. So maybe those kindergartners and first-graders really *should* be more careful in their choice of sex partners.

Unbelievable.

Said Rehkemper: "No one ever says anything about what the role of the parents was in all this. . . . Parents have the prime responsibility to look after their kids. I don't want to judge them one way or the other, but it doesn't appear they were very concerned about their kids."

Of course they weren't concerned! They allowed their children to spend time with a Roman Catholic priest, Rudolph Kos, who is God's representative on earth. Why on earth should they have been concerned? I am sure they felt thankful and possibly honored that a priest would spend so much time with their children. What a betrayal of trust.

Fortunately, more and more of these horrible stories are coming to light, and the Catholic Church's oft-repeated "solutions" to the molestations—sending the pedophile to another parish—are receiving the sharp criticism they deserve. They are finally being challenged—in court no less—on their ostrich-position approach toward pedophile priests. That two-dollar white collar cannot be allowed to shield evil men from their responsibilities.

HUMAN LITTER

Seven babies. Imagine. Seven. All at once. Well, perhaps "underdone fetuses" would be more accurate. Every so often you read about such unusual births. Those tiny two-pound entities are somewhere between zygote and viable human being, but just *where* along that spectrum is hard to pinpoint. And, because of that, normal health is a rarity in such cases.

There must be a compassionate compromise between giving birth to seven premature babies and simply enduring infertility. Fertility drugs commonly result in multiple embryos for the obvious reason that they are designed to overstimulate the ovaries, which cooperate by disgorging eggs like a gumball machine. Those sperms must think, Bonanza!

This naturally creates the dilemma of implanting a human uterus with anywhere from four to nine embryos, which it was never intended to accommodate. As a rule, dogs and cats and pigs have litters, but humans have one baby at a time. Even twins are rare, and it is only medical advances, such as C-sections, that have made it possible for so many successful twin births. One generation ago it was not at all uncommon for only one twin to survive the rigors of full-term pregnancy and childbirth. Today successful twinning is a happily frequent event.

But what do you do when your fierce desire for children results in a womb crammed full of hopefuls, which have zero chance of coming to full term? And there is no disagreement on this issue. All agree. No human female can carry six or so embryos to full term. It can never happen, and when the uterus finally decides enough is enough, it ejects its burdensome passengers long before they are ready for the light of day.

The tragic results are lungs, hearts, kidneys, and so on that are not fully developed. One or two of these tiny creatures usually die at birth, and those remaining often require major surgery, long-term care, or both. They just aren't quite "done." So, is there a solution? Happily, there is. Unhappily, the powerful Roman Catholic Church is dead set against it. The term used by doctors is "selective reduction."* The term used by the Catholic Church is "murder." Here we go again.

I remember watching a poignant television documentary on this reduction procedure. Two married, childless couples were featured. They had both been faced with the same problem. They had used fertility drugs, resulting in eight embryos in one woman, and seven in the other. Children they wanted, but not like this!

The first woman stated clearly and unequivocally that she would play no part in what she called "murder." Her church had spoken on the matter—it was just plain murder to "reduce" the number of embryos—and she obeyed. She allowed all eight embryos to work out their own destinies inside her. Her husband was in total agreement.

The second woman barely struggled at all with her decision. Knowing the impossibility of delivering seven healthy, full-term babies, she opted to remove five of them and allow the remaining twins to grow inside her. Her husband was in total agreement.

The results were sadly predictable. Of the eight premature babies born to the first woman, three died the first day, and the other five were woefully malformed. One little girl had lungs that were not developed and would require a respirator, just to breathe at all, for the rest of her life. One of the boys had a brain only half the normal size, even for his tiny body, and one of his brothers had only a partial spine. And so on.

---

*"Reduction" means just what it says. The number of embryos is reduced by means of injections, and those eliminated are resorbed back into the mother's body.

The second couple was thrilled to be parents of a healthy set of twins, a girl and a boy. At the time the documentary was filmed, the children in both families were one-and-a-half years old. There were scenes showing the twins giggling and being pushed in their swings in the backyard; then scenes as they played on a beach and splashed in the shallow water.

Then, suddenly, the scene shifted to a large "family" room that looked more like a hospital ward. One little girl was attached to a respirator by a lengthy hose, allowing her to walk at least that far. The tube in and around her neck, attached to the hose, made her look eerily like a dog tethered on a leash. She will have to use a respirator for as long as she lives.

One boy was slouched in a highchair, glassy-eyed and drooling. He had a drastically undersized brain and would never have a measurable IQ. Another boy was lying in a crib, where, because of his spine, he would always remain. There were no surgeries available to allow him ever to walk or sit up.

The other two children had less serious problems, but one had a back brace and the other wore very thick glasses and could barely see. It was like a horror movie come true. And it was heart-wrenching to watch.

But when they cut back to the other family's twins, greedily eating their pudding, grinning, red-cheeked, and obviously healthy, it was also impossible not to be angry. Both women had been offered the same options. They both could have ended up with one or two healthy children and neither needed to end up with a sick room full of permanently disabled babies. Once again, the Catholic Church's intractable, unreasonable stance had caused unimaginable suffering.

The martyred mom gushed about how much she loved each and every one of her five babies, and how precious their lives were. She also said she wished the other three had survived as well. Somehow I doubt that. But what I found most maddening was her repeated references to abiding by "God's will." Over and over she prided herself on accepting "God's will." Her priest was interviewed and he too complimented her on obeying "God's will."

It occurs to me that "God's will" was that she remain childless. Taking those fertility drugs is as "unnatural" as is the process of reduction. Why was that first action deemed permissible under "God's will," while the second was not? The strained logic that fertility drugs help people to "be fruitful and multiply" while reduction has the opposite effect, is most unconvincing. Surely giving birth to twins is being fruitful. But of course if the church approved aborting under any circumstances, even one as extremely unusual as this, it would find itself balanced precariously at the top of that famous slippery slope.

In order to be consistent about its insistence that *all* abortion is murder, the church today is in a preposterous position. It must accuse a woman, who wants to give birth to healthy twins, of violating God's law about being fruitful and multiplying. This is a classic example of the kind of cruelly bizarre predicament created when archaic, inflexible laws are applied to the modern age. Those laws don't work any more, if they ever did. What could the writers of the Bible know about fertility drugs, embryo reduction, and C-sections? But the bottom line remains. The Catholic Church is mired somewhere in the tenth century, refusing to acknowledge today's world, and millions of people suffer for it.

Historically, the Catholic Church has tried to sweep its multitudinous problems under the carpet. The Vatican must have the lumpiest carpets in the world. From exhuming pontifical corpses to the Crusades to the Inquisition to molesting children to condemning loving parents to nightmarish "litters" of babies, the church's is a most sordid history, especially when you consider the fact that it is still one of the largest religions in the world. Its biggest problem, though, seems to be that it is hamstrung by its own theory of "infallibility" which makes change and reform so very difficult. How can you say a previous pope was wrong about something if that pope was supposedly speaking ex cathedra, meaning he was speaking infallibly?

Occasionally, though, popes are forced to make changes. In

1979, Pope John Paul II declared that the Roman Catholic Church had been mistaken when it sentenced a seventy-year-old Galileo to house arrest (with threats of the tortures of the Inquisition) for insisting that the Earth orbits the Sun, not vice versa. *Mistaken?!* No, not mistaken. A mistake is when you slip the wrong key into your front door. The church's treatment of Galileo was viciously cruel and betrays the unenlightened, progress-impeding attitude that has dominated the church since its inception. And they were as wrong as it is possible to be.

In 1996, John Paul announced that the scientific theory of evolution could be said to be valid.[24] That message was received with enthusiastic approval in many circles throughout the world. Warm congratulations were offered to John Paul. But why should the pope be congratulated for reluctantly acknowledging evolution? Would the same admiration be extended if the pope announced that the scientific theory of gravity could be said to be valid?

"POPE ANNOUNCES THAT GRAVITY EXISTS!"

VATICAN CITY—Catholic admirers of Isaac Newton were jubilant today to hear the news that gravity is no longer just an unproven theory, as had been taught by the Catholic Church. Today, at last, when Catholics accidentally knock a combination pizza off the dinner table, they will be allowed to acknowledge the mess on the floor and clean it up.

"I'm ecstatic!" cried Patricia O'Rourke of Philadelphia. "All these years I've had to pretend that those spills and broken dishes didn't exist. And when our one-year-old was learning to walk, and she fell down, I had to just leave her there, in a little crumpled heap on the floor, crying," mourned O'Rourke. "What else could I do? It was gravity that made her fall, and as an observant Catholic I couldn't acknowledge gravity. Now all that has changed!"

O'Rourke's candid confession prompted an angry scowl and a tight-lipped rejoinder from Mr. O'Rourke. "So *that's* why our little

Mary Frances didn't learn to walk until she was three!" hissed an agitated Francis Xavier O'Rourke.

Elsewhere, Catholics all over the world are celebrating, throwing confetti into the air and rejoicing as they are finally permitted to concede that it does indeed fall back to the ground.

"Gravity has been a stumbling block in my true faith for years," admitted one anonymous Catholic priest. "I remember spilling the Communion wine one Sunday, and having to pretend that it hadn't splashed all over my Gucci loafers. I'm glad those days are behind us."

With this new sense of détente in the air, so to speak, the faithful are hoping that soon the pope will acknowledge heavier-than-air flight. "It has been extremely difficult," agreed Vincent Valenti, "to be an airline pilot and a good Catholic at the same time. I do fly 747s, and I know that they work, but I've been unable to reconcile that fact with my unswerving faith. If only His Holiness would reconsider. But with his decision about gravity, I have new hope!"

The paradox involved in this controversial topic of heavier-than-air flight is that the pope flies all over the world in modern jets. However, an earlier statement released by the Vatican explained why the pope is taking so long to make up his mind about official recognition. "The Holy See is aware of the grave importance of the Articles of Faith and their effect on the Faithful. Decisions such as these must be weighed carefully. What if His Holiness officially recognized heavier-than-air-flight, and then it turned out *not* to be possible? Such rash decisions could prove disastrous."

Nevertheless, there is speculation that several other similar announcements are currently being considered. Security has been tight surrounding these possible proclamations. But reliable sources have confirmed that in a bold move, during his traditional New Year's speech, the pope plans to concede the following: The existence of more than five planets in the solar system; the spherical shape of the Earth; E really does equal mc^2; water runs downhill; plants are capable of photosynthesis; and you can lead a horse to water but you can't make him drink.

The photosynthesis debate has raged for centuries in the Catholic hierarchy. Based on the "only God can make a tree" theorem, prelates have insisted that photosynthesis must be the work of the devil. Angry ecclesiastical voices have been heard to shout, "Grass grows because God causes it to grow!" while others have countered with, "No it doesn't! It's the chlorophyll!" This may remain an unresolved issue for the present. But the other items on the agenda appear to have already received the green light.

In addition, in a daring attempt to catapult the Roman Catholic Church into the twenty-first century, the pope plans to take the most drastic steps yet toward this end. Kept under wraps for months, but now considered an open secret, is the pope's plan regarding possible life forms on other planets. Should any be discovered, he will baptize them remotely, from Rome, making them Catholics in good standing. The College of Cardinals objected strenuously to the possibility of Catholic microbes, but the pope was adamant. He wants to demonstrate the universal nature of the Roman Catholic faith, and its willingness to embrace sinners on any planet.

Those in the inner circle are split in their opinions. "Well, I can understand the reasoning behind wanting to show the world that the Mother Church is no longer mired in the fourth century," explained one archbishop, who asked to remain anonymous. "But there's something eerie about the idea of microscopic Catholic organisms on another planet. And besides, how would they go to confession?"

Whether or not there will be spiritual kin on other worlds remains to be seen. But spirits are high here in Rome as people become aware of the church's new, progressive stance. No longer will critics be able to point to the Roman Catholic Church's somewhat backward view of the world. The papacy will truly have come of age. Except for the photosynthesis thing.

© *The Heretical News*

TAKING THOSE VOWS

In addition to the enormous suffering inflicted on its members by the Catholic Church's cruel and intractable position on birth control and abortion, the emotional toll exacted from its own servants is appalling. Their rules regarding celibacy and chastity for priests and nuns have led to centuries of such nightmares as pedophilia; alcoholism; furtive sexual affairs and the accompanying anguished guilt; unplanned pregnancies and the desperately unhappy choices between abortion, out-of-wedlock births, and/or leaving the church in shame to marry in a civil ceremony; and years or decades of intense, often obsessive sexual frustration. And, more recently, AIDS. Such an unnatural, unhealthy lifestyle is surely more distracting for the clergy than a normal, healthy family life—which is forbidden ostensibly because a family would be too distracting!

Actually, the real reasons for the ban on marriage are more distasteful—the desire to control and dominate their clergy, and a view of women and sex that historically has been nothing short of misogynistic, phobic, and bordering on hatred.

By forbidding marriage for their religious ("religious" meaning priests, brothers, and nuns) the church has absolute power over their lives. Those religious have no other family *but* the church. With no spouses or children to consider, they can be sent wherever the church decides to send them. And if they don't want to be sent to Backwater, Uruguay, they'd better toe the line. Most of them try to, but at a great price in self-esteem and emotional maturity.

And, in addition to the loneliness, sexual frustration, and guilt, a new nightmare now stalks the members of the Roman Catholic priesthood—AIDS. Exact figures are difficult, perhaps impossible, to come by, for obvious reasons. If ever secrecy shrouded a pressing issue, the Catholic Church's position on priests with AIDS is a dreadful example. Silence is the last thing young priests need in struggling with this life-and-death dilemma. Yet when it comes to sex the church's seminaries have done little more than say, in essence, "Don't engage in it." And people are now dying because of it.

On January 30, 2000, when the *Kansas City Star* broke the story about priests with AIDS, the most common reaction was shock. Except for people like me. Having read so much about the impossible situation young Catholic seminarians are put in, I figured that AIDS was an inevitability, not a reason for astonishment. Sadly, I was right.

According to the story, AIDS has caused hundreds of deaths of priests in the United States, although other causes of death may be listed on some of the death certificates. An example offered was a bishop in New York who died of AIDS, even though his death certificate attributed his death to "unknown natural causes" and his occupation was listed as a "laborer" in the manufacturing industry.[25]

When interviewed, *one* epidemiologist in *one* city stated that he had treated around twenty priests with AIDS, all of whom had kept it a secret. There's no telling how many AIDS-infected priests are currently suffering in silence; but the *Star* estimated that the death rate of priests from AIDS is at least four times that of the general population.[26]

This is not only tragic and sad; it is absurd. The Catholic Church requires vows of celibacy and/or chastity. At the same time, its priests are dying of AIDS, which means priests are having sex. So some seminaries are addressing this problem. For example, a residential treatment program for priests in Maryland conducts one- and two-day seminars on human sexuality, claiming it is part of being a "healthy" person. But wait a minute. There is a serious contradiction involved here. The church is trying to say two things at the same time: (1) You are forbidden to have sex, but (2) since we know you're doing it anyway, and it's part of being a "healthy" person, we'll give you some needed training on "safe" sex.

If sex is part of being a "healthy" person, then why does the church continue to forbid sexual activity for its clergy? Do they not want "healthy" humans serving as priests? Bishop Raymond J. Boland of the diocese of Kansas City–St. Joseph, summed up this whole contradictory, confusing mess when he said that AIDS deaths show that priests are human. "Much as we would regret it, it shows that human nature is human nature," Boland said. What on earth does that mean? Does he regret that humans are humans? That priests are humans?

Further, any seminars teaching safe sex for priests are implicitly approving of homosexual activity, which the church officially condemns. It's a vicious circle, deadly and self-contradictory, where everyone loses. There are no winners. It also highlights, in a ghastly way, the outrageous demands put on young men entering the priest-hood. They are now literally dying because of the church's cruel, inexcusable inflexibility on something as natural as human sexu-ality. How long will the church allow men to *die* at the altar of its own haughty, thoroughly unrealistic strictures?

The Catholic Church has a long history of negative pronounce-ments about sex (although that never prevented popes of the early church from fathering a great many children by a great many women) and those negative views on women and sex are still echoing in today's church. It is difficult to overcome a thousand years of teachings such as the following.

From St. John Chrysostom (d. 407), whose name, "Chrysos-tom," means "golden-mouthed":

> It does not profit a man to marry. For what is woman but an enemy of friendship, an inescapable punishment, a necessary evil. . . .[27]

From St. Augustine (d. 430), unarguably one of the most influ-ential of the early church fathers:

> For if that [birth of children] is taken away, husbands are shameful lovers, wives are harlots, marriage beds are bordellos, and fathers-in-law are pimps.[28]

> I don't see what sort of help woman was created to provide man with, if one excludes the purpose of procreation. If woman is not given to man for help in bearing children, for what help could she be?[29]

> [I]ntercourse . . . is a sin when the spouses surrender to lust.[30]

From Peter Lombard (d. 1164), bishop of Paris, on practicing birth control:

> She is her husband's harlot, and he an adulterer with his own wife.[31]

From St. Thomas Aquinas (d. 1274), probably *the* most influential thirteenth-century Catholic theologian:

> In sexual intercourse the human being becomes similar to the beast.[32]

> Women find it all the harder to resist sexual pleasure since they have "less strength of mind" than men.[33]

> Nothing drags the mind of man down from its elevation so much as the caresses of a woman. . . .[34]

Agreeing with Aristotle that a woman is a mutilated or imperfect male, Aquinas understood a woman to be "something that is not intended in itself, but originates in some defect." He elaborated by saying that women do not correspond to "nature's first intention," which aims at perfection (men), but to "nature's second intention (to such things as) decay, deformity, and the weakness of age."[35]

From Albert the Great (d. 1280), another dominant theologian:

> Woman is less qualified [than man] for moral behavior.[36]

> Woman knows nothing of fidelity.[37]

> Woman is a misbegotten man and has a faulty and defective nature in comparison with his.[38]

> [Intercourse is] filthy, defiling, ugly, shameful, sick, a degradation of the mind . . . debasing, corrupted, depraved. . . .[39]

> A Master Clement from Bohemia told me that a certain monk, already graying, had gone to a beautiful woman, like a ravenously hungry man. Up until the ringing of matins he lusted for her sixty-six times. But in the morning he lay sick in bed, and he died on the same day. Because he was a nobleman, his body was opened up. And it was found that his brain had been quite drained out, so that what was left was only the size of a pomegranate, and the eyes were as good as destroyed.[40]

> Explaining why dogs follow people who have sex, Albert said,
> "Dogs love strong smells and run after cadavers, and the body of
> a person who has a great deal of intercourse approaches the con-
> dition of a cadaver because of all the rotten semen."[41]

This blatant, woman-hating abhorrence for sex was firmly established in the church when the rules for its clergy were being carved into granite, and it shows. These degrading attitudes could not possibly lead to a wholesome view of human sexuality and marriage; and they didn't. This phobic disdain for all things sexual paved the way for one of the biggest mistakes the Catholic Church could ever have made. It was called the Council of Trent.

The Catholic Church's sixteenth-century Council of Trent, which took place a mere twenty-five years after Martin Luther ignited the wildfire known as the Reformation, was undoubtedly a backlash—an overreaction to that very Reformation. The church was shaken by this sudden religious rebellion after centuries of absolute, unchallenged authority; and it is probably no coincidence that at the same time this council—which resulted in strengthening the church's control over its clergy through celibacy—convened, the Spanish Inquisition was in full sway controlling "heretics."

The council was determined to set its clergy apart from the marrying Protestants. While celibacy had been mandated in the twelfth century by the Second Lateran Council, it had also been largely ignored. Clergy from parish priests to popes kept women and fathered children that were passed off as nieces and nephews. The Protestant joke about why there is always an orphanage next to a convent had a kernel of truth in it. Despite this, or perhaps because of it, the Council of Trent insisted on genuine, compulsory celibacy, and the human suffering that has resulted in the intervening centuries can only be guessed at.

Perhaps the most telling example of the early church's intense loathing of human sexuality is one of Augustine's theological conundrums. He was very much troubled, it seems, about the sexual goings-on in the Garden of Eden. It was clear to him that Adam and Eve had been created with sexual organs because they were going to have to "be fruitful and multiply." Therefore, he reasoned, they must have had sex before the Fall.

However, since pleasure is a sin, a truth held to be self-evident by this playboy-turned-ascetic, and Adam and Eve were sinless before the Fall, there could not have been any pleasure in their sex. It follows, then, that their intercourse had to be achieved without any lust or excitement. And how was that accomplished? Augustine, ever the determined pleasure hater, thought he had figured it out. Adam must have had full control of his penis, being able to control it by his will alone. No unbidden, lustful, sinful desires for Adam! "Why shouldn't we believe that before the Fall men could control the sex organs just as they could the other limbs?" asked Augustine. And to shore up his theory he offered, "Some people can even move their ears, either one at a time or both together."[42] See? Proof! It's logic itself. Adam's member performed at his bidding. No desire, no lust, no sin. But nothing is said about whether or not Adam could wiggle his ears.

It's hard not to see some sheer spiteful envy in this man's fanatic determination to separate humans from sexual pleasure. Augustine's younger years had been spent in wild sexual revelry. He had a son by his first mistress, and took a second mistress while waiting for his chosen bride to come of age. His nickname was the "Great Sinner."[43] When he finally "saw the light," and became a devout member of the Catholic clergy, he had to change his ways.

After proclaiming loudly and proudly that he was renouncing, forever, all sins of the flesh (as they were called), perhaps Augustine found that he didn't have Adam's gift of penis-control. Since he was still a young man, in his late thirties, when he made the change, it's highly probable that his private organ expressed some vehement objections to the new order of things. If so, he couldn't go back to his old ways without losing face and disgracing himself. And he may have taken out his frustrations on others by preaching against *all* sexual pleasure and making others feel guilty if they experienced it—thereby ruining some or all of their pleasure.

I, of course, have no way of confirming this. But if you look at it the other way around, it seems to make sense. Try this thought experiment. Assume the following:

(1) Augustine *had* in fact suffered from (secret) regrets at his choice in becoming ascetic.

(2) His regrets stemmed from his own sexual yearnings, now unfulfilled.

(3) As a man with experience he would know exactly what he was missing out on.

(4) He would also have recognized those around him who were enjoying themselves sexually.

(5) Witnessing that enjoyment would further exacerbate his own sexual frustration.

Now, assuming all that, how would you expect such a man to behave—a man who was by then a highly influential Catholic theologian? In my opinion he would have behaved precisely the way he actually did. He would rail against the sins of sexual pleasure, making everyone else *pay*, with guilt, for *their* pleasure, a pleasure now denied him. The only characteristic you have to endow him with to make this scenario plausible is envy, which is unfortunately a *very* common human emotion.

A more generous interpretation would be that Augustine sincerely believed in the sanctity of things spiritual, and strove to help his followers to achieve the same ecstatic spirituality he had achieved. And, in order to help them achieve it, they had to be discouraged from wallowing in the carnal. I'll leave it to the reader to decide which seems more likely, especially in light of the following quote from Augustine:

> Husbands, love your wives but love them chastely. Insist on the work of the flesh only in such measure as is necessary for the procreation of children. Since you cannot beget children in any other way, you must *descend to it against your will*, for it is the punishment of Adam. . . . A man should yearn for that embrace in which there can be no more corruption.[44]

Whatever the motivation, however, Augustine was highly influential. Some consider him the greatest Catholic theologian who ever lived. I don't know if that's a compliment to Augustine or an insult to Catholic theology. But he cast a long shadow indeed, and his forbidding, punishing hand reaches through the centuries and touches lives today.

As recently as 1951—repeat, 1951—Catholic theologians were still haggling over the degree of sinfulness that was attached to the practice of *coitus reservatus*, which is different from *coitus interruptus*. In *interruptus*, the penis is withdrawn from the vagina before ejaculation, but ejaculation occurs after that. Often used as a form of birth control, it is always a mortal sin for strict Catholics. In *reservatus*, there is the same withdrawal, but no ejaculation follows. So the degree of sinfulness in that case is difficult to determine since the husband is forgoing the pleasure of orgasm, but may also be preventing a pregnancy. See the problem? What a dilemma!

For over nine hundred years Catholic scholars have wrestled with the weighty issue of how much sin to assign to pulling out without climaxing. Since pleasure is the sin, the woman might be having too much fun even if her husband denies himself his orgasm; making it worse, he might even have some fun himself. An uneasy compromise was finally reached wherein priests are supposed to counsel against *reservatus*, but mildly and vaguely.

This whole thing would be silly except that this irrational, extreme obsession with sex has brought untold misery to countless millions. And making it a tragicomedy is that *priests* are the ones who are supposed to dispense this utterly foolish advice to married couples. What could be more inappropriate? How can a supposedly virginal, totally celibate priest offer sexual counseling? The absurdity of it is exceeded only by the unhappiness that must surely be the result of such a misalliance.

This history of bristling hostility toward human sexuality still hovers over the church like a foul, malodorous cloud. The most obvious manifestation of it is the policy on celibacy. Demanding celibacy and chastity from its religious is not only wildly unrealistic, but betrays the punitive approach that the church has adopted toward sex: If you do those nasty, naughty, disgusting things, your immortal soul is at risk.

Wholly ignored in Catholicism's rigid, self-defeating stance on celibacy is the undisputed fact that Protestant ministers manage to tend their parishioners *and* their families with no problem at all. Not being hampered by incessant sexual frustration, which can become obsessive, or the often unbearable loneliness from a lack of a companion, such ministers unquestionably will be *better* able to offer their congregations the compassion and support supposedly being sought by the Catholic hierarchy. The church has literally cut off its nose to spite its face on this issue, as priests and nuns have been leaving in droves for decades.[45]

But the Catholic clergy are living, breathing human beings. Statistics tell you nothing about the human suffering endured by the men and women who are forced to live a twilight existence as nonsexual beings, in celibacy and/or chastity. (*Celibacy* literally means not being married; *chastity* means refraining from genital sexual activity.[46] Question: Do French kissing and breast fondling violate vows of chastity? That I can even pose such a question reveals the church's inane policies on sexuality.)

Making it more tragic is the age at which most young people "feel the call" and commit themselves naively—completely unaware of what it will mean when they take their vows of celibacy. These all-important, lifelong commitments are usually made in the mid-to-late teens, before young people have any comprehension of sexual maturity or adult needs. They have no idea what they're getting into. It's as foolish as getting married at sixteen. We all had wild, grandiose plans for ourselves as teenagers; but how many of those plans were realistic?

So try to imagine the tragic impact on these committed young people when they finally realize, as they grow up, what they have let themselves in for. The sense of being trapped must often be near panic. The loneliness must be heartbreaking. And the guilt as their bodies demand what nature intended must be intense. But there is no way out that does not involve shame and trauma. If the church really cared about the health and happiness of their religious, they would not *allow*, let alone encourage, any youth to begin training for a *lifelong* commitment before the age of twenty-one.

On the other hand, if the church's true goal is to indoctrinate, dominate, and control, then grabbing teenagers makes perfect sense. A caring approach, however, would preclude such recruitment.

This of course is not to say that all Catholic religious are miserable, trapped creatures. But if the available statistics are correct (and they are probably underestimations, since many would not feel comfortable admitting their unhappiness) then there are scores of thousands of hopelessly unhappy people who wanted to serve their God, but instead ended up being indentured servants—pawns of the King of Rome.

Recognizing this unhappiness, a bit of the clergy's in-house gallows humor refers to liquor as a "celibacy vaccine."[47] It would be funny were it not for the fact that it is not at all funny. It is truly sad. While I often criticize, rather harshly, the Catholic Church's policies and popes, I have nothing but sympathy for the men and women who enter religious orders and seminaries with the best of intentions, only to end up frustrated, lonely, and lost. So on this issue, too, I *strongly* disagree with the church's adamant refusal to rescind the unworkable, cruel requirement of lifelong celibacy for their religious. But my heart goes out to those religious who do indeed suffer because of that heartless requirement.

NOTES

1. Peter de Rosa, *Vicars of Christ* (London: Corgi Books, 1988). All references to the early popes are from this scholarly study by de Rosa.

2. "Catholic Bishop Kills Self in Protest," Associated Press [online], www.msnbc.com/news/ [May 7, 1998].

3. "Pope Cracks Down on Dissidents, Changes Target Advocates of Women Priests, Contraception," Reuters [online], www.msnbc. com/news/ [July 1, 1998].

4. "Bishops Debate Return to Meatless Fridays," *Lodi News-Sentinel*, November 12, 1997, p. 11.

5. Carl Sagan, (The Estate of), *Billions & Billions* (New York: Random House, 1997), p. 166.

6. Christopher Hitchens, *The Missionary Position* (London: Verso, 1995), p. 11.

7. Ibid., p. 30.

8. Ibid., p. 57.

9. Ibid., p. 48.

10. Ibid., p. 58.

11. Carl Sagan, *The Demon-Haunted World* (New York: Random House, 1995), p. 10.

12. "Disaster in India," editorial, *Ottawa Citizen*, October 2, 1993.

13. John F. Burns, "India's Facade of Democracy," *Ottawa Citizen*, January 25, 1995, p. A11.

14. Sagan, *The Demon-Haunted World*, p. 362.

15. Hitchens, *The Missionary Position*, p. 41.

16. Sagan, *Billions and Billions*, p. 215.

17. Hitchens, *The Missionary Position*, p. 41.

18. "Saint Teresa?" *Stockton Record*, September 6, 1997, p. A7.

19. Ibid.

20. Clark Morphew, "Mother Teresa, Her Order Come Under Criticism," *Saint Paul Pioneer Press*, January 17, 1998.

21. "Mother Teresa," *Columbia University Press Encyclopedia* 1995.

22. "Did PTL's Jim Bakker Get a Fair Trial?" Evangelical Press News Service [online], www.excite.com/news/ [August 27, 1998].

23. "Ex-monsignor: Parents, Victims Must Shoulder Blame," *Houston Chronicle* News Services" [online], www.excite.com/news/ [August 8, 1997].

24. "Evolution Is God's Work, Pope Agrees," *News and Observer* Publishing [online], www.news-observer.com/ [February 21, 1997].

25. Judy L. Thomas, "Seminary Taught Spirituality, Liturgy and Latin—Sexuality Was Taboo," *Kansas City Star* [online], www.excite. com/news/ [January 30, 2000].

26. "Report: Priests Dying of AIDS," Associated Press, [online], www.excite.com/news/ [January 30, 2000].

27. Uta Ranke-Heinemann, *Eunuchs for the Kingdom of Heaven* (New York: Penguin Books, 1991), p. 236. Ranke-Heinemann, with a Ph.D. in Catholic theology, was the first woman ever to become a lecturer and then a professor of Catholic theology at the University of Essen, West Germany. This scholarly, passionate, detailed book is a scathing indictment of the Catholic Church's notoriously misogynistic history.

28. Ibid., p. 83.

29. Ibid., p. 88.

30. Ibid., p. 93.

31. Ibid., p. 205.

32. Ibid., p. 178.

33. Ibid., p. 187.

34. Ibid., p. 188.

35. Ibid.

36. Ibid., p. 178.

37. Ibid.

38. Ibid.

39. Ibid., p. 181.

40. Ibid., p. 182.

41. Ibid.

42. Ibid., p. 90.

43. de Rosa, *Vicars of Christ*, p. 443.

44. Ibid., p. 445; emphasis mine.

45. David Rice, *Shattered Vows* (Tarrytown, N.Y.: Triumph Books, 1992), p. 3.

46. Ibid., p. 35.

47. Ibid., p. 32.

3

THE HUMAN
IN HUMANISM

*Grief can take care of itself, but to get the full value of a joy you
must have somebody to divide it with.*
—Mark Twain, *Following the Equator*

I REALLY MISS THE MUSIC. Church music was mother's milk to me.
Since my father was the (excellent) pipe organist in the Lutheran
church of my youth, I was doubly lucky. I also got to hear that glorious music at home while Dad practiced for services. And often I'd
tag along on Saturday afternoons as Dad "worked up," on the
church organ, his selections for Sunday. It was just my father, me,
some magnificent Bach, and beautifully backlit stained-glass windows. Oh, yes—and God.

These are powerful memories for me. My sense of awe and reverence was palpable as those marvelous strains filled the church,
with me as the only audience. I would gaze up at the multicolored,
leaded-glass image of Jesus on the cross, which graced the wall
above the altar, and contemplate the wonder of it all. Just imagine.
Jesus died for me.

I had memorized every piece of stained glass in every other
window also, and I knew which Bible story each window depicted.
But not a one of them could hold a candle to the huge, brilliantly-

colored image of Jesus, thorny crown in place, hanging on that cross at the front of the church. It was a dominating, intimidating sight.

But church or no church, I was still just a kid, your basic rug rat, and on those Saturdays, along with enjoying the music, I reconnoitered the entire building. Top to bottom, I knew every square inch—except for the altar. My father made it very clear that the altar was strictly off-limits. All else, though, was fair game. I can still recall my tickled delight when I brazenly explored the men's room in the basement. It was like discovering an alien life form. I had never seen a urinal before, and, having only a vague notion of male anatomy, could not figure out how it worked. Ah, the things you can learn from going to church!

Then of course we were back again Sunday mornings, me in my Mary-Janes and best dress, only now surrounded by scores of other people. But nothing ever touched me as deeply, or reinforced my unquestioning faith so strongly, as those special, sparkling Saturdays.

When I was old enough to graduate from Junior Choir to Senior Choir, the music was even more fun. Singing a high soprano descant to "I Know That My Redeemer Lives" on Easter Sunday was a thrilling experience. The church was always packed on Easter, and there were lovely, fragrant bouquets of flowers filling every nook and cranny. Booming male voices, lilting female voices, and the powerful voices of the organ pipes all blended into a magnificent, moving expression of joyful celebration. It always gave me goosebumps.

And at Christmas, in addition to the regular church music, there was the added fun of caroling. We'd all meet at various neighbor-hoods, on many different evenings, and walk, arm-in-arm, merrily singing "Joy to the World" or "Hark the Herald Angels Sing." Cheeks pink from the cold night air, and sometimes carrying can-dles, we were welcomed with smiling faces wherever we went. Afterward, we'd meet back at the church for warm cider and Christmas cookies. These were fun times.

Then there were those long, lazy summer afternoons spent at the church picnics. They were at various parks throughout the area. These were, without a doubt, some of our most family-fun days. Relaxed and informal, some of the men would get a softball game going. Others would be playing volleyball, and many would just lounge on blankets spread on the grass. The kids played kickball and tag and jumped rope, but mostly we stuffed ourselves with the free ice cream. If our parents had known how much ice cream actually found its way into our stomachs, they would have been horrified. But we all survived.

I remember at one of those picnics my father actually pitched in a softball game. He had a pretty good wind up and delivery. He was no Roger Clemens or Jim Palmer, but then what do you expect from a pipe organist?

I've often suspected that it is these kinds of activities, more than religion itself, that attracts many churchgoers. I know such activities are certainly part of *my* fond memory collection. Quite possibly the most important offering of religion is that sense of community and bonding. If you take away the music, singing, stained-glass windows, solemn rituals, church picnics, charity work, cake sales, Christmas pageants, and on and on, all very *enjoyable* activities, and leave only the praying, what would you have? Well, Quakers, actually. But my point is that it is the comforting, bonding trappings of religion that attract people. Remove those and church attendance would plummet.

It is difficult to overestimate that warm, secure feeling of fellowship. It was often smug and condescending, to be sure, but it was also comforting almost beyond description. To know, with infallible certainty, that you are part of a community of Christians who will spend eternity with your personal Savior is no small thing. It could ease the sting of most, if not all, of life's slings and arrows.

So now I'm a godless atheist. Whatever happened? Like many of us, I just asked too many questions. But in addition to losing an irrational belief in the eternal significance of a bloody, sacrificial death, I lost a lot more. I lost my sense of belonging. Talk about a security blanket! I still mourn the loss of that comfort. It left a void in me that has yet to be filled.

Intellectually, of course, I grew by leaps and bounds when the restrictive blinders of religious faith were finally removed. But *emotionally*, I was a little girl again, reaching out for a new security blanket that was nowhere to be found. I think I understand why Unitarians go to "church" meetings. A great many Unitarians are really just atheists. But so what? Good Christians will scoff and tell you that Unitarians don't believe in much of anything. Good atheists will scoff and tell you that Unitarians are just cowardly atheists, afraid to come all the way out of the closet. I can agree with both opinions without scoffing at either.

There should be no shame attached to the very real human need for human companionship. Churches provide people with that strong sense of *community*. It's hard to beat those pot luck dinners in a church basement. With adults chatting over coffee and children giggling and chasing each other around, the feelings of interconnectedness are powerful. They are also necessary in any healthy human group. Activities such as picketing town hall to have the Ten Commandments removed from public property, for example, don't even come close.

Fortunately there are many local as well as national humanist groups, where you can socialize with like-minded people. Unfortunately, most of these groups are scattered and not linked to other groups. Consequently, they are financially strapped and this means they usually must rent small banquet rooms for their meetings. The cold, impersonal feeling of a rental hall can't begin to compare with the sense of permanence and community provided by a church building.

I do enjoy, very much, the humanist discussion groups on the Internet, as well as my correspondence with humanists all over the world. I believe ardently in separation of church and state. I take pleasure in my writing and the feedback from it. I feel a true sense of intellectual freedom now that I have thrown off the shackles of religious superstition. I am still *The Happy Heretic*.

Yet every now and again there is a small voice in me that asks plaintively, "But where is the music?"

ON THE OTHER HAND . . .

There is an old saying: "Out of everything good comes something bad; and out of everything bad comes something good." This was forcefully brought home to me when a friend, a humanist activist, fell ill suddenly and required major surgery. After the initial shock wore off I thought, What can I do to help? Living two thousand miles distant, I obviously couldn't take over a casserole or anything.

But I wanted to do *something. Now.* And, being a writer, my first thought was to write something. But what? *Get well soon?* Then I hit on the idea of putting together a "Get-Well Album" and began soliciting contributions from humanists all over the country. As it turned out, it was one of my better ideas.

I received cards and letters and e-mails from everywhere. The results were truly remarkable. People who had already sent their own personal get-well wishes to our mutual friend nevertheless sent me additional contributions for the album. There were pithy quips, lovely poems, and heartfelt wishes—a sincere portfolio of *caring.* People really *cared,* and were willing to express their thoughts through me. My "please-pass-the-message-along" request was obviously taken to heart, as I ultimately heard from people I had never heard of. These were total strangers, but we had a common bond—concern for a good friend.

Without realizing it, I was conducting a kind of experiment. My little album project was in effect testing "atheist compassion," a trait theists claim does not exist. I confess that I had the briefest twinge of worry. What if no one responded? What if only a handful did? Would I send *that* along? After all, I was asking people to do what was, for most of them, a duplication of effort. I could just hear, "But I already *sent* flowers!"

However, I needn't have worried. I think everyone understood my desire to have all these wonderful messages put into one pretty package. I had actually said in my appeal that I wanted to create the world's largest humanist get-well card. I have no way of knowing if that happened, but the messages rained in like a spring shower on a bed of buttercups. People were wonderful. After I added some colorful artwork (a carousel, roses, and so on) the finished product was a great big pretty bundle of love. Precisely what I had hoped for.

As I read through and assembled the heart-warming messages, it struck me that all of those thoughtful people were responding to my appeal not because they felt their God would frown on them if they didn't, not because they were trying to earn merit badges that would be redeemable in some afterlife, and not because they had been extorted into it with threats of hellfire. They responded simply

because they *cared*. They were motivated solely by human compassion and love. It was wonderful to see.

Even when I was still a believing Christian, lo these many years
ago, I often thought the "I'll pray for you" line was overworked and
a bit of a cop-out. It's a lot easier to pray for someone than to do
their laundry, or clean their house, or baby-sit. Robert Ingersoll's
Hands that help are better than lips that pray has real meaning
when there is real human suffering around you. I often wondered
back then, budding heretic that I was, if all those hours spent
praying for sick people might have been better spent by, say,
washing someone's hair for her, or taking someone's dog to a vet
appointment. Why pray, when the thing your bedridden friend perhaps needs most is a gentle backrub? These were undoubtedly
heretical thoughts, but they also seemed to me to ring out with
common sense. They still do.

On a much larger scale, during the devastating ice storms in
Canada in the winter of 1998, which caught everyone off guard, I remember seeing messages fly back and forth on the Internet discussion
list hosted by the Humanist Association of Canada (HAC). Normally
devoted to the usual discussions of religion and atheism, the list took
on a whole new, urgent life. There were messages instructing people
where they could go to seek warmth and food. There were so many
lengthy power outages, and the frigid temperatures were so unre-
lenting, people stood the very real chance of freezing to death. For
those who were "iced in," messages announced that so-and-so needed
firewood—*now*. Those with rugged ATVs delivered firewood and
food to those in desperate straits. Those who hadn't "checked in" in
a while were "checked on" to see why.

It was a glowing testament to human compassion, all carried out
by atheists, with no reward but the tremendous satisfaction of
knowing that friends were being taken care of. It was heartwarming
to behold.

We've all heard, *When the going gets tough, the tough get
going.* I learned something much more important. *When humans
are in real need, there is no better place to turn than to humanists.*

WHAT IS A HUMANIST?

For a long time Christians have claimed that secular humanism is a religion and therefore cannot be mentioned in public schools. This is disingenuous. The definition of "secular" should be our first clue. How can something "not related to religion" be a religion? Obviously, it can't.

Humanism is simply the affirmation of the value of the human condition and the acknowledgment that we have only ourselves to rely on in our quest for a better world. It is simplicity itself.

The Council for Secular Humanism has published a wonderful one-page document titled "The Affirmations of Humanism: A Statement of Principles." It is a marvelous testimonial to reason, compassion, morality, and tolerance. It speaks of moral excellence, scientific discovery, pluralistic societies, justice, the arts, and just about every other noble concept imaginable. It refers to human beings as citizens of the universe. So true! It also clearly refutes the idea of the existence of the supernatural. It's a lovely document.

So what, then, is a "religious" humanist? Good question. I've scoured the literature and find that defining religious humanism is a tricky and elusive business. For all the words that have been thrown at it, there is very little to show for it in the end. Perhaps this should tell us something—and that is, like trying to describe a square circle, the thing doesn't exist. Religious humanism makes about as much sense as secular Christianity.

Some insist that what makes religious humanism religious is that it represents a specific set of ideals and values. Well, then, that would make environmentalism a religion. Others say that it is the promoting of a moral code that qualifies it as religious. But moral codes can be, and certainly have been, formulated using careful reason alone, with no religious appeals of any kind.

Obviously the major stumbling block in understanding this issue is in the definitions of "religion" and "religious." Religion is almost universally understood to recognize some sort of supernatural realm and/or being. When someone says he brushes his teeth religiously, there is no confusion about what he's talking about. No thoughts of churches or gods come to mind. The same holds true if you say, "She's a deeply religious woman." We all know what that means.

A philosophy, though, is a bit more slippery. Harder to get a handle on. In trying to separate religions from philosophies, a good litmus test might be to ask the question, "Is worship involved?" If people worship a god, trees, or volcanoes, they are part of a religion. No worship? No religion. Worship is, of course, subject to its own definition problems, but, again, *most* of us would agree on what it means. We use the word in a tongue-in-cheek way when we say, "She worships the ground he walks on!" But there's a general consensus as to its meaning.

And humanists do not *worship* humanity. We simply cherish it.

Here's a good thought experiment. Go about this thing backwards. Imagine that you're trying to recruit new members to your new religion. In describing your religion, explain that there is no belief in a god; no belief in devils, angels, or demons; no belief in a human "soul"; no belief in heaven or hell; no belief in an afterlife of any kind; no belief in reincarnation; no belief in miracles; and no prayer. People would laugh in your face and say, "That's no religion!" And they would be right.

Without that essential object of veneration, a deity of some kind, there can be no religion. We all understand this. This is not a revolutionary notion. Religion = a god concept = religion. But there are still those who insist on arguing that humanism is religious, even though it fails to conform to any of religion's definitions. The first group, Christian, is anxious to paint humanism with a religious brush so that if the word is even mentioned in classrooms, Christians proselytizers can rush in demanding equal time.

The second group consists of humanists themselves who run from the word "secular" like scalded cats. This is a shame because secular is not a dirty word. We should be proud that we have arrived at a lifestyle that strives toward reason and compassion without being motivated by the fear of eternal damnation or promises of paradise after death. We are motivated solely by our recognition of human dignity and worth.

Mason Olds, in *Free Inquiry* magazine, spent over three thousand words trying to define religious humanism.[1] This should be our first clue that perhaps we're chasing rainbows. He firmly believes it exists. He explores the empirical method of understanding the universe and in doing so casually mentions that religious humanists repudiate "the supernatural realm." Well, there goes "religious." He also claims humanists do not affirm or deny the existence of God. But then he goes on to offer humanist "reconstructions" of God. Two "constructs" are presented: (1) God is a "force within the universe that enables it to evolve from one state to the next" and (2) "God is an ego-ideal that embodies the highest values to which humans aspire." If these vague, nebulous concepts can be considered to be definitions of God, then I'll throw in one of my own: God is that force which enables us to create new and interesting chili recipes.

"Religious" humanism seems to be nothing more than a slightly desperate ploy to cling to that socially acceptable and therefore overly prized adjective, "religious." But humanism needs no softening, no dressing up, and no apologies. It is a fine and noble philosophy unto itself. It asserts unambiguously that we human beings are quite capable of making this life a more pleasant experience for everyone; and we can embark on this challenging journey without any supernatural prodding of any kind.

THIS IS HUMANISM

A one-year-old child is trying to take her first steps, alone, with no helping hands. Surrounding her are seven adults, all family. Seven pairs of eyes are glued to the child, transfixed, accompanied by seven daffy, involuntary grins, eagerly awaiting the outcome of the swaying toddler's struggle against gravity. She loses the battle and topples unceremoniously, face-first onto the living room carpet. A chorus of sympathetic sighs augments Amy's cries of frustration. Swift arms scoop her up, with kisses of commiseration. Not to be deterred, the tiny tot wriggles mightily to be let loose, once more to do battle with the forces of nature. This time she takes three steps, shakily to be sure, but steps they are. Her proud smile is ear-to-ear—as are all the other smiles in the room. Then, weary from her efforts, she plops down on her bottom and graciously accepts the expected cheers and applause. This is humanism.

Amy and Ned face each other on a flower-bedecked lanai, dressed in old lace and scratchy tuxedo material, as they say their vows. In front of people they love and honor, they vow to love and respect each other as they begin their lives as husband and wife. Their love and commitment bind them; their vows are solely between each other; there are no gods to obey or appease. Just love. A kiss for luck, and it's time to celebrate. The music is wonderful, the refreshments are wonderful, the dancing is wonderful, and life is wonderful. This is humanism.

Something has gone horribly wrong. The tiny embryo insider her will never turn into a normal human being. The test has been redone, twice, but with the same result: there will be multiple deformities. There will be no chance ever for this child to live outside a hospital setting. Never.

Amy and Ned agonize over their decision. This planned pregnancy had been eagerly hoped for. But in the end they both agree that a life with no possibility of happiness was not a life at all. A weeping Amy has an abortion.

Seven months later Amy is again pregnant. And joyous. She ultimately delivers a healthy eight-pound baby girl—Melinda. The baby talk begins. Ned is conversant immediately. Three-way baby gibberish begins. The proud parents are giddy and silly. This is humanism.

About three years later a boy child, Jason, is born. Ned says seriously that if the boy becomes a poet he will be delighted. Amy says that if he becomes a football star she will be delighted. They are both lying. But they are not lying about their love for this tiny new child. Jason's big sister, Melinda, has an equally sincere love for the baby, but decides to call him Roger Dodger. No one ever figures out why.

While still in the maternity ward at the hospital, Amy watches as her nearest roommate, who had a long, difficult labor and finally a C-Section, is handed her baby. Foggy at best, but smiling weakly, the roommate seems not to be aware that her newborn baby son has just had the tip of his penis cut off. Though they had been urged to allow it, Amy and Ned were firm about refusing this archaic religious practice that possesses no medical validity whatever. But Amy is quiet about her beliefs and convictions when talking to her roommate. Now is not the right time. Instead, she simply offers encouragement and sympathy to this young woman, who seems to be in a great deal of pain. This is humanism.

"Mommy, who is Santa Claus?" There is a long, awkward silence. Amy sighs and clears her throat. This question has been long anticipated. "Well, Honey, Santa Claus is just a fun, pretend person that some people say puts all the presents under the tree on Christmas morning."

"Don't those come from you and Daddy?"

"Yes, they do."

"Then who is Santa Claus?!"

"Well, a lot of Mommies and Daddies like to play a game and pretend that a magical man with a big white beard and flying reindeer sneaks into everyone's house in the middle of the night and puts presents under their trees. It's just a game. It's pretend. See?"

"Sort of. But why do they do it?"

"Oh, just to have fun, I guess."

A thoughtful silence, then, "I think it's silly."

"We do too, but remember something. It's very important to keep this a *secret*. *I* know there's no Santa Claus, and *you* know there's no Santa Claus, but a lot of your friends think there *is* a Santa Claus. If you go and tell them there is no Santa Claus, you'll spoil their game. So don't tell them, all right?"

"I guess so. But I still think it's silly. Is there any ice cream left?" This is humanism.

"Daddy, who is Jesus?"

It is now Ned's turn on the hot seat. "He is what some people think of as a god. Like the Hindu god, Vishnu. Or—"

"Fishnu?!"

"No. Vishnu. In different parts of the world, people believe in different gods. They believe the gods live up in the sky or some-place invisible, and Jesus is one of those gods."

"Jody said he prayed to Jesus for his dog not to die, but he died anyway."

Ned thought, Bingo! What he said, though, was, "Jody and a lot of your friends believe in a god and they pray to the god to help them." As a preemptive strike he added, "Even though they don't usually get any help."

"Then why do they pray?"

"That's a good question. Most people pray to feel better. They want to believe there is someone watching over them, taking care of them."

"Do we believe in a god?"

"No."

"Why not?"

"Well, have you ever seen a god?"

"No."

"Neither have I. Have you ever heard a god or talked to a god?"

"No, but I've seen a picture of Jesus."

"That was a drawing, not a picture. People can draw anything—like Donald Duck. Is he real?"

Smiling, "No. But why do people believe something that's not real?"

"It makes them feel better. They don't understand where the planets and the sun and stars came from, so they figure it must be from some kind of god."

"Where *did* they come from?"

Sigh. "There are some things we may never understand. But enough for now. We'll talk about the universe tomorrow. I promise. Okay?"

"Okay. Is there any ice cream left?" This is humanism.

Racing into Amy's study, Melinda sputters breathlessly, "Danny just told me that if I don't believe in Jesus I'll go to hell and I'm gonna burn forever and scream and everyone around me will be screaming and—"

Amy turns away from her computer and keels on the floor, hugging her frantic daughter. "Now calm down, Melly."

"But Danny said I won't ever stop burning and there'll be flames coming out of my mouth and—" Tears flow down her cheeks as she gasps for air.

"Shhh. Quiet now. Listen to me, okay? I want you to listen to me."

A slow nod, a few more tears, then silence.

Staring down into the huge, frightened eyes, Amy says, "What Danny told you is what some people really believe. But we don't believe it, and a whole lot of other people don't believe it either. Your friend Sandra doesn't believe it, does she?"

"No. She said she was Jewish."

"See? We all believe different things."

"But Danny says if you kill someone or steal something God will send you to hell."

"Do you want to kill someone or steal something?"

Indignantly, "No!"

"I don't either. Grandma and Grandpa taught me to love other people, not to be afraid of a god. And that's what we want for you. So the next time Danny tries to scare you, you tell him you don't believe in hell and you don't want to talk about it any more. All right?"

The response is a slow nod and a look of relief. This is humanism.

The unmistakable paraphernalia of life-supporting equipment is everywhere. Respirators, feeding tubes, heart monitors . . . it's a fever dream gone terribly ugly. Ragged breathing, tortured moans, restless motion. A cancer ward. It's a waiting game, and Amy has had enough. She knows her cancer has metastasized, and she knows there will not be another remission. She wants to go home.

Against doctor's advice, she checks herself out of the hospital and goes home to the faces she loves: her beloved Ned, her sweet Melinda and Jason, her four grandchildren, and myriad other faces that, as the days pass, are becoming increasingly difficult to differentiate. But it doesn't matter any more. She is surrounded by love. She has lived with love and she is now preparing to die with love. Amy knows her life has been full and happy; she has been more fortunate than most; and she has no fear of death. She fears no hell and anticipates no heaven. She knows this is the end, and she has made her peace with it.

The pain is steadily getting worse, and she wants to say her good-byes before it becomes unbearable. She has the pills to end her life when she is ready. Strangely, that knowledge is comforting. She feels in control. She plans to be alone with Ned when the time comes for her final, dreamless sleep. But right now she is enjoying the reminiscing, the photo albums, and the hugs. Everyone knows they are saying a final good-bye. This is humanism.

The casket is closed and the first speaker stands in the front of the room. She absentmindedly smoothes her thinning gray hair, and begins to talk. Her voice is quavering, but determined. "You know, when I was a teenager, I was there in that crowded living room, so many years ago, when a very tiny Amy fought to take her first steps. I was also there with her, at the end, when she fought the pain as she said good-bye. There is no doubt the first was more fun than the second." Nervous laughter. "But if ever there was a loving child and a wonderful woman, Amy was it. She was a delight to be around, and I remember once when. . . ."

This is humanism.

HUMANIST TOLERANCE

Perhaps the most striking difference between secular humanism and so many religions is *tolerance*. Many of the world's largest religions have incredibly complex dietary laws, accompanied by dire consequences if broken. The Judeo-Christian Bible is packed with complicated rules and laws and forbidden behaviors, as well as very long lists of people who are to be shunned or killed. Among many others on the death list are witches (a very sensible precaution), idolaters, adulterers, anyone who curses their parents, anyone doing work on the Sabbath, anyone who lets a dangerous ox roam about freely (?!), anyone having sex with the wrong in-laws, any girl not found to be virginal on her wedding night, and . . . homosexuals. This is hardly a description of tolerance.

Most humanists would agree that allowing a dangerous ox to roam around is not a good idea, as people could definitely get hurt. But the death penalty for such carelessness is outrageous. And the treatment of witches is obviously a subject for another century—a long-ago century. The other "sinful" activities mentioned, however, are sinful only to religious fundamentalists. Fundamentalists include voluntary euthanasia as one of those "sins." "Death with dignity" is scoffed at and referred to as nothing more than a euphemism for "murder."

The subject of physician-assisted suicide is highly controversial. Yet the arguments against it are specious. Pressing these arguments is the Roman Catholic Church, trying to intrude in yet another public policy matter while flexing its considerable muscles.

Any compassionate person who has ever seen a loved one, or even a total stranger, suffer insufferable pain in the course of a terminal illness, cannot bear to witness it. Even doctors and nurses, who necessarily become accustomed to a great deal of human suffering, are moved to pity when the agony is great and the hope for survival is nil. And this brings up the first specious argument.

What if a cure for a patient's disease is discovered shortly after a suicide?

In a way, this would be a wonderful problem to have, wouldn't it? "Damn! We've found a cure for cancer! But it was just a bit too late for recently euthanized Jane!" This cure would normally signal a joyous day indeed for humankind, were it not for the unforgivable obscenity of the various worldwide Janes and their loved ones. Or so says the live-no-matter-what camp.

But they are wrong in their portrayals of Jane. The overwhelming majority, if not all, of terminal cancer patients, for example, *would not be helped by a cancer cure anyway.* Why? Because by the time they reach the end stage, their kidneys, lungs, liver, or other organs have been so ravaged by the disease that simply killing the cancer cells would be of no help. Those organs are beyond repair. So unless a cancer cure *and* a means of organ reconstruction could be discovered simultaneously (and we should all be so lucky) this particular hold-on-till-the-last-possible-moment argument is wholly invalid.

There are other equally destructive diseases that are similarly irreversible at a certain point, whether or not a "cure" is found for the original disease-causing agents. And these are the very diseases that cause the unbearable pain that sufferers beg to be freed of.

What's to prevent greedy relatives from knocking off their wealthy kin?

This is most disingenuous. Every physician-assisted suicide law thus far proposed has carefully crafted safeguards built in that would render such happenings impossible. The Greedy Relative argument implies that the following absurd scenario would be possible:

Greedy Relative: We think Aunt Helen is suffering way too much, and she's going to die anyway, so let's put her out of her misery.

Doctor: I guess you're right. So go ahead and kill her.

Greedy Relative: I brought along a revolver just in case you agreed. Okay?

Doctor: Good grief, no! You'll wake the other patients! [Begins preparing syringe.] Come on, let's go give the old lady her hot shot.

And the rest, as they say, is probate history.

This preposterous Greedy Relative argument ignores the very name of the procedure in question—physician-assisted *suicide*. This means that Aunt Helen must *want* to die, relatives or no relatives, and that physicians (*s*!) will help her do so only if no possible relief is available. Every proposed plan mandates that at least *two* doctors must agree that death is imminent and that all treatment options have been exhausted.

What's to prevent HMOs or insurance carriers from killing patients to save the staggeringly high medical costs involved in end-stage illnesses?

Once again, safeguards would be in place requiring family members to agree to the *patient-requested* procedure. If no family members are available, then a disinterested third party (or two) would be appointed to act as patient advocate. This important decision could *never* be made by any single individual—doctor, relative, *or* patient. It is practically an abuse-free plan.

What if the diagnosis proves incorrect and Aunt Helen wasn't terminal after all?

Well, what if the diagnosis proves incorrect and Uncle Henry didn't need to have his (prostate, lung, kidney, whatever) removed after all? Misdiagnosis is always a possibility, because people are not perfect. But should the *possibility* of misdiagnosis then prohibit *all* surgery? There was a time when male physicians were not allowed to function as obstetricians or gynecologists because of the distasteful possibility of sexual misconduct. That possibility is still alive and well today, but would anyone seriously suggest that men should be barred from that profession? The amount of suffering that could be prevented with euthanasia so overwhelmingly outweighs the remote possibilities of abuse that there is no reason, other than religious ones, not to use it.

There is no question that in a case of euthanasia the consequences are obviously as permanently irreversible as it is possible to be. However, very few doctors fail to recognize *end-stage* terminal illness. The possibility of two doctors making such a colossal mistake is extremely remote.

In any case, we're not talking about immediate euthanasia upon diagnosis. The following could never happen:

Doctor: I'm afraid your cancer is inoperable. You have maybe six months to live. I'm very sorry.
Patient: No! It can't be! I don't believe you!
Doctor: Please get a second opinion, but I'm afraid it will be the same.
Patient: Then I want to die now. I don't want to die in agony.
Doctor: Okay. Which would you prefer? A shot or some pills?
Patient: I'd rather have the shot and be done with it.
Doctor: Okay. You're outta here.

The live-no-matter-what camp would have us believe such ludicrous occurrences are likely if assisted suicide is legalized. They are not.

What if a patient's death wish is just a temporary thing, and it's acted on too soon?

All the safeguards proposed so far include the requirement that the desire for death must be *durable*. Assisted suicide may not be a spur-of-the-moment activity. The desire for death must continue for weeks, not mere hours.

In a published letter to a local humanist group, a woman wrote about her opposition to euthanasia. She said that she had suffered years earlier from suicidal depression, and she was grateful that none of her relatives was "kind" enough to have her "put out of her misery" at that time.

Well, lady, I'm glad no one killed you either. But what does this story have to do with physician-assisted suicide? This woman had no terminal illness. No doctor anywhere, let alone two of them, would ever even consider suicide in a case of depression *only*. Like many others trying to hide their religious motives, this woman was just throwing up another straw man. Opponents of euthanasia are either being disingenuous or are simply unwilling to educate themselves about the carefully designed safeguards in euthanasia proposals.

All things human are subject to abuse, which is why weighty issues demand stringent laws. Critics of euthanasia like to present it in a vaguely Wild West, cowboy atmosphere. A patient in pain cries, "I wish I were dead!" and someone promptly pulls out a six-shooter and blows him away. But now back to the real world.

Suicide used to be a *felony* in many jurisdictions in the United States, which clearly betrays the religious origins of such a ridiculous statute. I don't know offhand what the penalty was for the successful lawbreaker in this case. I'll have to look that up. But the fact that the Roman Catholic Church considers it a sin is their business only. The rest of us, in a democracy, should have the right to view our lives *and deaths*, differently.

It is worth noting that active euthanasia has been practiced in the Netherlands for two decades, involving fifty thousand patients, without one single report of abuse.[2] It would appear that safeguards can and do work.

New technology has made amazing recoveries possible. But it has also made amazing suffering possible, well beyond anything Mother Nature ever intended or would have allowed. In medicine, as elsewhere, high technology is truly a double-edged sword. Diseases that would normally have carried us off rather swiftly can now sometimes be cured, but too often are only prolonged. Often it is not really life that we prolong, but rather just the suffering.

When someone has expressly requested *not* to have his life end with feeding tubes and IV tubes and unbearable agony in the face of certain death, that request should be respected and honored. It is *his* life, not yours, or mine, or the Catholic Church's. If we see our loved ones in hopeless torment, we can and must help them end it, if that is their choice. We do it for our pets. Surely our human loved ones deserve as much.

Death with dignity is a valid, compassionate concept. And for many of us, the day will come when it is definitely time to say good-bye.

Another aspect of human behavior that is seldom the beneficiary of tolerance concerns our sexuality. Human sexuality is probably the single most conspicuous example of the contrast between religion and humanism. Humanism holds the position that a person's sex life is none of society's business. As long as no one is victimized (as in rape or child abuse) sexuality is a strictly private affair. But fundamentalists, especially Christian fundamentalists, spend an inordinate amount of time haranguing about sex. They seem almost obsessed with it. And their obsession with homosexuality can have tragic consequences.

In October of 1998, the country was shocked to hear about a young man named Matthew Shepard, the twenty-one-year-old Wyoming college student who was savagely beaten, tied to a fence post, and left for dead on a freezing night. In fact, he died a few days later from his injuries.[3] And why did this horror take place? Shepard was gay. That's it. He was gay.

Never in my life have I heard of anyone wanting to protest a funeral. Never. Who on earth would want to interfere with anyone burying their dead? But it happened. This obscene, heartless action was carried out by a group of Christian fundamentalists. Obviously extremists, they were nevertheless Christian fundamentalists. They staged a vocal protest outside the church where Shepard's funeral was being held. More than a dozen adults and *children* staged an antigay demonstration.

The explanation offered for the demonstration was that the

funeral was being used as a "platform for gay rights." Using a funeral as a platform? I thought they were just trying to bury their dead son. But the rabid bigots insisted that "the homosexuals are using it [the funeral] to demand new laws." What?!

Shepard's parents, obviously grief-stricken, had to endure not only the death of their son, but the ordeal of this nightmarish demonstration. They showed remarkable restraint. Mr. Dennis Shepard offered these words: "We should try to remember that because Matt's last few minutes of consciousness on earth might have been hell, his family and friends want more than ever to say their farewells to him in a peaceful, dignified, and loving manner." His sorrowful eloquence was heartbreaking.

Some of the placards displayed during the demonstration said things like "Fear God Not Fags" and "God Hates Fags" and "Heaven Won't Take Fags—Hell Has Him Now." It was so Nazi-like in its venomous hatred that it was frightening. Free speech is one thing, but . . .

The terrible irony in all this is that the Bible itself is the reason fundamentalists are fanatically, maniacally homophobic, and they can quote you chapter and verse to prove it. So can I.

> If a man also lie with mankind, as he lieth with a woman, both of them have committed an abomination: they shall surely be put to death; their blood shall be upon them. (Lev. 20:13)

There can be no doubt about what that means. "Surely be put to death" can't be more clear. The New Testament (Rom. 1:26–32) reinforces that edict. Children are naturally going to grow up hating homosexuals if their Bibles and fundamentalist parents constantly refer to gays as "abominations" and people who need "help."

Jerry Falwell, one of the most influential fundamentalist preachers ever, claimed he "loved" homosexuals, and would do everything in his power to help them return to "normalcy." Normalcy? Gays aren't freaks or lepers requiring "treatment." All gays require is to be left alone to live their lives as they see fit. And this is the humanist position.

We can only hope, though we will never know, that uncon-
sciousness came quickly to Matthew Shepard. Such viciousness is
difficult for the average person to comprehend, and just trying to
imagine it is very painful. But we must address the origins of such
violent acts. And there can be no doubt that the Religious Right,
with its ceaseless haranguing about the evils of homosexuality, per-
meates the air with an ugly tension that is bound to incite such violence eventually. If you keep spewing hateful words incessantly,
hateful actions will follow. And such bigoted rhetoric undoubtedly
played a part in the horrific death of an innocent young man.

If you take the gay-positive position to its logical conclusion, as the
humanist position does, there is no earthly reason why same-sex
marriage should not be allowed. Marriage is such a familiar feature
in our society that we barely take notice of it. It's difficult to
imagine a time in Western history when marriage did not exist. For
all the jokes we make about it, we still marry. In droves.

There is a common misperception about the nature of marriage.
Almost everyone would say that it is a union between a woman and
a man; and many would add that the union is blessed by God. But
God or no God, they would be wrong. In this country, marriage is
an uneven three-way partnership, and the state has the controlling
hand. The state, not the loving couple, dictates who may marry, and
when and where. In many states, it requires a blood test beforehand,
taking a bit of the romance out of the occasion. You must purchase
a license to get married, just as you must to go fishing or to drive a
car. It is a licensed event.

The state has the sole power to dissolve a marriage, and to dis-
tribute the assets tied to that marriage. Child custody and child support payments are determined by the state. Marriage is about inheritance, insurance benefits, powers of attorney, and tax exemptions.
Somehow the rose-covered cottage gets lost in the paperwork.

With this in mind, the idea of same-sex marriage seems suddenly less alien. Conservatives denounce gay marriage, claiming

that it is "unnatural" in the eyes of God. Pension-plan survivor benefits, though, to pick just one example, seem rather "unnatural" if you view marriage as a holy union between woman, man, and God. Yet there is no conservative clamor to remove any of the crass financial aspects from the sacred bond of holy matrimony. Community property laws are alive and well in Christian circles.

Church/state entanglement is probably nowhere more pervasive, though less readily apparent, than in our laws about marriage and reproduction. From wife beating to birth control to abortion, our "family" laws have been molded by religion.

So much of our historical baggage is religious baggage that we often overlook this point. We say to ourselves, if we think about it at all, that there must have been good reasons for laws to have evolved or else they wouldn't have become laws. Well, there are always reasons, but they don't necessarily have to be good ones. The old Jim Crow laws of the South speak volumes on that subject.

We owe an incalculable debt of gratitude to Margaret Sanger for her extraordinary bravery in fighting for reproductive freedom in the early decades of this century. It's almost inconceivable that people were actually sentenced to *jail* for the *crime* of sending birth control literature through the mail. And this was happening during the time period that my own grandmothers were in their reproductive years. The reason for the unreasonable ban? Religion.

And this brings us to gay marriages. The societal prejudice against such unions is firmly rooted in religion. If you look for any other reasons to be against it, you'll have a difficult time of it. I tried. And I failed. Trying to articulate both sides of a debate is an excellent exercise. I tried to argue both sides of this issue, but I couldn't do it. I could not come up with one valid, nonreligious reason to oppose gay marriages.

While a few tentative steps have been taken, for example in the state of Hawaii, the future of gay marriage remains unclear. But the objections to such marriages are difficult to nail down. For example, if it is true that procreation is the sole purpose of marriage, as so many religionists insist, then of course gay marriage is out of the question. However, if procreation is really the only reason for marriage, then the following people should not be allowed to marry: men who have had vasectomies; women who have had hysterectomies; postmenopausal women; and men and women who are sterile, for whatever reason, whether from injury, illness, or causes unknown. Further, fertility tests should be required before marriage licenses are issued, and if either party proves infertile, no marriage should be allowed. Marriages that do not produce children after some specified period of time should be declared null and void.

These radical suggestions are merely the logical end result of the marriage-must-equal-babies policy. If such measures seem preposterous, then the primary objection to gay marriages (lack of offspring) is preposterous. If we agree that forcing people to have babies is beyond the pale, meaning marriage may exist without children, then what precisely is wrong with gays marrying? Consensual, adult, gay sexual activity hurts no one. So what is all the fuss about?

Religionists claim that homosexual activity is "unnatural." The Bible refers to it as an "abomination." But just who is going to define "natural" sexual practices? Many "normal," heterosexual marriages include many "unnatural" sexual activities—oral, anal, and otherwise. Ask any marriage counselor. Or psychologist. Or bartender. Or just look in the mirror. Our bedrooms are our own business—not the state's and not the church's. The absurdity of the whole bedroom discussion serves to highlight the absurdity of the Religious Right's melodramatic expressions of horror regarding homosexual activity. Their righteous denunciation of gay sexual activity seems to echo from another century. And maybe that's because it does. The Bible is thousands of years old.

Sadly, the religious harping about gays is as strong in Muslim communities as it is in Christian enclaves. The primitive, superstitious cultures that spawned our religions are clearly reflected in this nonsensical taboo. One leader of an African nation announced that the spread of AIDS in his country was 100 percent heterosexual. How did he know that? Well, his country was Muslim, and Islam forbids homosexuality. Therefore, there were no gays, not one, in his entire nation. You can only shake your head and sigh. Or pound a table, depending on your mood.

Diversity is one of the driving forces behind beneficial social change, and the idea that we must all resemble peas in a pod is antiquated and stifling. For example, as hard as it is to believe, some people actually like lima beans. *Lima beans.* However, when I meet someone in this category, I do not feel the urge to scream and go running off in another direction. Well, maybe I feel it a little—we *are* talking about lima beans. Nevertheless, I recognize these people as fully human and deserving of any respect that goes with that status.

And so it must be with all of our social diversities, from stodgy bookworms to party hounds. Tolerance must be the hallmark we all strive toward. Gays should have the same rights as anyone else to experience the bliss of marriage and the agony of divorce. If two gays love each other and want to formalize their commitment with the official stamp of marriage, so much the better. The world can always use more love and commitment.

Until we outgrow our bigoted, divisive religions, however, humanism is probably our only hope in spearheading this cause. Humanism recognizes the uniqueness in each of us. This is the beauty of secular humanism. Its wide, tolerant umbrella provides a generous, welcoming canopy of understanding and acceptance for us all. Even if you happen to like lima beans.

NOTES

1. Mason Olds, "What Is Religious Humanism?" *Free Inquiry* 16, no. 4 (fall 1996): 11–14.

2. Pieter V. Admiraal, "Euthanasia in the Netherlands," *Free Inquiry* 17, no. 1 (winter 1997): 5–8.

3. E. N. Smith, "Gay Wyoming Student Beaten, Tied to Fence and Left for Dead," *Stockton Record*, October 10, 1998, p. A1.

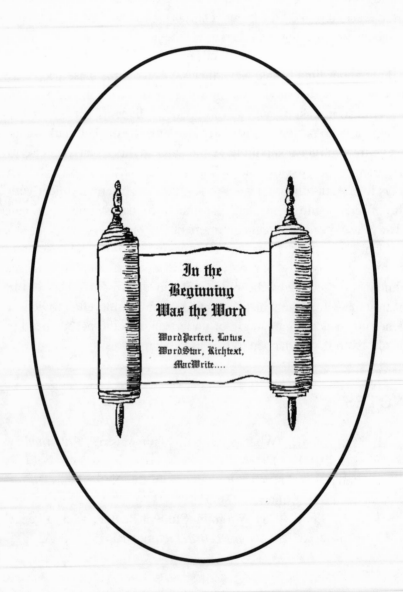

In the
Beginning
Was the Word

WordPerfect, Lotus,
WordStar, Richtext,
MacWrite....

4

THE ENTIRE BIBLE— CONDENSED

FOR THOSE OF YOU WHO ARE
ALWAYS ON THE GO
OR
JUST HAVE SLIGHTLY BELOW AVERAGE
READING SKILLS

Persons attempting to find a motive in this narrative will be prosecuted; persons attempting to find a moral in it will be banished; persons attempting to find a plot in it will be shot.
— Mark Twain, *Huckleberry Finn*

THE OLD TESTAMENT

Genesis

IN THE BEGINNING WAS THE Word. No one is certain which word it was, although scholars believe it was probably "spirit," "void," or "cranberry." After the Word came days and nights, which alternated nicely, and it's a good thing, too, or we'd never know when to go to bed. Then came all the stuff up in the sky, and all the stuff down here on the ground, like water and plants and animals and people. More or less in that order. And the whole thing happened in six days flat. The little animals ate the plants, the big animals ate the little animals, and the people ate anything they could get their hands on, often with mayonnaise on the side, unless they were watching their fat intake.

Now, the god who created all this had no real name, and just called himself "I who is Me" or something like that. But the people

117

wanted him to have a *real* name, like Jim or Juan, since they figured they'd be talking to him, you know? So they called him JHVWHW—which of course is impossible to pronounce. But that turned out not to be a problem because JHVWHW hit the roof when he heard about the name thing, and told them that if they *ever* called him by his real name they'd be dead on the spot. No one understood why he was so sensitive about this whole name business, but why take chances? So they simply called him God.

When God had created the plants and animals, he put them all in one garden. Every plant and animal on earth was in this *one garden*—Eden. It must have been one hell of a big garden. And one of the trees in this colossal garden was called the Tree of the Knowledge of Good and Evil—definitely an oddball name for a tree, but as we now know God had a real problem with names. Now this tree grew some kind of fruit, though no one knows which kind. It may have been apples or figs, or maybe even cranberries. But there was a hitch—if the people ate the fruit, they would learn things that only God was supposed to know, and evidently there were some things he just didn't want to share. He warned them loud and clear not to eat that fruit. So of course that's one of the first things they did. They ate the damn fruit. Wouldn't you know it? Here they had all the trees in the world to pick from but *nooooooo*, it had to be *that* one. Sheesh! Makes you want to slap 'em upside the head, doesn't it?

And worse, you know *why* they ate the forbidden fruit? A snake told them to. That's why. Now up until now this story has made perfect sense—except for the part about the whole universe being created in six days, and all the plants and animals fitting into one big garden, and that business about *names*, and the screwy tree with the magical powers. But other than that, it has been a straightforward, believable story. This talking snake, though, is pushing it. Serpents do not talk. Except maybe in Mozart's *Magic Flute*.

Well, smooth-talking serpents or not, these people, Adam and Eve, who were named very nicely by Someone with a problem in that area, screwed it up for everyone. They got kicked out of the garden, had to start growing their own food, having kids became a real pain, which hasn't changed since, and then they went and raised a couple of real losers—Cain and Abel of sibling rivalry fame. Uncertainty shrouds the nature of the first parental words ever uttered, but a probable candidate is, "Whatever you do, don't call Him by name! He *hates* that!"

Remember now that there were only four people on the whole planet—Mom, Dad, Cain, and Abel. So what happens? Cain kills Abel, leaving only three. What the heck was *his* problem? Was the entire planet just not big enough for the four of them? There must have been a bad gene in this group right from the get-go. Anyway, Cain then follows up his murder with a marriage. However, since there were no other people in the world yet, anywhere, this bride is of unknown origin. It's also rather unsavory to contemplate her possible identity, so we'll skip over that part.

At this point, though, things really pick up. More and more people appear, people beget more people—there's a lot of begetting going on. They breed like jackrabbits. But these people must have been a real pain in the neck because one day, out of the blue (or more likely out of a cloudy sky—must have been clouding up by now) God went and killed them all. Just like that. Without so much as a warning. Except for one guy and his family—*one guy!*—he killed everyone. Drowned them all in this huge flood.

This part of the story is very sad. And very nauseating. In no time at all the world was awash in dead bodies, bloated and floating everywhere and smelling *horrible*. People, pigs, prairie dogs. Just a mess. And they stank to high heaven. So to speak. But this is definitely too gross to dwell on, so we'll skip over this part, too.

It turns out that the fellow with the winning lottery ticket was named Noah. God told Noah to build a very large boat because it was gonna rain till hell wouldn't have it. Or words to that effect. And it had to be a *huge* boat because it was going to have to hold at least two of every kind of animal on earth. Sort of like the garden thing. So Noah built this enormous boat, gathered up his family and the animals, and then sat on his boat while it rained. For forty days and nights. That's a lot of rain. And he sat with all the animals and their . . . droppings. That's a lot of droppings. But Noah and his group were safe. All the rest of the humans, though, were like a bunch of drowned rats—which, come to think of it, they must have looked like from God's perspective. According to Noah, God said that humans were acting like real dorks, and he had no choice but to off 'em all. What a temper.

The people did the jackrabbit thing again, though, and pretty soon there were people everywhere. Some of them tried to build a tower reaching all the way up to heaven (can you imagine what the blueprints looked like?) but God put a stop to that pronto. Seems he didn't want visitors any more than he wanted people calling him by name. Clearly God was basically antisocial.

After that, languages were created; circumcision was invented (ouch!); some kings had some wars; Sodom and Gomorrah, two real party towns, were destroyed; a lady was turned into salt (really!); Jacob's Ladder got invented (now available at Home Depot); the pharaoh had some dreams that needed interpreting; a famine followed; and then Jacob, who made ladder history, died. And that's the end of Genesis.

Exodus

This section opens with the Children of Israel being fruitful and multiplying. Seems we can't get away from the jackrabbit thing. Someone named Moses climbed up a mountain and talked to God, who was disguised as a burning bush. (See? Here we go again. The antisocial thing.) Moses turned a plain old stick into a serpent—but it's hard to understand why anyone would do that. Which would you rather have in your hand—a snake that might bite you or a stick that you could use as firewood? Or as a walking stick? Or maybe even a pogo stick? It makes no sense.

Anyway, after that the plagues came. One after another, plagues, plagues, plagues. There were frogs, lice, locusts, and flies everywhere. It was totally disgusting. People couldn't help but step on them, so there were squished vermin all over the place. And the flies were so thick people were accidentally swallowing them . . . we'll skip over this, too.

Passover gets going, and then the Israelites escape from Egypt.

This infuriates the pharaoh and he sends his soldiers after them. This next part is really cool. Moses lifts up his hands (it doesn't say whether he was holding a stick or a serpent) and the Red Sea splits right in half so they can run through! Is that cool? Charlton Heston did it great in the movie. Not only that, but the water closes right up behind them, like a zipper, and the Egyptians drown. Too cool! Except, of course, for the Egyptian soldiers. For them it was a real bummer.

Almost as cool is the food falling out of the sky. No kidding. The people are hungry and God drops food right out of the sky. The original fast food. Notice, though, how God doesn't come down himself, sit down, and share a nice meal with these people? Same problem as before.

Pretty soon God gives Moses the Ten Commandments, which Charlton Heston also did very well. But later on there are sickeningly detailed instructions about how to sacrifice a ram. All kinds of stuff about blood and horns and kidneys and liver and even *dung*. Yuck. All this stuff is supposed to be burned on an altar as a sacrifice to God. Don't read this part near mealtime.

Then the people build a golden calf, which apparently was quite attractive, but God didn't think so. Seems it threatened his ego. So he killed a whole bunch of people because of it, which seems a bit of an overreaction to one lousy golden calf, but by now it's clear there's no figuring this guy. And during a conversation with Moses, God said, "There shall no man see me, and live." See? There it is again. Well, finally a great big tabernacle is built, but no one can go in it because God is already in there and he doesn't want company. It just never ends. But this is the end of Exodus.

Leviticus

This book lists every possible thing humans can do that is wrong, and what kind of punishments they'll get for doing them. It is a very, very long book because there are a great many ~~fun~~ wrong things people can do. Dietary laws are also laid out here. For example, people are not allowed to eat bats, tortoises, Quiche Lorraine, warthogs, Fritos, or bratwurst. Or cranberries.

Numbers

This book is all about numbers. They counted the noses of all the Children of Israel and ended up with some very big numbers. This book has lots and lots of numbers in it. That's why it's called "Numbers." No one is certain who wrote this book, but rumor has it that it was a CPA.

Deuteronomy

This is where the Israelites, led by Moses, wander through the wilderness for forty years. Can you imagine? They obviously had no travel plan. A travel agent would have saved them a heck of a lot of time. Then the people are told they should take the first fruits and firstborn animals to the Levite priests as offerings to God. The priests will then put the offerings on the altar, and whatever God doesn't eat overnight they get to keep for themselves. (Nice little racket they had going.) This command about the offerings is accompanied by an equally forceful enjoinder:

> Take heed to thyself that thou forsake not the Levite as long as thou livest upon the earth. (Deut. 12:19)

This enjoinder is conveyed to the people by the Levite priests themselves—the guys who get to keep all the offerings. It was a *great* little racket. The only thing they wouldn't accept was cranberries.

Then there are more rules about what they can eat. They can eat meat, but not the blood. The blood must be poured on the ground . . . we'll skip this part, too. They can eat ox, sheep, goats, deer, and chamois, although it's hard to imagine eating anything you polish your car with. They can have fish as long as it has fins and scales. No fins, no scales, no dinner. Vultures and bats are forbidden, which seems prudent, but so are pigs. Pigs are out of the question. God never explained what he had against bacon. The people were also not supposed to seethe a kid in its mother's milk, though it's not clear why anyone would want to do that in the first place. Interestingly, no mention is made of Chateaubriand or truffles or pheasant under glass, so we must assume this was not an upscale community.

The people are again reminded to give their first fruits to the priests.

Then there is a whole collection of other laws. For example, they can't plow their fields with an ox and an ass together. You do have to wonder if the field would really mind. Nor can they wear wool and linen together, which definitely puts a crimp in their wardrobe choices.

Next is a long list of curses they will have to endure if they don't obey the laws. The Lord will smite them with consumption, fever, inflammation, extreme burning, mildew, scabs, blindness, madness, and the itch. Hopefully not all at the same time. And hopefully not just because someone inadvertently threw on her wool frock over her linen underwear one hurried morning.

The people are reminded yet again to give over their first fruits to the priests. The Levites knew how to keep a good thing going. Then Moses sings a long song, followed by several farewell addresses. They don't rank with Washington's farewell address, but they're not bad actually. Of course Moses is 120 years old at the time, so we shouldn't expect too much. Then he dies. Which we should expect.

Joshua

Here is where that famous battle takes place. The battle plan is simplicity itself. The Israelites, led by Joshua, surround the city of Jericho. Your basic siege. On the seventh day of the siege the priests blow their rams' horns, paid for with the money they got from all those first fruits, and at that signal all the people start shouting and singing. Obviously they were no Mormon Tabernacle Choir because their voices make the walls of the city crumble and fall on the spot. And that's how Joshua wins the battle.

In another battle, Joshua needs more time, so he asks God to have the sun stay put for a while longer so he can see who he's killing, you know? God obliges and the sun stays where it is for an extra day. Now there are some problems with this account. The sun does not move—the earth does. And even if the sun *did* stay in the same place for a whole day, any oceans facing it would begin boiling. Well, let's not quibble.

There are more battles, and people get hanged, and smitten, and conquered. There is an awful lot of this killing in the Bible. It's like watching a Clint Eastwood/Sylvester Stalone/Arnold Schwarzenegger movie marathon. Joshua kills the Hittites, the Jebusites, the Amorites, the Perizzites, the Samsonites, the Stalagmites, and the Stalactites. After that Joshua himself dies.

The people are then reminded to make their offerings to the priests.

Judges

This book is a list of all the judges who presided over Israel. It's quite a list. But they're all here. Everyone is accounted for, including Judge Roy Bean, Judge John Sirica, Judge Wapner, Judge Lance Ito, and Judge Judy.

This is also where you find the story of Samson and Delilah. They have this thing going, but Samson doesn't know Delilah is really a double-agent for the Philistines, the Israelites' sworn enemy. She asks Samson where he gets his extraordinary strength. He tells her that if he is tied with a special kind of rope he'll lose all his strength. So she ties him up. Three different times she ties him up. There's some S & M going on here. But none of the ropes can hold him. Finally he admits his strength is in his hair. His *hair*. So she cuts off all his hair, which eliminates his power. This is a very kinky story. Stripped of his power, Samson has his eyes gouged out by the Philistines. They tie him up yet again (definitely S & M) and toss him in prison. But Samson's hair grows out again, he gets his strength back, and he gets even by making this huge Philistine palace crumble, killing everyone inside. Trouble is, Samson is inside too. He didn't think this one through. So that's how he dies.

Ruth

This book contains the famous quote, "Whither thou goest, I will go." That's what the Israelites said to Moses, and look what *they* did for forty years. Like a typical male, Moses wouldn't ask for directions, so they wandered aimlessly through the wilderness for forty years. Anyway, this whole book is only three or four pages long—not a proper book at all. It should be called the leaflet of Ruth.

1 Samuel, 2 Samuel, 1 Kings, 2 Kings, 1 Chronicles, 2 Chronicles

Now this is truly padding. This is gilding the lily. There is no need for two of each. One each would have done very nicely, thank you. And it's not like the Bible needs padding. It's a hefty read, a bona fide long haul. Perhaps the writers didn't realize how long the whole thing was going to be when it was finished, and they felt the need to pad it out. You know, like we all did in high school when we were told to write essays. I remember once in American history we were supposed to write a report with a minimum of two thousand words. I was an A student, but I never got any feedback or comments on any of my reports. I was certain the teacher wasn't even reading them. So this time, after the first two pages about the Louisiana Purchase, I started waxing eloquent about pig farms. Then I wrote about how much I liked *Mad* magazine. I even quoted Alfred E. Neuman: *What, me worry?* I included a fan letter I had sent to Elvis Presley years ago. Then I rounded it out with a couple of terrific recipes, one for sauerbraten and one for apple strudel, and finished up with a page on the Louisiana Purchase. I made sure I had nice margins—neatness counts. I got an A+, with no comments, validating my theory. But I digress.

So maybe these biblical writers felt the same need to pad. But these "first" and "second" books meander all over the place. The only interesting stories are about David and Goliath, the Queen of Sheba, Jezebel, and Elijah. David is a little guy who beats the crap out of a big bully, which is always fun, since most of us root for the underdog. But the Sheba-Jezebel stories, reminiscent of the treacherous Delilah, get on your nerves after a while. The only women in the Bible seem to be strumpets. Like you can see on Pay-Per-View.

However, the part about Elijah ascending to heaven on a whirlwind, in a chariot of fire with horses of fire, must have been something to see! That's where the phrase "hold your horses" comes from. You hold on tight because you never know when your horses might just head on up to heaven . . .

After that the great temple is destroyed. And the people are reminded to make their offerings to the priests—but to hold the cranberries.

Ezra, Nehemiah, Esther

These books should really all be clumped together and called "Endless Lists of Names No One Cares About." Now Esther is a very pretty name. But can you imagine looking down at a sweet newborn baby and saying, "I know! Let's call him Nehemiah!" The razzing he'd take at school would be relentless. "And now at the plate, Nehemiah Johnson!" Snicker, giggle. Ezra isn't much better. But on with the story. Such as it is.

These three books all together don't have much to say. In Ezra there is a long, long list of all the Israelites who came back from captivity in Babylon. I'm sure they were excited about it, but who wants to read page after page of names? "The Nethinims: the children of Ziha, the children of Hasupha, the children of Tabbaoth, the children of Keros, and Siaha's children." More? "The children of Padon, the children of Lebanah, the children of Hagabah, the children of Akkub, the children of Hagab, the children of Shalmai, the children of Hanan, the children of Giddel, the children of Gahar, the children of Reaiah, the children of Rezin, the children of Nekoda, the children of Gazzam, the children of Uzza, the children of Paseah, the children of Besai, the children of Asnah, the children of Mehunim, the children of Nephusim, . . ." (Ezra 2:43–50). Sheesh! And that's only about a tenth of it.

Then there's talk about rebuilding the temple, which they

finally finish. To show you how slow this section is, on the top of
one of the pages, where many Bibles summarize the important
highlights of those very pages, there is this: "Ezra proclaimeth a
fast." Whoa! That sounds like riveting reading, doesn't it?!

Nehemiah isn't much better. It describes how they're going to
build a wall around Jerusalem. But we get right back into the lists
of names thing. I mean, who really cares?

> But the fish gate did the sons of Hassenaah build, who also laid
> the beams thereof, and set up the doors thereof, the locks thereof,
> and the bars thereof. (Neh 3:3)

Locks. They're talking about locks and beams and bars. Book
of the Month Club, stand by. But wait. There's more.

> Next unto him repaired Uzziel the son of Harhaiah, of the gold-
> smiths. Next unto him also repaired Hananiah the son of one of
> the apothecaries, and they fortified Jerusalem unto the broad wall.
> (Neh 3:8)

More lists of names. There are so many of these wall-building
credits that you just know the Carpenter's Union had a hand in it.
Not only that, but when they finally get the damn wall built, there
is *another* long list of the Israelites who fled captivity in Babylon.
Like we need this twice? And then there's a list of the people who
"sealed the covenant." Lists, lists, lists. There's another list of all
the priests of first fruits fame. And finally—a shopping list. I
wonder if Nehemiah remembered to bring home that loaf of bread
and a six-pack.

In Esther, there is the story of how she pleased a king and
became a queen. Then there is—guess what? Right! Another list!
These authors really needed a good editor. This time the list names
the enemies of the Jews who are then killed. Finally, it ends. And
not a moment too soon.

Job

By now we all know about God's recurrent temper tantrums. Sodom and Gomorrah, the people who made the golden calf, and the Flood are major examples. Remember that flood?! God unquestionably has an anger-management problem. But the story of Job is somehow even worse. It's so *personal*.

Here we have this guy named Job. He is an all-around nice person, runs an honorable household, keeps kosher, honors the Sabbath—the works. Of course he is extremely wealthy, which helps. But still, he's a nice fellow, taking good care of his family. So guess what happens to him?

Maybe you've seen that cartoon where this guy is standing on a street corner, hands in pockets, a vacant grin on his face. The image is dumb and happy. Just behind and above him, out of his sight, is this immense black cloud, filling half the sky. An equally enormous hand is reaching down from inside that cloud. The thumb is holding the middle finger back, in a tight circle, while the other three fingers are straight forward—the way you'd prepare to flick a small beetle off your picnic blanket. But this enormous finger is aimed straight at the back of the head of this hapless, unsuspecting man. He is about to be "flicked" from here to next Thursday. There is no caption because the image says it all. You have to laugh, even if you don't want to, because you can't help but identify with it, thinking there are days when you feel just like that. Like you've been severely flicked. Well, think of the guy in this cartoon as Job. Job was flicked like few of us have ever been flicked. But he was flicked by God. And through no fault of his own. Here's how it happened.

It seems God was taunting Satan about this guy Job, pointing out that Job was a perfect servant of his (God's), and what did Satan think of that? Satan answered that sure, it was easy for Job to be such a great guy since God had given him so much wealth. Job had seven sons and three daughters, seven thousand sheep, five hundred yoke of oxen, and five hundred asses. Oh, and camels. He even had camels—three thousand of them. So he was pretty well off, and he and his family feasted a lot. Well, wouldn't you?

So, God takes up the challenge and tells Satan that he's free to do whatever he wants to do to Job. God bets that Job will still remain faithful to him. Satan accepts the bet and begins his campaign of destruction. First he kills all of Job's oxen, asses, sheep, and the servants. Then he goes after the camels and kills them too. Not finished, though, Satan then kills all of Job's children. When Job hears about all this, you know what he does? He tears his coat, shaves his head, and falls to the ground worshipping God. I think I might have reacted differently, but then I'm not Job.

Well, anyway, God is laughing up his sleeve, and with a derisive grin says to Satan, "See? I told you! The guy's a gem! Look at him. Still worshipping me. I *told* you so."

Satan answers, "Well, there's a lot more I could have done to him!"

God responds, "Fine. Go for it. Do whatever you want to him, but don't kill him. Leave him alive."

You know, there's an unsavory undertone to all this. Think about it. You inflict punishment then ask, "Do you still love me?" Then you inflict more punishment and ask, "Do you still love me *now*?" And so on. Reminds me of one of those movies that feature women in black boots with whips.

Keep in mind that Job has done absolutely nothing to deserve this. Not to mention his blameless children, servants, oxen, sheep and camels. How could a camel offend anyone? But they were all killed, and all because of a childish schoolyard wager between God and Satan. The Bible doesn't say, though, if there was any money riding on this bet. But the odds-makers were giving eight to five, taking Satan.

Well, Satan has a go at Job's body next. He covers his whole body with boils from head to foot. Not only is the guy miserable, but he looks like the ferrets have been at him. So his wife finally complains and asks why Job doesn't curse God for the things he is doing to him. Job chews her out for doubting God; but frankly I'm surprised she didn't complain sooner. All those boils . . .

At long last, though, Job has finally had it. He wishes he were dead and curses the day he was ever born. Trouble is, he curses that day page after page after page. He won't give it a rest. And the descriptions of his suffering are unnecessarily graphic.

My bone cleaveth to my skin and to my flesh, and I am escaped with the skin of my teeth. [Another phrase accounted for.] (Job 19:20)

My bowels boiled, and rested not: the days of affliction prevented me. (Job 30:27)

Yet his meat in his bowels is turned, it is the gall of asps within him. He hath swallowed down riches, and he shall vomit them up again: God shall cast them out of his belly. He shall suck the poison of asps. . . . (Job 20:14-16)

We'll skip over the rest.

Well, Job and some friends argue and debate for days on end about things like righteousness, complaining, whether God can make mistakes (they can ask that with Job's boils and bowel problems?), human frailty, wickedness, and whether or not to invest in overseas mutual funds.

But in the end Job goes back to praising God and humbling himself. God is tickled, and rewards him with twice as much wealth as he had before. Camels and all. He even gives him seven more sons and three more daughters. Fat lot of good that does, though, for the ten dead children already in their graves. But at least now we know why Job's wife was allowed to live—to bear ten more children. I can't imagine she was all that thrilled. But apparently Job is satisfied, and he dies a contented old man.

What is not satisfying, however, is that the story ends without telling us who won the bet—God or Satan. Job started out great, but faded big time when the going got too tough, then seemed to pull it out again at the end—like a relief pitcher. So who won? After making us slog through this whole vile mess, the least they could do is tell us who won the stupid bet. Maybe, sensing a draw, and therefore to save face, they called the whole thing off on account of rain.

And what had poor Job done to deserve all this torment? He was just standing on a corner one day minding his own business, hands in his pockets, when the colossal hand of God reached down from out of a cloud . . .

The moral of this story? There are two. One, never stop looking over your shoulder, and two, know when to duck.

Psalms

This is one long, whining, grousing, hand-wringing, neurotic harangue. There are 150 chapters, each as depressing as the next. "O Lord, rebuke me not," and "Why standest thou afar off, O Lord?" and "Wash me thoroughly from mine iniquity," and blah, blah, blah. It never stops. Hear me cry, show me mercy, forget me not, don't turn away from me, don't kick me in the groin, and so on. In between these fretful worries there are praises offered to the God who is causing all this worry to begin with. At one point God is praised because "he shall pluck my feet out of the net" (Ps. 25:15). Actually I've never found that I needed much help in that area. In fact, I'm trying to figure out how you can get your feet caught in a net at all. Perhaps *rushing* the net. I don't know. Although I guess if you're hurling fishing nets out into the ocean while standing on shore, you might get your feet caught. Of course you'd have to be incredibly inept to have such a stupid thing happen to you, but it *would* give your fishing buddies a good laugh.

The most famous psalm is the twenty-third, where David talks about the Lord being a shepherd, and leading people beside the still waters. The last verse:

> Surely goodness and mercy shall follow me all the days of my life: and I will dwell in the house of the LORD for ever. (Ps 23:6)

But just one psalm before, in Psalm 22, David says:

> My God, my God, why hast thou forsaken me? why art thou so far from helping me, and from the words of my roaring? (Ps 22:1)

So which is it? Goodness and mercy or being forsaken?

Well, shortly after the complaint about being forsaken, David refers to himself as a "worm." He obviously has a decided self-esteem problem, and some serious issues to work through, such as his schizophrenic, love/hate relationship with God. The Psalms make it clear that a good shrink would do them both a lot of good.

Proverbs

C'mon, Baby Boomers! Don't tell me you don't remember this one! Sing along:

> Proverbs, proverbs, they're so true;
> Proverbs tell us what to do;
> Proverbs help us all to be
> Better Mouseketeers!

Although some of the authors of the Bible are said to have had prophetic powers, there is no actual proof that Proverbs was written with the future 1950s TV series *The Mickey Mouse Club* in mind. Anything's possible of course, but some of the proverbs don't sound like they would be suitable for little Cubby and Karen to be singing about. For example, "The memory of the just is blessed: but the name of the wicked shall rot" (Prov. 10:7). Or "For a whore is a deep ditch; and a strange woman is a narrow pit" (Prov. 23:27). Or "For the lips of a strange woman drop as an honeycomb, and her mouth is smoother than oil: But her end is bitter as wormwood, sharp as a twoedged sword" (Prov. 5:3-4). Her *end*? Well, this is not the stuff of Disney.

But there's some good stuff too. "A false balance is abomination to the Lord: but a just weight is his delight" (Prov. 11:1). This is wise guidance, especially if you plan to join the circus as a tightrope walker. A high-wire artist has to have good balance, *and* keep his weight under control. Definitely good advice here.

"Divers weights, and divers measures, both of them are alike abomination to the Lord" (Prov. 20:10). "A just weight and balance are the Lord's: all the weights of the bag are his work" (Prov. 16:11). This weight thing does wear a bit thin, though. I wonder if God has a weight problem—maybe belongs to Weight Watchers? Their success rate is extraordinary, by the way.

"The righteous shall never be removed: but the wicked shall not inhabit the earth" (Prov. 10:7). Which earth do you suppose they're talking about? Certainly not this one. The wicked are inhabiting big-time. Always have. So they got this one all wrong.

"Surely in vain the net is spread in the sight of any bird" (Prov. 1:17). "The wicked desireth the net of evil men: but the root of the righteous yieldeth fruit" (Prov. 12:12). "A man that flattereth his neighbour spreadeth a net for his feet" (Prov. 29:5). Jeez. We're back to the nets-and-feet thing. This sounds like some sort of fetish, so let's move on.

"Pride goeth before destruction, and an haughty spirit before a fall" (Prov. 16:18). So true. And women goeth before men, at least on the *Titanic*.

There are many lesser-known proverbs that have real meaning and depth. Here are some examples:

(1) An idealist is one who, on noticing that a rose smells better than a cabbage, concludes that it will also make better soup.

(2) Conscience is the inner voice which warns us that someone may be looking.

(3) Historian—an unsuccessful novelist.

(4) The holy passion of friendship is of so sweet and steady and loyal and enduring a nature that it will last through a whole lifetime, if not asked to lend money.

(5) She was not quite what you would call refined. She was not quite what you would call unrefined. She was the kind of person that keeps a parrot.

(6) Always do right—this will gratify some and astonish the rest.

(7) Man is the only animal that blushes. Or needs to.

(8) It takes your enemy and your friend, working together, to hurt you to the heart: the one to slander you and the other to get the news to you.

(9) If you pick up a starving dog and make him prosperous, he will not bite you. This is the principal difference between a dog and a man.

(10) Put all your eggs in the one basket and—*watch that basket*.

(11) A book is a man's best friend, outside of a dog; inside of a dog it's too dark to read.

(12) Once you've finally figured out what life is all about, you've probably already screwed yours up.

(13) You can't tell a book by its cover, but you can tell your hairdresser anything.

pla·gia·rize (plā′jə-rīz′) *verb*
pla·gia·rized, **pla·gia·riz·ing**, **pla·gia·riz·es** *verb, transitive*

(1) To use and pass off as one's own [the ideas or writings of another].

(2) To appropriate for use as one's own passages or ideas from [another].

Okay, okay, so they're not all mine.[1] The last two are, though. And all right, they may not be in Proverbs, but the point is they *should* be. They're certainly more wise and prudent than all that blather about weights and nets and feet.

Anyway, at the very end of the book of Proverbs the Israelites are again reminded to make their offerings to the priests.

Ecclesiastes

This book, one of the hardest to pronounce, was written solely for the purpose of providing the 1960s rock group The Byrds with a hit single. Which of course *proves* that the Old Testament prophets could see into the future. Pete Seeger wrote the song "Turn, Turn, Turn" and he called it that because he was talking about how there's a season for everything—everything in its turn—like it says in Ecclesiastes:

> To every thing there is a season, and a time to every purpose under the heaven: A time to be born, and a time to die; a time to plant, and a time to pluck up that which is planted; A time to kill, and a time to heal; a time to break down, and a time to build up; A time to weep, and a time to laugh; a time to mourn, and a time to dance; . . . (Eccles. 3:1–4)

It goes on and on like that. Seeger added all the "turns," so the song goes like this: "To everything, turn, turn, turn, there is a season, turn, turn, turn. . . ." He left out of few of the seasons, such as a time to drink and a time to pass out; a time to deal the cards and a time to ante up; a time to visit your dental hygienist and a time to eat sweets; and so on. But other than that, and the addition of all the "turns," it was a straight steal.

There is no mention of feet and nets together in this book.

Song of Solomon

This book has no mention of nets at all, and only two references to feet. But the rest of the body is covered, or should I say uncovered, in great detail. Presented as a collection of love poems describing God's love for Israel, no one buys that explanation. The Song of Solomon is an out-and-out erotic, sensual sex poem. Sometimes called the Song of Songs, it would be better titled the Song of Sex. It's hot stuff. "A bundle of myrrh is my wellbeloved unto me; he shall lie all night betwixt my breasts" (Song of Sol. 1:13). "Thy two breasts are like two young roes that are twins, which feed among the lilies" (Song of Sol. 4:5).

> How beautiful are thy feet [here we go again] with shoes, O prince's daughter! the joints of thy thighs are like jewels, the work of the hands of a cunning workman. Thy navel is like a round goblet, which wanteth not liquor: thy belly is like an heap of wheat set about with lilies. Thy two breasts are like two young roes that are twins. (Song of Sol. 7:1–3)

> This thy stature is like to a palm tree, and thy breasts to clusters of grapes. I said, I will go up to the palm tree, I will take hold of the boughs thereof: now also thy breasts shall be as clusters of the vine, and the smell of thy nose like apples; ... (Song of Sol. 7:7–8)

Well, okay, some of the imagery is less than perfect. The nose/ apple thing doesn't work. And there are a couple of other unfortunate choices of words here and there.

> Thy teeth are like a flock of sheep that are even shorn, which came up from the washing; whereof every one bear twins, and none is barren among them. (Song of Sol. 4:2)

> Thy neck is as a tower of ivory; thine eyes like the fishpools in Heshbon, by the gate of Bathrabbim: thy nose is as the tower of Lebanon which looketh toward Damascus. (Song of Sol. 7:4–5)

Teeth rarely look like a flock of sheep, and the shot about a nose looking like the tower of Lebanon is uncalled for in an otherwise arousing narrative. But when you're describing breasts, thighs, breasts, bellies, breasts, navels, and breasts, you're talking about sex. Solomon had a veritable obsession with breasts. But if someone tries to tell you all this breast-talk is about God's love for Israel or the "Church's love for Christ," direct them to:

dis·in·gen·u·ous (dĭs'ĭn-jĕn'yoo-əs) *adjective*
Not straightforward or candid; crafty:
— **dis'in·gen'u·ous·ly** adverb
— **dis'in·gen'u·ous·ness** noun

Isaiah

This is the famous book that supposedly prophesies the coming of Christ. But in addition it is filled with dire warnings and threats for any Israelites who misbehave. For example:

Woe unto them that join house to house, that lay field to field, till there be no place, that they may be placed alone in the midst of the earth! (Isa. 5:8)

Well, I should think so! Who would want to join houses and fields anyway? What evil, depraved mind could even contemplate such actions?! You start joining houses and fields and you end up with a city. Decadence!

Woe unto him that striveth with his Maker! Let the potsherd strive with the potsherds of the earth. (Isa. 45:9)

And I hope all potsherds are listening.

Woe unto him that saith unto his father, What begettest thou? or to the woman, What hast thou brought forth? (Isa. 45:10)

And what inane questions they are, too! Hey, Mom and Dad, did you ever have any children? Jeez.

The most frequently quoted verse that supposedly foretells the birth of Jesus is:

Therefore the Lord himself shall give you a sign; Behold, a virgin shall conceive, and bear a son, and shall call his name Immanuel. (Isa. 7:14)

But there's some background to this verse. If you go back just a few verses, you'll read that this guy named Ahaz (another great name, huh?) is smack in the middle of a war, and he's worried that God won't help him win it. So God tells Isaiah to go to Ahaz and tell him not to worry. Everything will be fine. But Ahaz is still worried, so God himself talks to Ahaz, personally. That's when the verse tells us, "Therefore the Lord himself shall give you a sign; Behold, a virgin shall conceive, and bear a son, and shall call his name Immanuel." *After* this verse, the Lord continues to reassure Ahaz, telling him that before this child named *Immanuel* is old enough to know good from bad, Ahaz's troubles will be all over, his enemies destroyed, and there'll be good times all around. How does this foretell the birth of Jesus some seven hundred years later? That's easy. It doesn't. They even got the name wrong. Hasn't anyone noticed that Mary did not name her son "Immanuel?" She named him Jesus. Immanuel. Jesus. Not even close.

This problem with names plagues the entire Bible. Right from the start, if you recall the JHVWHW debacle, and the tree called "the Tree of the Knowledge of Good and Evil," names are a glaring obstacle.

Anyway, before long there are more "Woe unto them" verses. There are just *so* many things people are not supposed to do. Here are some of them:

Woe unto them that:

- Drink straight from the milk carton.
- Hog the remote control.
- Forget to floss.
- Lose their lottery tickets.
- Spill coffee on the carpet—unless it's a StainMaster, which cleans up quite nicely as long as you get cold water on the stain immediately and remember to *blot*, not *rub*.
- Eat that peppermint-tasting paste in kindergarten. It tastes great, but you'll get a tummy-ache. I always wondered why the manufacturers of that kind of paste made it smell and taste so yummy. Why not make it smell like cabbage, or sewage, or my Aunt Bertha's fruitcake? Then no one would ever be tempted to eat it, and tummy-aches would be avoided for millions of children. Not to mention the money saved by schools, as the paste supplies would really hang in there. But I digress.

This book contains many more supposed references to the coming Jesus, but they are all even more vague and nebulous than the one about someone named Immanuel. If you can believe it. Then there are more "woe unto them" threats, and finally it ends.

Isaiah has only a couple of references to nets, but it is positively awash with references to feet. Well, we can assume the feet were washed.

Jeremiah

A guy named Jeremiah was an ordained prophet before he was even born. Really! After he's born, one of the first things God tells him is:

> See, I have this day set thee over the nations and over the king-doms, to root out, and to pull down, and to destroy, and to throw down, to build, and to plant. (Jer. 1:10)

Yes, it's going to be one of those. Up or down, in or out, back-ward or forward—what are they trying to say? Of course that's why I've taken the time to condense this for you. Studying the Bible is like holding a live trout in your hands—a slippery, elusive business. Unless you have a net. But there are no nets in Jeremiah.

Well, Jeremiah has a vision, and God asks him what he sees. Jeremiah says he sees "a rod of an almond tree." God tells him that he has seen well, and that he, God, will "hasten my word to perform it." Perform it? How do you perform the rod of an almond tree? You know, this Bible is actually one long Zen koan. No one really knows what the hell it's talking about. Still, we'll keep plodding along as best we can.

After Jeremiah sees the almond tree rod, he has a second vision. This time he sees a seething pot. The pot is facing north. Don't even ask. We'll just move on.

In the now-familiar pattern, there are chapters filled with threats from God. In one he says, "And I will make Jerusalem heaps, and a den of dragons; and I will make the cities of Judah desolate, without an inhabitant" (Jer. 9:11). In another, "Behold, I will feed them, even this people, with wormwood, and give them water of gall to drink" (Jer. 9:15). And: "But the Lord is the true God, he is the living God, and an everlasting king: at his wrath the earth shall tremble, and the nations shall not be able to abide his indignation" (Jer. 10:10).

There's that temper again. It goes on and on like this, page after page of graphic, grisly threats. I wonder what gall tastes like?

But then, out of the blue, after all the ranting and haranguing, comes a bizarre narrative about a girdle. Yes, a girdle. Read for yourself:

> Thus saith the LORD unto me, Go and get thee a linen girdle, and put it upon thy loins, and put it not in water. So I got a girdle according to the word of the LORD, and put it on my loins. And the word of the LORD came unto me the second time, saying, Take the girdle that thou hast got, which is upon thy loins, and arise, go to Euphrates, and hide it there in a hole of the rock. So I went, and hid it by Euphrates, as the LORD commanded me. And it came to pass after many days, that the LORD said unto me, Arise, go to Euphrates, and take the girdle from thence, which I commanded thee to hide there. Then I went to Euphrates, and digged, and took the girdle from the place where I had hid it: and, behold, the girdle was marred, it was profitable for nothing. Then the word of the LORD came unto me, saying, Thus saith the LORD, After this manner will I mar the pride of Judah, and the great pride of Jerusalem. (Jer. 13:1–9)

A morality lesson using a linen girdle. I'm trying to think of a sillier allegory. I can't. I almost expected a reference to a Cross-Your-Heart bra, but we're spared that one. This is one of the worst books we've come across so far, isn't it? Well, later on, Jeremiah is arraigned for some kind of rabble-rousing, but acquitted. Much later, he is again taken, but this time he's thrown into prison. Then he's released. Then he's again put in prison. And again he's released. Not to wish ill on someone I don't even know, but I think prison was a deserved fate for putting us through such a tiresome book.

The people are again exhorted to make their offerings to the priests. And we're finally done with Jeremiah.

Lamentations

Well, not quite. These are the lamentations of *Jeremiah*. If you thought the book Jeremiah was a Valium, Lamentations is a cyanide capsule. Grief, misery, desolation, devastation, calamities, gloom, despondency. It never ends!

> My flesh and my skin hath he made old; he hath broken my bones. He hath builded against me, and compassed me with gall and travail. He hath set me in dark places, as they that be dead of old. He hath hedged me about, that I cannot get out: he hath made my chain heavy. (Lam. 3:4–7)

What a downer. Jeremiah must have been the life of the party, huh?

> He hath filled me with bitterness, he hath made me drunken with wormwood. He hath also broken my teeth with gravel stones, he hath covered me with ashes. (Lam. 3:15–16)

Fortunately for all concerned, Lamentations is only four pages long. Any more and you'd be putting your head in an oven.

> From above hath he sent fire into my bones, and it prevaileth against them: he hath spread a net for my feet, he hath turned me back: he hath made me desolate and faint all the day. (Lam. 1:13)

Oh, for cryin' out loud, here we go again. The net and the feet thing.

fet·ish also **fet·ich** (fĕt'ĭsh, fē'tĭsh) *noun*

(1) An object of unreasonably excessive attention or reverence: *made a fetish of punctuality.*
(2) An abnormally obsessive preoccupation or attachment; a fixation.

Ezekiel

This is where that song comes from: "Leg bone connected to the knee bone; knee bone connected to the thigh bone; thigh bone connected to the hip bone; now hear the word of the Lord! Dry bones, dry bones, dry—*dry* bones; now hear the word of the Lord!" and so on. Not great on lyrics, but most of us sang parts of this when we were children. I never remembered what the hip bone was connected to. Anyway, this story is about God taking a huge pile of dry bones, from dead people, and putting flesh back on them and bringing the bones to life. The details are most distasteful, including sinews and all, so we'll skip over that part.

There are quite a few references to the Levite priests, and what they should and should not do. Example:

> They shall enter into my sanctuary, and they shall come near to my table, to minister unto me, and they shall keep my charge. And it shall come to pass, that when they enter in at the gates of the inner court, they shall be clothed with linen garments; and no wool shall come upon them, whiles they minister in the gates of the inner court, and within. They shall have linen bonnets upon their heads, and shall have linen breeches upon their loins; they shall not gird themselves with any thing that causeth sweat. (Ezek. 44:16–18)

Hmmm. That wool and linen thing again. God never explains his aversion to the combination of wool and linen. I wonder how he felt about polyester?

Well, a short while later there is this:

> They shall eat the meat offering, and the sin offering, and the trespass offering; and every dedicated thing in Israel shall be theirs. And the first of all the firstfruits of all things, and every oblation of all, of every sort of your oblations, shall be the priest's: ye shall also give unto the priest the first of your dough, that he may cause the blessing to rest in thine house. (Ezek. 44:29–30)

Sound familiar? Those priests weren't about to let you forget those offerings. They were looking out for Number One. And doing a first-rate job of it.

There are some more threats, intermixed with promises of mercy, another familiar and by now *boring* feature of the Bible. How many times do you have to threaten someone before you're sure they get the message? The Bible is nothing if not redundant. Nothing much else happens in this book, so—onward.

Daniel

This opens with some more spiffy names—Daniel, Hananiah, Mishael, and Azariah. But King Nebuchadnezzar of Babylon has them renamed when he conquers Jerusalem. He calls them Belteshazzar, Shadrach, Meshach, and Abednego. You have to wonder if he honestly thought that was an improvement. He then chooses these four to have positions of importance in his kingdom. But Daniel/Belteshazzar would not turn away from the God of the Jews, so he doesn't eat the king's food, not even the cranberries, or drink the king's wine. Apparently Nebuchadnezzar's "prince of the eunuchs" was in charge of these four guys. "Now God had brought Daniel into favour and tender love with the prince of the eunuchs" (Dan. 1:9). I'm not going to touch that one.

But the king was having bad dreams, and he wanted someone to tell him what they meant. "Then the king commanded to call the magicians, and the astrologers, and the sorcerers, and the Chaldeans, for to shew the king his dreams" (Dan. 2:2). You know, he approaches this thing scientifically. But when these guys ask the king what his dream was, the king says he forgot, and wants *them* to tell *him* what the dream was and what it meant. "The thing is gone from me: if ye will not make known unto me the dream, with the interpretation thereof, ye shall be cut in pieces, and your houses shall be made a dunghill" (Dan. 2:5). No pressure or anything. Well, they can't do it, so it's going to be death and dunghills all around.

Why didn't they just *make something up?!* Who'd know? Duh. But at the last minute, Daniel comes to the rescue—like the Lone

Ranger. Daniel does the dream thing just fine, no one gets killed, and Daniel receives some nifty gifts from the king for doing such a good job. He gets a Rolex watch, a Canon digital camera, and a Sony Walkman.

But Nebuchadnezzar can't leave well enough alone. He builds this enormous gold statue, which is a new god to worship, and commands everyone to bow down to it. But three of our four Jewish heroes, whose names we can't pronounce, won't do it. Daniel is conveniently elsewhere at the time. So the three are thrown into a fiery furnace. But God protects them from the flames and they're just fine. At this point a new king, Darius, takes over.

It turns out that some of King Darius's officials, jealous of Daniels's Rolex, set a trap so that Daniel breaks the worship laws too; and, reluctantly, because Darius likes the guy, he throws Daniel into a lion's den. But Daniel is protected by God's casting choices in lions. Now this would be a nice happy ending, but when King Darius finds out about the guys who set the trap, he throws *them* into a *real* lion's den.

But check this out: "And the king commanded, and they brought those men which had accused Daniel, and they cast them into the den of lions, them, their children, and their wives; and the lions had the mastery of them, and brake all their bones in pieces or ever they came at the bottom of the den" (Dan. 6:24). What's with the wives and kids?! *They* didn't do anything! Well, we *are* talking about the Bible, so we ought to be used to such things by now.

There are several mentions of feet in Daniel, but no nets. Anywhere.

The end of this book is filled with visions. Daniel has visions about beasts and horns and lemmings and all manner of wildlife. This goes on interminably. At one point Daniel says, "And I Daniel alone saw the vision: for the men that were with me saw not the vision. . . ." (Dan. 10:7). Sounds like Daniel finally started drinking the king's wine.

Hosea

This starts off very strangely. "And the LORD said to Hosea, Go, take unto thee a wife of whoredoms and children of whoredoms: for the land hath committed great whoredom, departing from the LORD" (Hos. 1:2). After that, the LORD never stops punishing the people for their "whoredom." How do you win in a situation like that?

Hosea contains three mentions of harlot; eight of whoredom; one of whore; three of adultery; one of adulteress; two of whoring; two of lewdness; one of "strip her naked"; and one of nakedness. And the whole book is only five-and-a-half pages long. Someone is utterly besotted with the idea of whores and whoring. Makes for ugly reading.

The old, familiar theme—obey me or else—is yet again trotted out and examined in ominous, repulsive detail. God tells the people they shall not have any other gods but him; and for those that do: "Therefore I will be unto them as a lion: as a leopard by the way will I observe them: I will meet them as a bear that is bereaved of her whelps, and will rend the caul of their heart, and there will I devour them like a lion: the wild beast shall tear them" (Hos. 13:7–8).

Of the 610,577 words in the Old Testament, Hosea contains only 5,175 of them. (By comparison, Daniel contains 11,606.) So pound for pound Hosea is probably the *ugliest* book in the whole Bible. As if to prove that, one of the last verses in this book says:

> Samaria shall become desolate; for she hath rebelled against her God: they shall fall by the sword: their infants shall be dashed in pieces, and their women with child shall be ripped up. (Hos. 13:16)

In the synopsis in the front of my Bible, each book is represented by a few brief, clipped descriptions of the contents. One regarding Hosea says, "God's patience with the unfaithful nation." Say again? I feel like we've somehow wandered through the looking glass. Let's get out of this book. It offends.

Joel

Joel isn't much better than Hosea, but at least it's shorter—by half. And it doesn't have any nets or feet either. But the sun will be turned to darkness, the moon turns into blood. Edom shall be a desolate wilderness. Yes, we know. Been there. Done that. Next?

Amos

Here we have death and destruction, fire and devouring palaces. I'm not clear on how one goes about devouring a palace. Nevertheless, faithful to its theme, the Old Testament provides us with yet more examples of the Lord smiting people. For some reason, though, fire is definitely his weapon of choice in Amos. "But I will send a fire on the wall of Gaza, which shall devour the palaces thereof" (Amos 1:7). "But I will send a fire on the wall of Tyrus, which shall devour the palaces thereof" (Amos 1:10). On and on it goes. God sends fire to Ben-ha'dad, Teman, Rabbah, Moab, Judah, and the house of Joseph. Oh, and I think the Seattle Space Needle was also targeted. So along with everything else, God seems to be an arsonist.

However, once again my Bible's synopsis describes Amos, in part, as showing "God's patience with Israel." Now. I think it's fair to say that I've been objective, unbiased, and generally fair-minded in my rendering thus far. But this boils my water. After tens of thousands of words of nasty, revolting, obscene threats, all spelled out in sadistic detail, this "God's patience" stuff really pisses me off. Sorry about the language, but after reading enough of this rubbish you begin to pick up the lingo. It also makes you quite testy and irritable. And I'd love to have a sit-down chat with whoever wrote the synopses in my Bible. We clearly have entirely different understandings of some basic English words—like crush, make bleed, set on fire, and dash to pieces. You know, stuff like that. To me they seem like rather nasty things to do. To the Great Synopsis Writer, they show God's patience.

Oh, to have that chat.

Obadiah

Well, at least we get a break here. This tiny book is only 670 words—of gibberish. Nonsense. It can't offend anyone because no one could possibly know what it's talking about.

> All the men of thy confederacy have brought thee even to the border: the men that were at peace with thee have deceived thee, and prevailed against thee; they that eat thy bread have laid a wound under thee: there is none understanding in him. (Obad. 1:7)

No understanding here, either. We're in agreement.

Jonah

Finally, some comic relief! This guy Jonah is told by God to go to Nineveh and chew those people out because they're being evil. This part is old hat. What's new, though, is Jonah decides he wants no part of Nineveh, and instead runs away to Tarshish. He hops on a ship and thinks he's made a clean escape. Wrong. God sends a furious, hair-raising storm that threatens to overturn the ship. The sailors figure that God is ticked off at Jonah, so they heave him overboard. The storm stops, the sailors relax, and Jonah gets swallowed by a big fish.

Three days later he is still inside that fish. I wonder what he did all that time. It would have been too dark to read or weave a basket, or do anything useful. Or anything at all. I guess he just sat there. I can't imagine there was anything to drink or eat either. He was on the wrong side of those fish bones. And it's highly unlikely that there was room service. Was there a bathroom, do you suppose?

But three days of this is enough. Jonah knows the score. He begins praying and begging and scraping and humbling himself—God's favorite behaviors. And that does the trick. "And the LORD spake unto the fish, and it vomited out Jonah upon the dry land" (Jon. 2:10). Not the greatest imagery, but at least Jonah is out. I'll bet he wanted a shower.

So God again directs Jonah to go to Nineveh. And guess what? This time he *goes*. Wouldn't you? Funny, though, with all this talk about fish there is no mention of nets. Or feet. And for some reason tuna fish does not appeal. I usually like tuna sandwiches.

Micah, Nahum, Habakkuk, Zephaniah, Haggi, Zechariah

These books are nothing more than a smart-alecky challenge to English-speaking people. *No* word should have three *K*s in it. However, I refuse to take the bait so we're going to skip over these books. Altogether they're only fourteen pages, so we're not missing anything. There are a few nets and feet here and there, but other than that it's just a bunch of threats and fighting. Same old song.

Then the people are reminded to make their offerings to the priests.

Malachi

This is the book we've all been waiting for. It's the *last* book in the Old Testament. About time, too. It's only three pages long, but it ends on just the right note. The very last verse in this very last book is as follows:

> And he shall turn the heart of the fathers to the children, and the heart of the children to their fathers, lest I come and smite the earth with a curse. (Mal. 4:6)

Same old song.

THE NEW TESTAMENT

Matthew, Mark, Luke, John

These four books are all the same in that they claim to be telling the same story about Jesus' life, but they all tell it so differently, disagreeing on so many things, large and small, that they aren't really the same at all, and even though so many people insist they *are* the same, they are not—they're different. If that sounds confusing, try reading the books. They inaugurate what is called the New Testament, but they do a haphazard, slipshod job of it. It's like listening to a quartet singing out of tune. Or watching jugglers who keep dropping the plates. You wish they'd get their act together before climbing up on stage.

You read Matthew and think, well, that was an interesting story. Rather spectacular, too. Then you read Mark and think, that was sort of an interesting story, but it left out almost all of the spectacular stuff. Then you move on to Luke and throw your hands up in the air. This isn't like either of the previous two. By the time you get to John, you have given up altogether and start to think about maybe rereading *Treasure Island*.

Mark, generally agreed to be the earliest of the four books, makes no mention of John the Baptist's birth; Jesus' genealogy; the angels announcing Jesus' birth to the shepherds; the visit by the Three Wise Men; the circumcision of Jesus; Herod's murder of the innocents, or Jesus' making his preaching debut, so to speak, at the age of twelve, in the temple. Oh, and Mark also fails to mention *the birth of Jesus at all*.

Now think about this. You're going to tell the story of the Savior of the world, sent from heaven to save all humankind from eternal damnation, but you don't bother mentioning his birth. Don't you think people might be interested? Did he just fall out of the sky? Was he shot out of a volcano? Born in a cave? Left in a basket on someone's doorstep? How could you think the birth wasn't *important*? The only real reference Mark makes of Jesus' origins is just before Jesus begins preaching, when he's already around thirty years old.

> And it came to pass in those days, that Jesus came from Nazareth of Galilee, and was baptized of John in Jordan. (Mark 1:9)

That's it.

Because of the discrepancies between the Gospels, scholars disagree about the date of Jesus' birth (if in fact there was a historical Jesus at all). It could have been anywhere from 17 B.C. to 7 A.D. According to the Gregorian calendar, B.C. means before Christ, and A.D. means "anno Domini" which means anytime after the birth of Christ. So Jesus was born several years before, or after, his birth. There's a delicious irony in that.

But even leaving aside for the moment the many discrepancies between these supposedly inerrant, divinely inspired books, the narratives are incomplete. Unsatisfying. Sketchy. You jump from town to town, year to year, hitting only the highlights of what should be the most meticulously detailed biography in the history of the world.

There are many miracles attributed to Jesus. For example, in John (but not in Matthew, Mark, or Luke) Jesus turns water into wine at a wedding (John 2:1–11). For this the world needed a Savior? A great deal of wine had already been consumed, but they wanted more. I wonder if Jesus said to himself, "I'll worry about the world's starving children later. Right now these drunks need some more *booze*!"

In Matthew, Mark, and Luke (but not John) Jesus walks on the water. This is one compassionate, altruistic miracle! Hold back the tears if you can, but such a benevolent, heartwarming act of charity toward humankind is difficult to fathom. Feeling the lump in your throat?

Then of course we get back to the nets again.

"And Jesus said unto them, Come ye after me, and I will make you to become fishers of men. And straightway they forsook their nets, and followed him" (Mark 1:17–18). "Again, the kingdom of heaven is like unto a net, that was cast into the sea, and gathered of every kind" (Matt. 13:47). "And he said unto them, Cast the net on the right side of the ship, and ye shall find" (John 21:6). And so on.

The one thing that all four Gospels *do* agree on is—feet. There's the washing of feet where people wash their own as well as other people's, and the anointing of feet, a great deal of kissing of feet, and wiping of feet—it's endless.

And stood at his feet behind him weeping, and began to wash his feet with tears, and did wipe them with the hairs of her head, and kissed his feet, and anointed them with the ointment. (Luke 7:38)

But we'll definitely move along. Enough is enough already.

During his preaching years, Jesus tells some parables. One of them, in Matthew (not in Mark, Luke, or John) tells the story of ten virgins (Matt. 21:5), all of whom are planning to marry the same man on the same night. The groom-to-be has ordered that they all dress up in skimpy outfits from Victoria's Secret and Frederick's of Hollywood. He is planning himself one heck of an evening. But *ten* virgins to deflower? Not taking any chances, he prudently has oysters for dinner.

While the bridegroom is feasting, the brides-to-be are fiddling with their outfits, and using a great deal of their lamp oil so they can see what they're doing. Five of them dress faster than the other five, saving a lot of oil. So when the time comes to meet their groom, five don't have enough oil to light their way, and they miss out on the wedding-night revelry. Secretly the groom is relieved. He now has complete confidence in his oysters.

However, when the groom shows up wearing nothing but a black Zorro mask and black leather boots, a couple of the virgins are understandably frightened. Nevertheless, the moral of the story shines through. And just what is that moral? Make sure you have enough oil in your lamps so you can see your groom's wedding-night finery.

Another parable, found in Luke (but not in Matthew, Mark, or John), concerns the so-called prodigal son. There were these two sons, and the younger one asks his father for his share of his inheritance—now. Dad gives it to him, and he takes off for a "far country" and blows it all. "And not many days after the younger son gathered all together, and took his journey into a far country, and there wasted his substance with riotous living" (Luke 15:13). Which means he had a ball.

When he finally decides to straggle back home, he figures Dad will read him the riot act, but he's so hungry he doesn't care. To his surprise, though, Dad not only doesn't yell at him: "But the father said to his servants, Bring forth the best robe, and put it on him; and put a ring on his hand, and shoes on his feet: And bring hither the fatted calf, and kill it; and let us eat, and be merry: For this my son was dead, and is alive again; he was lost, and is found. And they began to be merry" (Luke 15:22–24).

Hearing the music and laughter, the older son, who had stayed home helping Dad all this time, asks a servant what all the celebrating is about. "And he said unto him, Thy brother is come; and thy father hath killed the fatted calf, because he hath received him safe and sound" (Luke 15:27). Well, Older Brother is pushed out of shape and tells his father so. He works hard, his brother plays, and they're celebrating because of his playboy brother! He says to his father, "But as soon as this thy son was come, which hath devoured thy living with harlots, thou hast killed for him the fatted calf" (Luke 15:30). So his father explains all about the "wayward son who was lost but now is found" business, and everything's fine. Everyone's happy. Except the fatted calf.

One of the miracles performed by Jesus is recorded in Matthew, Mark, and Luke (but not John) and is about a guy who is filled with demons. Bunches of them. Jesus orders the demons to leave the man and enter a herd of swine. The demons obediently do so, and then they run off a cliff and drown in the sea. Really. I am not making this up (Matt. 8:30; Mark 5:11; Luke 8:33).

Well, more stuff like this happens. There are more miscellaneous miracles, some isolated healings here and there, and then we get to the meat of the story. Jesus is hauled away to a Roman jail, and from there he is led away and crucified. He dies. Then a couple days later he raises from the dead, and ascends into heaven. And no one's seen him since.

Quite a story, isn't it? But before all that happens, Jesus, in preparation for his final ordeal, goes out into the wilderness to be tempted by Satan. "Being forty days tempted of the devil. And in those days he did eat nothing: and when they were ended, he afterward hungered" (Luke 4:2). Well, I guess he'd be hungry. Jeez. I get hungry if I skip lunch. I remember once when I was working for the phone company in the Budgets & Results Department, and I had skipped breakfast because I was running late. We got the news that the big shots wanted a brand new report, not one of the regular monthlies, and they wanted it by *tomorrow*. It's always like that, isn't it? Everyone wants everything today. Or yesterday.

And not only that, but this special report was to be distributed from Division Level down, which meant to all the district supervisors, all the second-level supervisors and all the first-level supervisors. For all of northern California! I don't *think* so, fellas! Well, we got to working on the numbers, all of us running around like crazy, and before we knew it, it was five o'clock. Overtime tonight, gang. I hadn't even noticed that I had skipped lunch. Most of us had skipped. Then all of a sudden I looked at my friend, Laura, and said, "I think I'm going to faint." She grabbed me, and someone handed me some fruit, and I slowly rejoined the world. I can't remember what kind of fruit it was, though. I think it was a banana, but it might have been an apple. I just know it was some kind of fruit. The point is—it's foolish to skip meals. You always end up paying for it. But I digress.

So Jesus was in the wilderness for forty days, being tempted by Satan. What do you suppose they did all that time? What did they talk about? Football? Microsoft versus Macintosh? The best way to remove a splinter? Who was funnier—Fred or Ethel Mertz? Whether to hit a sixteen when the dealer is showing a king? Who's on first?

Anyway, after successfully resisting Satan's temptations, Jesus has another unpleasant experience to go through before his death. He has a Last Supper with his twelve disciples. They never say who paid the check, but it must have been a tension-filled event. "Hi, guys. Glad you could all be here. Too bad one of you is going to double-cross me later on this evening, and the rest of you are going to skedaddle right at my moment of crisis. But enough for now. Simon, would you please pass the mustard?"

Rise, let us be going: behold, he is at hand that doth betray me. (Matt. 26:46)

> But all this was done, that the scriptures of the prophets might be fulfilled. Then all the disciples forsook him, and fled. (Matt. 26:56)

Last Supper. Kind of ghoulish. Sounds like that last meal they give to condemned prisoners—which in a way I guess it was. What all did they eat, anyway? Gefilte fish? Lox and bagels? Wheaties? Pizza? Cranberries? Peanut butter sandwiches? And whatever they had, did they have fries with it? Also, did they say grace before eating? Did Jesus thank himself for the food he was about to receive?

Finally, though, the time has come, and Jesus is condemned to die. "Then delivered he him therefore unto them to be crucified. And they took Jesus, and led him away. And he bearing his cross went forth into a place called the place of a skull, which is called in the Hebrew Golgotha: Where they crucified him . . ." (John 19:16–18). Now this is the part I don't get. They're going to kill him. It's a done deal. So he has to carry his own cross to the place where they're going to do it?! *Why does he do it?* How could they punish him if he refused? I'm trying to imagine what could be worse than being nailed or impaled on a piece of wood and left to die. Other than being forced to listen to a CD of spirituals sung by a country-and-western singer, I can't think of a thing.

So, when a Roman soldier ordered him to pick up his cross, why didn't he just say, "Pick it up yourself, you knock-kneed, donkey-loving pail of penguin piss!" Or something like that. What did he have to lose?

At last, though, he dies. Supposedly he's alive again after three days, so it really isn't a proper, bona fide death, is it? Graves are usually reliably permanent abodes. However, "And go quickly, and tell his disciples that he is risen from the dead; and, behold, he goeth before you into Galilee; there shall ye see him: lo, I have told you" (Matt. 28:7). But I have a real problem with this part too.

You're going to raise yourself from the dead. You are going to become undead. This is not your everyday occurrence. This is spectacular, sensational, history-making. Search for superlatives, but they won't be enough. Now, who does Jesus choose to witness this breath-taking event? A couple of women. Maybe only one—the Gospels don't even agree on that. In one account, a lone women finds the empty tomb and thinks the *risen Jesus* is the *gardener*.

> Jesus saith unto her, Woman, why weepest thou? whom seekest thou? She, supposing him to be the gardener, saith unto him, Sir, if thou have borne him hence, tell me where thou hast laid him, and I will take him away. (John 20:15)

She thinks he's the gardener. Well this news will travel like lightning! I can see the headlines: "Woman at Tomb Mistakes Dead Close Friend, Now Risen from the Dead, for Gardener!" A publicist. Just like Moses needed a travel agent, Jesus needed a publicist. You don't perform these kind of wondrous miracles with one or two witnesses! You get the word out. *Beforehand*. Then people will believe. And you won't have to wait sixty or seventy years for someone to write about it, either. You'll be in all the papers.

After this ill-conceived stunt, it gets worse. Jesus plans to ascend into heaven. Does he tell anyone about it beforehand? *Noooooo*. Matthew and John don't even *mention* this astonishing event. According to them, they talk a bit with Jesus after he rises from the dead, and then they end their accounts. Mark and Luke only give the event a couple of sentences. "So then after the Lord had spoken unto them, he was received up into heaven, [yawn] and sat on the right hand of God" (Mark 16:19). That's it? That is the description of someone levitating himself up into the sky until he disappears into heaven?! Harry Houdini got more attention when he escaped from a locked safe that had been pitched into the water. All in all, the story of the resurrection and ascension of Jesus is truly a case of going out with a whimper instead of a bang. Maybe that's why so many people find it difficult to believe. There was no fuss made about this miraculous event at all. How can you have a no-fuss ascension into heaven?

Oh, and here's a note for biblical literalists: Ever noticed how often the word "forty" is used in the Bible? It's somewhere in the neighborhood of 150 times. Think about it. How long was Moses in

the wilderness? Forty years. How long did it rain in the Flood?
Forty days and forty nights. How long was Jesus in the wilderness
with Satan? Forty days. How long was Moses on the mount with
God writing down commandments? Forty days and forty nights
(Exod. 34:28). The Bible is literally packed with time periods that
just happen to be in increments of forty. To pick just one book,
Ezekiel, look up these: chapters 4:6; 29:11; 29:12; 29:13; 41:2; and
46:22. They are all time periods, and all *forty* of whatever periods.
"Forty" simply means a very long time, and this point alone
destroys the doctrine of inerrancy and the *literal* truth of the Bible.
Which is why I brought it up.

Now, before leaving the four Gospels, in fairness I should point
out some of the attractive, pleasing parts. Jesus' Sermon on the
Mount is often quoted as being one of the wisest, kindest speeches
ever made. In it are the "beatitudes." These epigrammatic platitudes
are often referred to as the *beauty* of the Bible. The most famous of
course is Matt. 5:5: "Blessed are the meek: for they shall inherit the
earth." In the Broadway musical, *Camelot*, a tune declares, "It's not
the earth the meek inherit—it's the dirt!" Indeed. But there are
many other beatitudes that most people are unaware of. And here
they are:

Blessed Are They Who . . .

- Have the correct change at a toll booth.
- Never say "irregardless."
- Put down the seat when they're finished.
- Don't tell you "your call is important to us" while you're on hold.
- Choose not to describe the details of their recent surgery.
- Know how to program a VCR.
- Never write checks or redeem coupons at the supermarket.
- Can open a tamper-proof bottle without using a knife.
- Don't have a long, cutesy message on the home phone answering machine.
- Don't try to sell their kid's candy at the office.

- While standing behind you in line, don't describe the entire plot and ending of the movie you are about to see.
- Merge onto a freeway at something over 28 m.p.h.
- Don't end every e-mail with a pithy quote.

Acts

Known as "The Acts of the Apostles," this book is not quoted as often as the four main Gospels. And it's easy to see why. There were quite a few acts, but they weren't all great. The sword-swallower was only so-so. You could see the sword retracting in increments as he pretended to shove it down his throat. On the other hand, the dancing bear act was first rate. And the bareback rider was fantastic. As the horse rode in circles, she sat on top of him, calmly brewing a cup of tea on a small coal burner. Never spilled a drop of the tea! She was great. The clowns, though, were pathetic. No funny noses, no baggy pants, no seltzer-spritzers, no floppy feet. They just stood there and told some old, worn out knock-knock jokes. Terrible. However, the closing act was stupendous. This guy told a story about how another guy had *walked on water*. Can you believe it? Walked on water! And the crowd *bought it*! He was some story-teller. He had the crowd mesmerized, in the palm of his hand. He brought down the house. Nice closing Act.

Romans, 1 Corinthians, 2 Corinthians, Galatians, Ephesians,Philippians, Colossians, 1 Thessalonians, 2 Thessalonians

These are some of Paul's epistles. He wrote a lot of them. They're sort of like letters. Actually, that's exactly what they are. Chain letters. Paul tried to get this chain letter game plan going. It was something like the strategy of those pyramid schemes. You tell everyone to send some money to the first ten names on the list, and then tell them to forward the letter to ten *more* people, and so on. But it never got off the ground. The Ephesians screwed it up.

1 Timothy

This letter to Timothy starts off rather nicely, saying things like "grace, mercy and peace from God our Father" and so on. In no time at all, though, Paul starts pontificating A *lot*. By the tenth verse in the first chapter, he's off on a tirade about whoremongers. He blasts liars and blasphemers, but then he has a real go at women. All women. First he condemns women who braid their hair, or wear any gold jewelry, or pearls, or anything elegant (1 Tim. 2:9). Then he really puts women in their place:

> Let the woman learn in silence with all subjection. But I suffer not a woman to teach, nor to usurp authority over the man, but to be in silence. For Adam was first formed, then Eve. And Adam was not deceived, but the woman being deceived was in the transgression. (1 Tim. 2:11–14)

Yeah, right. Like Adam didn't eat the cranberries, too! So, according to Paul, women should sit down and shut up. Paul had a real problem with women. In one of his earlier chain letters to the Corinthians, he wrote:

> For I would that all men were even as I myself. But every man hath his proper gift of God, one after this manner, and another after that. I say therefore to the unmarried and widows, It is good for them if they abide even as I. But if they cannot contain, let them marry: for it is better to marry than to burn. (1 Cor. 7:7–9)

Well, that's a nice healthy outlook! Stay away from sex. It's icky-poo. But if you can't do that, like I can, then at least marry the hag. Nice. Maybe Paul was asexual. Some people are, you know. I don't know what his problem was. Maybe he should have seen a urologist.

2 Timothy, Titus, Philemon, Hebrews

In these epistles, Paul again tries to get his pyramid thing going. He may have had a hang-up about women, but he was an industrious fellow. Alas, he seems to have been a man before his time. No one took him up on his scheme. But you've got to give him points for tenaciousness.

James, 1 Peter, 2 Peter, 1, 2, 3 John, Jude

These are the by now familiar exhortations to stay away from evil things and do good things. Stay away from harlots, don't blaspheme, remember to call your mother on Mother's Day, don't spit on the sidewalk, and always recycle. Jude gets on his high horse a bit about sinners who "walk after their own ungodly lusts." Echoes of Paul. But we're all used to this stuff by now. And weary as well. But don't lose hope. We're heading into the homestretch now. Because what follows is *the last book in the whole blasted Bible!*

Revelation

This book is truly a revelation. I haven't read anything like it since Timothy Leary waxed eloquent about LSD in the 1960s. I don't see how anyone can make any sense out of it at all. Unless you're stoned. Officially called "The Revelation of St. John the Divine," I think "St. John the Toker" might be more appropriate. Whatever he was smoking, it must have been expensive. People have claimed to receive many a "revelation" while whacked out of their skulls. But, no matter what the source of the inspirations, here are some of the results:

> And out of the throne proceeded lightnings and thunderings and voices: and there were seven lamps of fire burning before the throne, which are the seven Spirits of God. And before the throne there was a sea of glass like unto crystal: and in the midst of the throne, and round about the throne, were four beasts full of eyes before and behind. And the first beast was like a lion, and the second beast like a calf, and the third beast had a face as a man, and the fourth beast was like a flying eagle. And the four beasts had each of them six wings about him; and they were full of eyes within: and they rest not day and night, saying, Holy, holy, holy, Lord God Almighty, which was, and is, and is to come. (Rev. 4:5–8)

Ahem. Need I say more? Well, here are a couple of other examples, and then I won't bother you with any more:

> And there appeared another wonder in heaven; and behold a great red dragon, having seven heads and ten horns, and seven crowns upon his heads. (Rev. 12:3)

> And I stood upon the sand of the sea, and saw a beast rise up out of the sea, having seven heads and ten horns, and upon his horns ten crowns, and upon his heads the name of blasphemy. And the beast which I saw was like unto a leopard, and his feet were as the feet of a bear, and his mouth as the mouth of a lion: and the dragon gave him his power, and his seat, and great authority. (Rev. 13:1–2)

> And I saw another sign in heaven, great and marvellous, seven angels having the seven last plagues; for in them is filled up the wrath of God. (Rev. 15:1)

It goes on like this, chapter after chapter. There are over *sixty* mentions of the number seven. John is fixated with the number seven. Ten to one he was a superstitious gambler. There are seven angels, seven candlesticks, seven seals, seven plagues, seven heads, seven mountains, seven crowns, seven thunders, seven stars, and even some 7-Up. In chapter 17, John "sees" one of seven angels, who shows him a whore. This whore has written on her forehead, "MYSTERY, BABYLON THE GREAT, THE MOTHER OF HARLOTS AND ABOMINATIONS OF THE EARTH." She must have had one hell of a big forehead.

In his closing, John says, "For I testify unto every man that heareth the words of the prophecy of this book, If any man shall add unto these things, God shall add unto him the plagues that are written in this book" (Rev. 22:18). Hmmm. Does that mean me? You know, I do feel like I'm getting a sore throat. . . .

❈   ❈   ❈

Well, we did it! We got through the whole Bible! You can now say with justifiable pride that you have read the entire Bible. *And*, you did it in less than an hour and a half! Not bad. We got through the wool and linen problem, the cranberries, the feet, and the nets.

I hoped you've learned something from all this—and that is, don't forget to make your offerings to the priests.

NOTES

1. List of quotations:
(1) H. L. Mencken, "Sententiae," *A Book of Burlesques* (1920).
(2) H. L. Mencken, "Sententiæ: The Mind of Men," *A Mencken Chrestomathy*, (1914).
(3) H. L. Mencken, "Sententiæ: The Mind of Men," *A Mencken Chrestomathy* (1949).
(4) Mark Twain, *Pudd'nhead Wilson* (1894), chap. 8.
(5) Mark Twain, *Following the Equator* (1897), chap. 57.
(6) Mark Twain, Message to the Young People's Society, New York City, February 16, 1901. President Harry S. Truman had this remark framed behind his desk in the Oval Office.
(7) Mark Twain, *Following the Equator*, chap. 27.
(8) Mark Twain, *Following the Equator*, chap. 9.
(9) Mark Twain, *Pudd'nhead Wilson*, chap. 16.
(10) Mark Twain, *Pudd'nhead Wilson*, chap. 15.
(11) Anonymous (possibly Groucho Marx).
(12) Author.
(13) Author.

5

GODS AND GOVERNMENTS

It could probably be shown by facts and figures that there is no distinctly native American criminal class except Congress.
—Mark Twain, *Following the Equator*

WHAT DO GODS AND GOVERNMENTS have in common? They share the same first two letters. Other than that—nothing. Yet human history is replete with theocracies of every conceivable variety. And they were all dismal failures. From the bloody sacrifices of the Aztecs, to the bloody Roman Catholic Inquisitions, to the bloody jihads of the Muslim Middle East, we have proved time and again that theology and government don't mix. Combining religion and government is like repeated incestuous unions—aberrations are bound to result. You'd think we'd have learned by now.

Even in classical Greece, at the dawn of democracy, when great minds combined to pass on a most impressive legacy, Socrates was sentenced to death for "refusing to recognize the gods of the state." He died willingly, rather than try to escape, viewing death calmly and philosophically. "For anything that men can tell, death may be the greatest good that can happen to them: but they fear it as if they knew quite well that it was the greatest of evils."[1] You have to admire his poise and acceptance, but his death was senseless. A true tragedy. Gods and governments don't mix.

In our ancient past, when we were understandably frightened by nature's truly intimidating, harmful twists and turns, looking into the heavens for some help may have seemed perfectly logical. After all, it was those very heavens that kept sending us wind and storms and that terrifying thunder and lightning. Maybe someone lived up there. And maybe they were mad at us. And whoever they were, they must have been very powerful, and they must have lived high above the clouds because we couldn't see them. It must be beautiful up there—above those threatening clouds. It must be heaven.

In addition, the earth itself seemed to have some evil goings-on down below. Volcanoes are frightful things. And what *was* all that fire and brimstone, anyway? Where was it coming from? Well, wherever it was, it was a place no one would ever want to be! It must be a fiery, never-ending inferno. It must be hell.

In the Bible's Old Testament there are so many references to mountains and fire and smoke and God that volcano worship/ appeasement may have been the origin of the Hebrew religion. A few examples:

> And it came to pass on the third day in the morning, that there were thunders and lightnings, and a thick cloud upon the mount, and the voice of the trumpet exceeding loud; so that all the people that was in the camp trembled. And Moses brought forth the people out of the camp to meet with God; and they stood at the nether part of the mount. And mount Sinai was altogether on a smoke, because the LORD descended upon it in fire: and the smoke thereof ascended as the smoke of a furnace, and the whole mount quaked greatly. And when the voice of the trumpet sounded long, and waxed louder and louder, Moses spake, and God answered him by a voice. (Exod. 19:16–19)

> And ye came near and stood under the mountain; and the mountain burned with fire unto the midst of heaven, with darkness, clouds, and thick darkness. And the LORD spake unto you out of the midst of the fire: ye heard the voice of the words, but saw no similitude; only ye heard a voice. (Deut. 4:11–12)

> In my distress I called upon the LORD, and cried unto my God: he heard my voice out of his temple, and my cry came before him,

even into his ears. Then the earth shook and trembled; the foundations also of the hills moved and were shaken, because he was wroth. There went up a smoke out of his nostrils, and fire out of his mouth devoured: coals were kindled by it. (Ps. 18:6–8)

There is much, much more of this, and the imagery is hard to ignore. But it is not hard to understand. The prescientific world was a dangerous, mystifying place. *Something* had to be causing all those disasters. And those "somethings" became known as gods. All over the world, as laws and rules were codified, it would have been natural to incorporate your gods into them. Why shouldn't we kill each other? Because the gods will punish us. From volcanic eruptions to floods to famines to (then-)unexplainable diseases, the gods showed just how good they were at punishing. Better not take any chances. And thus worship was born.

So the origins of religions are more or less understandable. But we have since made so many discoveries, in so many different fields, that it is difficult to understand why religions still have such a powerful grip on most of us. No one today really thinks volcanoes erupt because the gods are mad at us, or that comets foretell evil events. But we still flock to our churches and temples and mosques as if we *did* believe such things. Why? Why do we do this?

I believe that people worship today for precisely the same reason they worshiped millennia ago—fear. The fear of death is probably as old as the appearance of our fully evolved cerebral cortexes. No one wants to stay dead. It's not exactly appealing, is it? And we can't all be as pragmatic about it as Socrates apparently was. That fear, combined with our dogged determination to discover the Meaning of Life, may explain the tenacious, enduring hold of our religions.

Even the sects of Buddhism that do not believe in reincarnation nevertheless strive to provide life with a meaningful goal—to try to achieve "the Enlightenment." The attempt alone is considered to imbue life with value and purpose. And it reflects our puzzled wonderment about the world around us, which can be felt early on. Even a twelve-year-old, during a rare moment of contemplation, perhaps lying on the grass, gazing up at the clouds, will ponder the *meaning* of it all. Why are we here? We humans have enough intelligence to pose such insightful questions, but we don't seem to have enough to answer them. Our religions have helped to fill that knowledge void.

So, today, instead of fearing thunder and lightning, we fear death and the ego-deflating possibility that life has no meaning beyond life itself. Our ancient ancestors had those same fears *in addition* to having to worry about lightning bolts being intentionally hurled at them by angry gods. They must have worried *a lot*.

The logical commingling of gods and government, way back then, took the same toll then as now—the excesses and corruption that inevitably result from that very commingling. They follow like day after night. When the people making the rules can anchor their authority in the gods, how can you challenge them? You can't, that's how. You were brought up correctly, you know which gods are what, and you will behave accordingly or pay a big price. It could be a mysterious ailment or ostracism or even death. So you toe the line like everyone else.

But here's the problem. Since there's little disagreement that absolute power corrupts absolutely, most people who are placed in the position of having spiritual *and* worldly control over their fellow citizens are going to give in to the temptations that go with the job. It's almost inescapable. Our friend Socrates was actually the victim of political motives, and had his enemies not had the ability to persecute and punish for religious heresies, he undoubtedly would not have met his unpleasant fate, resigned though he may have been to that fate.

However, Socrates died in 399 B.C.E. Now let's jump ahead twenty-four hundred years. I'd like to be able to say we've come a long way, baby. In some ways, of course, we have. Most of us no longer do dances to bring rain, or sacrifice humans to appease an active volcano. But still to be found among us today, along with other horrors, are *fatwas*, which are literally religious contracts for death, like a Mafia contract for a hit, directed against anyone who is held to have blasphemed against Islam. "Honor killing" is also alive and well.[2] Directed only against women (now there's a surprise) "honor" killings punish women who have lost their virginity before marriage—even if they have been raped. In the Near and Middle East, rigid Muslim fundamentalists take such things seriously, and consider death the proper punishment. Such deaths have taken place, and are made possible only because the line between church and state is either hopelessly blurred or nonexistent. We have walked on the moon, built space stations, mastered gene splicing, linked the entire globe with the Internet—and still, some of us believe it is morally correct to murder women because of their hymens. We still have a long, long way to go. Baby.

In chapter 4, where I condensed the entire Bible, I intentionally emphasized the exhortations to remember to make "offerings to the priests." In part, I did it because it *is* mentioned so often in the Bible; and in part I did it to make clear the point that in the business of religion, one group always fares quite well—the leaders. The popes of the Middle Ages took it to wild extremes with their mistresses, vast wealth, and riotous living—although a tour of today's Vatican will still reveal *staggering* wealth. And even my own grandfather, who was a Lutheran minister during the Depression, never did without. Not that I ever would have begrudged him the food on his plate, but he never missed a meal. The same could not be said for many in his congregation.

In later years I did indeed begrudge. As a teenager I remember clearly feeling outrage as the collection plate was passed, Sunday after Sunday, and weathered hands reached into threadbare pockets for what small change they could afford to give. Those same collection plates paid for our minister's (not my grandfather at this point) trip to Europe. What is wrong with this picture?

But the point remains. The priests have always done as well as any in their congregations, and usually better. When they were in a position of being able to enact secular laws as well, they *always* did better. And here is the temptation. Pass a law demanding a tithe. Why not? Tax households for the number of people in them (Peter's pence) and deposit that money into your already overflowing vaults of treasures. Why not? Absolute power . . .

England's Henry VIII was a spectacular example of abuse of absolute power. When he broke with Rome and set himself up as both secular *and* spiritual leader of the country, heads began to roll—literally. If he was wild and headstrong before his dual supremacy, he was insane with power afterward. Not only did he kill his many inconvenient wives, but if any clergy of what had been the Roman Catholic Church but was now the newly created Church of England, did not recognize Henry's authority as head of the church, it was off with their heads, too. The wise and honorable Sir Thomas More was just one notable example. His death was tragic proof that gods and governments don't mix.

Yet here we are today, in this, a new millennium, at least if you reckon time by the Gregorian calendar. And here, in the United States, the world's superpower, the Religious Right is still trying in earnest to break down that wall of separation between church and state that has served us so well for so long. Their hue and cry is always based on some rhetoric about restoring this country to its "original Christian foundation," a myth that ranks with some other common misconceptions. George Washington chopped down a cherry tree and would not tell a lie about it. Abraham Lincoln freed *all* the slaves. John Kennedy ushered into the White House all the glory of King Arthur's Camelot. And I know how to turn iron into gold.

We so often believe what we want to believe, ignoring clear-cut evidence as we do so. This is especially true of our country's supposed Christian origins. You can find this topic almost daily in op-ed pages all across the country, as Christian fundamentalists strive mightily to turn America into the Christian nation they claim it once was. The rhetoric flows fast and thick, and after a while some of us begin to believe it. A lie told often enough . . .

But we must look at our history objectively and resist the temptation to rewrite it to suit our opinions of what our heritage *ought* to have been. This admonition applies to atheists as well. If our nation indeed has Christian roots, then we'll just have to accept it and move on from there. So—does it?

The obvious first step in seeking out our nation's origins is to read its founding documents. In doing so, one is struck immediately by the total absence of any mention of Jesus, Christ, or Christianity. There is also no reference to any Christian church—Catholic, Baptist, Lutheran, Episcopal, Calvinist—nothing. Not a word, not a hint. If our Founding Fathers did intend to make this a Christian nation, they could not have hidden that intention more completely.

The Declaration of Independence refers only to "Nature's God," "divine Providence" and a "Creator." All of these terms are so vague that they could be used comfortably by any faithful Muslim. Moreover, "Nature's God" was part of a passage that reads, ". . . the separate and equal Station to which the Laws of Nature and of Nature's God entitle them. . . ." You'll notice "God" got second billing. And not only did the founders feel that the word "God" required an adjective, but the modifier they chose, "Nature's," couldn't be further removed from Christianity, and is in fact a *precise* definition of the God of Deism.*

The U.S. Constitution, with its Bill of Rights, fares even worse in the Christian-roots theory. No deity at all is mentioned, let alone a Christian one. The wildest, broadest interpretations imaginable cannot make the Constitution a Christian document. Its only mention of religion at all is where it forbids Congress from making any laws establishing or prohibiting it,[3] and where it forbids religious tests for holding public office.[4] So the Constitution's two brief mentions of religion strictly emphasize the need to keep it *out* of government.

So, then, where did all this "Christian nation" stuff come from? Our founders went out of their way, very wisely, to avoid religion altogether. When atheists point to this shrieking silence about religion, Christians often counterattack that point by calling it an "argument from silence," one of the weakest arguments available. Generally speaking, arguments from silence *are* weak. In this case, though, it is one of the *strongest* arguments available. Other than bluntly and specifically repudiating Christianity, which they were also wise enough to avoid, the founders could not have made more

---

Deism is the belief that an unknowable God created everything, and then just walked away from it all, leaving all things to work out their own destinies, from atoms to apples.

plain their desire to separate their new government from religion. Their silence about Christianity rings out loudly and clearly. If they had wanted to mention it, they would have. But they did not.

Deathbed and trauma-induced Christian conversions of historical figures are very popular grist for Christian mills. They are also offered as peripheral evidence of our Christian origins. But are they true? The first *Life of Washington*, for example, from which we received the ridiculous cherry-tree story, was written by Mason Weems, a Christian minister and therefore hardly an objective observer.[5] Weems presents Washington as a devout Christian. However, Washington's own diaries record that in 1769 he attended church only ten times, in 1770 nine times, in 1771 and 1772 six times, and in 1773 five times. Devout? Hardly. Such sporadic church attendance reflects, at best, a halfhearted attempt at conforming to social proprieties. It does not reflect a devout Christian.

John Adams was a Unitarian and flatly denied the doctrine of eternal damnation—obviously not a Christian. John Quincy Adams was likewise a Unitarian. The brilliant Thomas Jefferson was an out and out freethinker, and even urged his nephew to "Question with boldness even the existence of a God." These are not the words of a Christian.

James Madison early on studied to become a minister, but inexplicably did not. He expressed his indignation that people were being *jailed* in Virginia merely for criticizing the Episcopal Church, then the established Church of Virginia. The state laws of the time called for the *death penalty* for the following:

- Speaking impiously of any articles of Christianity
- Blaspheming God's name
- Incorrigible cursing

Surely this is a lesson in why *not* to allow theocracies. But why is it, anyway, that as soon as religions get a foothold, they immediately begin to persecute other religions? Is oppression a necessary component of religious belief? It certainly rears its ugly head often enough to make you think so.

Madison, of course, went on to become a fierce advocate of

church/state separation, and as an adult he simply refused to discuss religion at all. This fact alone makes his Christianity highly unlikely, living as he did in a society that smiled favorably on it.

Abraham Lincoln was a Deist in his youth, but was subsequently, and probably wisely, advised against advertising that fact if he wanted to succeed in politics. Legend has him converting to Christianity, though Lincoln himself never bothered to mention it to anyone. No one else mentioned it either until long after Lincoln's death. And no one agrees on where or when this supposed profound life-change took place. Depending on the source, it was either in Illinois or Washington, in 1848, 1858, 1862, or 1863. Such large discrepancies make "never" the most likely.

Lincoln's closest friend and law partner for over twenty years, William H. Herndon, claimed that Old Abe had no religious beliefs at all. Lincoln's own silence on the subject makes his friend's observation seem probable.

Benjamin Franklin, Ethan Allen, and Thomas Paine were thoroughgoing freethinking Deists. Though not presidents, they were strongly influential in forming our early republic. Thomas Paine was a champion of reason. Highly praised for *The Rights of Man*, he was equally vilified for *The Age of Reason*. A glittering testimonial to freedom of thought, *The Age of Reason* excoriated Christianity. Paine bravely put pen to paper in a way that guaranteed censure in the year of 1795. He was praised for glorifying political freedom, but cursed for applauding religious freedom. It is to history's shame that this beacon of reason and rationality suffered so tragically at the end of his life. He was a man ahead of his times.

What most of us fail to recognize in these discussions, however, is that it wouldn't matter if every single president since Washington had been a Bible-toting, evangelical Christian. They weren't, of course, but even if they *had* been, it still would not change the secular foundation of our republic. Christians like to quote various presidents or Supreme Court justices who (quite incorrectly) have referred to our "Christian nation." But what do those quotes prove? I could quote Richard Nixon, but would that prove that ours was intended to be a nation of crooks?

Our founders clearly created a secular government that was carefully separated from religion. You can peer and probe and dissect to your heart's content, but you will never find Christ or Christianity referred to, even obliquely, in our admirable founding documents. It is because of those documents that Christians are free to worship as they please, a priceless freedom enjoyed in precious few countries throughout history. Christians should be grateful for that freedom and stop trying to force their beliefs, posthumously, on our founders (and on the rest of us—today). *We the People* are truly a diverse group, and this has always been one of our greatest strengths.

Very shortly after the founding of our government, its secular nature was reaffirmed in a document known as the Treaty with Tripoli. Negotiations began in 1785, and the treaty was adopted by the United States government in 1797. During this period almost all of the original Founding Fathers were still very active in government. The Treaty with Tripoli resolved many issues involving maritime trade and piracy, but of the twelve articles contained in it, one is quite fascinating. Article 11 reads, "As the government of the United States of America *is not founded in any sense on the Christian religion*—as it has in itself no character of enmity against the laws, religion or tranquility of Musselmen [Muslims]—and as the said states have never entered into any war or act of hostility against any Mahometan nation, it is declared by the parties, that no pretext *arising from religious opinions* shall ever produce an interruption of the harmony existing between the two countries."[6]

The treaty itself is less important that the thunderous silence it met with in the U.S. Senate when it was read aloud on the Senate floor, and when printed copies were provided for the senators.[7] There is no record of any discussion or debate about the treaty by the Senate, and it was passed *unanimously*. There was not a word of protest. Any senator who truly believed that the United States was founded as, and intended to remain, a Christian country, would have exploded with outrage at the wording, ". . . the United States of America is not founded in any sense on the Christian religion. . . ." But there were no explosions, no outrage, no debate, no nothing. It passed unanimously without a word of dissent. And that fact alone speaks volumes.

We never were, were never intended to be, and hopefully never will be, a "Christian" nation.

ONWARD CHRISTIAN SOLDIERS

When a young friend of mine acquired her first teaching job, as a third-grade teacher, it was in a rural school district. Starry-eyed and idealistic, she was bubbling about all of her glorious plans for guiding these young, impressionable minds. When I asked what she would do if she were forced to lead those young minds in a daily morning prayer, she looked stunned, then amused, then quickly dismissed the whole idea with a derisive chuckle and that supreme confidence found only in the young. It could never happen here, she assured me. (Didn't Americans say that same thing just before the McCarthy witch-hunts in the 1950s?) When I pressed for an answer, though, my young friend responded confidently that she would simply refuse to lead prayers in her classroom. And if her refusal meant her dismissal? Her confidence wavered, she looked thoughtful and puzzled, but she had no reply.

Many of us forget the fact that teachers are not in charge of their classrooms. School boards are. And these were systematically and successfully targeted by the Religious Right all across the country in the last decade or so. Because of the Christian fundamentalists' success in many areas, voucher plans for private, religious schools; "creationism" being offered as an alternative to evolution in public classrooms; and prayers being allowed in those same classrooms all became issues where no issues should have existed. What should have been settled law decades ago, *true* separation of church and state, meaning true separation of religion and tax-supported schools, was exhumed and challenged. And, unhappily, it was often challenged successfully.

Many insist that such examples are rare and isolated, so there is no need to worry. If ever the phrase "slippery slope" could be applied properly, this is it. To say that these examples are the exceptions, not the rule, is the same as saying that there are only a few ants on the picnic basket. Choose your metaphor, pick your analogy—slippery slope, foot in the door, only the beginning—they all work. One outlandish example was an Alabama county judge, Roy Moore, who insisted on displaying the Ten Commandments on his courtroom wall as well as conducting Protestant prayers before jury sessions. Defying a court order, he was solidly backed by Alabama governor Fob James, who threatened to call out the National Guard and state troopers if necessary to keep those Christian displays and practices in a public courtroom.[8] James was voted out of office in 1998, but is this not insanity?

The ego-blinded Christians pushing for school prayer fail to consider that there are other religions. Shall a Jewish minority be forced to listen to Christian prayers in a public school? Shall a Protestant minority be forced to listen to Hail Marys? Shall Christian minorities be forced to listen to Muslim prayers? Let's follow this through. To begin with, "student-sponsored" prayers are a laughable smoke screen. Most students don't even want to be in school, let alone pray in it. But if "religious expression" may not be discriminated against, then in a multicultural school, Protestant students will have to be allowed to offer their prayers, Catholics theirs, Jews theirs, Hindus theirs, and Buddhists theirs. Muslims must be allowed to answer their many calls to prayer during the school day. Native Americans must be allowed their forms of worship. And so on.

Schools would dissolve into chaos if such a thing ever came to pass. One U.S. senator said this problem could easily be solved just by letting the "majority" rule. But wait a minute. In a democracy such as ours, we are fond of saying that the majority always rules. But this is not true. It rules, but only up to a point. If a state were to decide, by "majority rule," that slavery should be reinstated, the Supreme Court would tell that "majority" just what it could do with its votes.

The same must hold true for school prayer and all other church/state entanglements. They fly in the face of our Constitution, and it doesn't matter if you get 100 percent of the vote on the issue, you can't have it, any more than you can have slavery, unless we amend the United States Constitution. It is not a local issue. Why is this so difficult to understand?

But Christian fundamentalists keep on trying. And trying. And trying. They are *very* trying. They are pushing for the marriage of God and government. I wonder how they'd feel, though, if the marriage turned out to be a Muslim ceremony? Gods and governments don't mix. Our secular democracy is one of the most successful in history. Why can't we leave it alone?

The famous McCollum court case was decided *back in 1948.*[9] The case involved a grammar school boy in Champaign, Illinois, who was being coerced to take a class, in a public school, sponsored by the Council of Religious Education. The boy's mother, Mrs. McCollum, did not want to sign the permission slip for such a class. But her son was pressured, both by his peers and by teachers, and she ultimately signed. She was then outraged to discover that the class was not at all about "education." It was outright Christian proselytizing, Jesus' miracles and all. The children made posters of Jesus' resurrection.

When McCollum moved her son to a different public school in the same city, the same thing happened—only this time she held her ground and refused to sign the permission slip. Her son was forced to sit by himself, in a small anteroom next to the teachers' bathroom, during the hour his classmates took religious "education." He was the only one not taking the class, and he suffered the inevitable social ostracism because of it. Galvanized, McCollum challenged this policy in the courts. It went all the way to the U.S. Supreme Court. The Supreme Court decision, by an eight-to-one margin, was unambiguous. Public schools may not be used for religious instruction of any kind. McCollum won.

Yet today, a half-century later, we're *still* haggling over these same issues. And too often, because the Religious Right *does* control such a massive voting block, elected officials often pander to them, and President Clinton was no exception. In one of the pervasive twists and turns of political life, President Clinton issued the following White House press release in 1996. In light of the ultimate clash between that same Religious Right and Clinton, it positively *defines* irony. The official press release read, in part:

For Immediate Release

April 4, 1996
EASTER, 1996

. . . In this age of great challenge and even greater possibility, Easter's timeless message strengthens us for the tasks before us. As we celebrate in churches and cathedrals, at sunrise services and in family gatherings, we remember that our lives have great purpose and value. We recognize that the life and words of Jesus call us to works of caring and compassion, to giving more than receiving. His death *and resurrection* are powerful reminders of how God's grace is still at work in the world in which we live today. Hillary joins me in extending best wishes to all for a wonderful Easter celebration. [Italics mine.]

WILLIAM J. CLINTON

Well. That's fairly specific. Jesus rose from the dead. We have it on the authority of none other than the president of the United States. Suppose, though, that Clinton had said, "You Jews are all wrong. Your religion does not recognize Jesus Christ, our Redeemer. Your worship is useless and just plain *wrong*." The outraged cries of anti-Semitism would have echoed through the capitol for months. Yet isn't that exactly what Clinton *did* say?

Such messages are a slap in the face to every non-Christian, American citizen. Jews, Muslims, Buddhists, Confucianists, Hindus, atheists—all are excluded from that official statement. All presidents obviously have the right to worship any way they choose. But they do *not* have the right to use the powerful office of the presidency to proselytize for Christianity. Clinton was not just wishing Christians a happy Easter, which certainly would have been appropriate. Rather, he announced, unequivocally, that Jesus had risen from dead, a fact which should give meaning to all of our lives. There's a world of difference between those two deeds, as Clinton very well knew.

President Clinton's ultimate fate, impeachment, which had the full backing of the very Religious Right that he was trying to indulge with his Easter message of 1996, would be comical if the resulting constitutional crises were not so grave. Time is the mother of perspective. Since enough time has elapsed between now and the madness that was known as the impeachment of President Clinton in 1998, we can look back on that nightmare with a great deal of justifiable alarm.

THE CRUCIFIXION OF CLINTON

There will ultimately be many books written about the Clinton impeachment, and I don't intend to go into detail about it. But the tantalizing links have already been established between the Religious Right, the Paula Jones lawsuit that inaugurated the impeachment process, and the Republican-controlled 105th Congress that did the impeaching.

For example, in the sexual harassment suit against Clinton not begun until three years *after* the alleged incident, Jones's first lawyer, Daniel Traylor, sought help from lawyer Cliff Jackson, who had earlier been retained by two Arkansas state troopers to help them peddle their stories about Clinton's sexual peccadilloes. Then Jones and her husband agreed to be videotaped for a vile video titled *The Clinton Chronicles.*[10] Peddled on Jerry Falwell's *Old-Time Gospel Hour* TV show throughout 1994 and 1995, the video makes outrageous, unsubstantiated charges against Clinton. Among them are accusations that Clinton is a drug addict, a murderer, and a participant in a drug-smuggling ring in Arkansas. No proof is offered.[11]

Jones also appeared on Pat Robertson's *700 Club* TV show on the Christian Broadcasting Network.[12]

Jones hired news lawyers who withdrew from her case after a disagreement about a settlement.[13] She replaced them with lawyers who were recruited by the Rutherford Institute, a right-wing Christian organization based in Virginia. Rutherford is known for taking on cases defending protestors at abortion clinics, such as Randall Terry's Operation Rescue. Here are a couple of quotes from John Whitehead, founder and president of Rutherford: "The Christian faith is not reducible to the level of every other religion. Christianity offers the only path to the one true God. To hold that the Christian religion is no better than Buddhism or Judaism is blasphemy. . . ." Whitehead referred to public schools as "satanic imitations of the true God's institutional church."[14]

Shortly after Jones hired Rutherford's lawyers, that mysterious, "anonymous" phone call arrived at Rutherford, suggesting that Jones's lawyers should look into the relationship between Clinton and a White House intern named Monica Lewinsky. The rest, as they say, is history. And a sorry history it is.

During both the House and Senate impeachment debates (if you could really call them debates, since the Republicans dominated and thereby controlled the outcome of every motion) the one thing you could always count on was religious rhetoric. I watched almost all of the proceedings, and there were times when I wasn't sure if I was watching a political impeachment or a good old-fashioned tent revival. The repeated references to "family values" and the Holy Bible and the Ten Commandments had me wondering if they were considering whether or not obstruction of justice had taken place, or if it was time for everyone to confess their sins to Jesus. It also infuriated me.

My atheism was not the sole source of my fury, though obviously it played a large part. But I kept trying to put myself in the position of being an American citizen who also happened to be, say, Buddhist or Muslim. Buddhists and Muslims *are* allowed to be American citizens—at least thus far. Viewed in that light, the constant religious references were very offensive. During all their self-righteous pontificating, I wished just one of them would have answered this simple question: What makes the Religious Right the right religion? If the One True God favors conservative Christianity, he forgot to inform the majority of the world's population about it.

From the very beginning of the impeachment proceedings, the American public made it very clear that we were against the whole thing, and wanted it to end. Our anger and impatience only increased as the impeachment proceedings dragged on into a new year—and a new Congress. (That in itself was an extremely *odd*, if even legal, part of the whole thing. The 105th Congress impeached, and the 106th Congress, with a much altered political makeup, voted on the articles. Something doesn't sound right about that.) Americans voiced their anger about the impeachment in the midterm elections of 1998. Everyone was astonished on that November 3.

The Republican Party, which of course was spearheading the impeachment of the Democratic president, was sharply rebuked by the electorate. Instead of *gaining* twenty to twenty-five congressional seats, as they expected, they *lost* five seats. And this happened with a six-year, opposition-party president in office who was in the process of *being impeached*. The people had spoken. Not only that, but poll after poll, month after month, showed that a full two-thirds of us approved of Clinton's performance as president, and *opposed* the impeachment. But the Republicans were not listening. They charged ahead with righteous determination. Our country was being torn apart, our federal government was completely paralyzed for the better part of a year, and why? Because of an adult, consensual sexual affair that was no one's business in the first place.

Generally speaking, we had far too much prurient fun with this whole farce. Talk show hosts, who make a living booking guests who confess such things as, "I Pissed Off The Family Dog By Screwing My Neighbor's Cat!" went all somber and clucked their tongues about Clinton. But their glittering eyes betrayed their sheer glee. This was a booking agent's dream. Get a two-bit psychologist, ask her to analyze Clinton's sex life, and your ratings shoot through the roof.

WASHINGTON, D.C.—Kenneth Starr announced today that he was going to broaden the scope of his investigation to include the sex life of the Clintons' cat, Socks. Inside sources reveal that on many a night Socks went "over the wall" in search of illicit sex. The weighty issue of whether or not such activities rise to the level of impeachable offenses will have to be addressed by the House Judiciary Committee. "There can be no doubt about it," asserted Independent Counsel Starr, "that what we have on our hands is nothing less than an egregious abuse of power and possibly obstruction of justice. We subpoenaed Socks for the Grand Jury, but he simply ignored the subpoena. It was a feline no-show. Moreover, he failed to answer the eighty-one questions presented in an interrogatory. This reflects a flagrant disregard for the judicial process."

When asked to respond to the charges, a White House spokesperson said that Socks had "no comment" to make at this time.

Outside the White House, scores of protestors carried signs saying, "Socks Has the Morals of an Alley Cat!" and "No Catting Around in the White House!" Socks's defenders carried their own banners saying, "Privacy Rights for Cats!" and "It Was Just a Little Pussy!" The two factions jostled each other, shouting obscenities. The police were called to quell the escalating violence when the protestors began throwing Meow Mix at each other.

From Vicksburg, Virginia, Reverend Jerry Falwell added his voice to the growing chorus of denunciations. "It is no longer a matter of legality. It is a question of morality and leadership," stated the Baptist minister. "How can President Clinton continue to lead this country with his cat going 'over the wall' at all hours of the night? Such shocking behavior offends every decent American. The next thing you know that cat will be refusing to use his litter box. Socks has sullied the dignity of the White House. Clinton must step down."

Polls show that most Americans agree with Falwell's assessment. Forty-two percent of those questioned in an MSNBC poll believe that Socks's activities undermined Clinton's authority enough to require resignation or impeachment; 18 percent said Clinton should only be censured; 11 percent said they didn't give a damn one way or the other; and 29 percent said, "Who's Socks?"

Leaks from the Office of Independent Counsel have beltway insiders buzzing with speculation. Washington wags are all a-titter about some wanton goings on in the Clintons' tortoise tank. . . .

Earlier this week, in a related story, Attorney General Janet Reno appointed a second special prosecutor to investigate the office of the first special prosecutor. At that time Reno declared, "There are hints of impropriety about the manner in which evidence was gathered in the Socks Investigation." In today's press conference Reno announced that she, like Starr, will be expanding the scope of her own investigations. A third special prosecutor has been appointed to investigate the second special prosecutor who is investigating the first special prosecutor, who most people believe to be Kenneth Starr, but as the investigations broaden, confusion reigns.

When asked about this third prosecutor Reno explained, "Not only will he be investigating the second special prosecutor, who is investigating the first special prosecutor, whose name escapes me for the moment; but he will be investigating the sex lives of every president who ever lived. In addition, he will be leading a commission of inquiry which will probe the sexual dalliances and peccadilloes of every British monarch who ever reigned, going back to Henry VIII."

When asked if this was a wise use of taxpayers' dollars, Reno snapped, "What better use is there for tax dollars than investigating sex lives?!"

Asked what she thinks about these late-breaking stories, atheist Internet columnist Judith Hayes replied, "When the hell are our elected officials going to stop probing other people's sex parts and get back to the business of government? And as for Jerry Falwell's pontificating and insisting that the president of the United States *must step down*, you may tell Mr. Falwell for me that he is not an elected official, and I don't give a sh** what he thinks about anything."

The rest was not fit for print.

© *The Heretical News*

Did the Clinton travesty really get *that* out of hand? Yes, it did. Other U.S. presidents have had their affairs, but they didn't paralyze our government. For example, John Kennedy seemed to spend most of his time doing little else *but* have extramarital sex, yet he's still regarded as one of our better presidents. And if there had been a paparazzi around during Thomas Jefferson's day, he'd have been drummed out of office. His "traveling companion," a young slave woman named Sally Hemings, would have been fodder for the gossip mills and a tabloid editor's dream come true. And Jefferson was one of the most brilliant men to grace our country's history, as John Kennedy pointed out at a White House dinner brimming with the cream of the country's intelligentsia: "There has never been such a collection of talent and intellect gathered in this room since Thomas Jefferson dined here alone." Well said; and I would only add that Jefferson's sex life, like that of all our presidents, is none of anyone's business.

When the articles of impeachment against Clinton were finally voted on in the House, I sat, like many others I'm sure, transfixed—glued to the TV screen as the "yeas" and "nays" were counted. And, as I watched, it was with a sense of utter unreality. This couldn't be happening. This was not real. When the first-rate TV journalist Judy Woodruff of CNN announced the precise moment when the vote total meant that at least one article of impeachment had definitely been voted, her voice quavered. I had a lump in my throat, too, but I wasn't sure why. This was history in the making, and on a grand scale. After all the months of wrangling, pompous grandstanding, and just plain B.S., here we were. Watching the first-ever impeachment of an elected president of the United States. It was powerful, moving, poignant, and awful.

When it finally hit the Senate, that sense of unreality only increased. Toward the end of the sessions, as senators were making their play-to-the-crowd speeches, I heard the words "oral sex." From the floor of the Senate of the United States of America, one of the most influential institutions in world history, I heard "oral sex." Was I dreaming, I asked myself? Yes, in fact I was. But it was a nightmare come true.

I have always been a big time fan of democracy. As human inventions go, it was one of our better efforts. And for two hundred years we've done a pretty good job of it. Our democracy has survived a bloody civil war, two world wars, the Great Depression of the 1930s, McCarthyism, presidential assassinations, and Watergate. And the music of the Beach Boys.

But what we witnessed in this impeachment chills me to the marrow. We crossed a dangerous line and set a frightening precedent. While partisan politics has always been part of our democracy, and has almost always possessed the scruples and decorum of a barroom brawl, this was new. This was scary. We allowed the president of the United States to be dragged to the dock to be publicly grilled, like a cheese sandwich, about the most intimate details of his sexual life. To our everlasting shame.

While it's true that Clinton was impeached by politicians, not religious leaders, the entanglement of religion and politics was glaringly obvious throughout. In fact, long before impeachment was even dreamed of, Jerry Falwell, famed conservative Christian minister and evangelist, decided to inject the so-called Moral Majority into politics. In mid-1979, Falwell gathered his key staff to announce his intention to get involved in politics in order to "reverse the moral decline" in America.[15]

Hmmm. Why are alarm bells going off? Oh, yes, now I remember. It's this:

INTERNAL REVENUE CODE
Sec. 501. Exemption from tax on corporations, certain trusts, etc.
TITLE 26, Subtitle A, CHAPTER 1, Subchapter F, PART I, Sec. 501
STATUTE
(c)
List of exempt organizations

The following organizations are referred to in subsection (a):

Corporations, and any community chest, fund, or foundation, organized and operated exclusively for religious, charitable, scientific, testing for public safety, literary, or educational purposes, or to foster national or international amateur sports competition (but only if no part of its activities involve the provision of athletic facilities or equipment), or for the prevention of cruelty to children or animals, no part of the net earnings of which inures to the benefit of any private shareholder or individual, *no substantial part of the activities of which is carrying on propaganda, or otherwise attempting, to influence legislation (except as otherwise provided in subsection [h]), and which does not participate in, or intervene in (including the publishing or distributing of statements), any political campaign on behalf of (or in opposition to) any candidate for public office.* [Emphasis mine.]

I guess Jerry's special. He has campaigned "in opposition to" Clinton since the day he was elected. This unambiguous church/ state entanglement was addressed in a book written by two of Falwell's former assistants, Cal Thomas and Ed Dobson. Titled *Blinded by Might: Can the Religious Right Save America?* the book acknowledges the dubious validity of such political actions by their heretofore leader. In an online review of this book by *MSNBC On Air Today*,[16] Dobson and Thomas are quoted as referring to what they call their "sins" for having believed that they could make things right through the "manipulation" of the political system. They candidly describe Falwell's unrestrained glee at having "influenced an entire election." They said they shared that glee, reveling in the fact that "our man" was in the White House and the Senate was "under our control."

Tax exempt indeed.

When the 1980 elections saw Reagan defeating Carter easily and the Republicans gaining important congressional seats, the media credited Falwell and the Moral Majority for the dramatic voting shift. The Religious Right was on its roll.

That roll continued into the 1980s and 1990s, with conservatives growing bolder every year. The heavy-hitting, powerfully influential Republicans pushing the 1998 impeachment train along the tracks all had high-profile conservative Christian ties. Henry Hyde, chairman of the House Judiciary committee, was an outspoken conservative Christian. Trent Lott, Senate majority leader, was a regular columnist for *Citizen Informer*, the newspaper of the Council of Conservative Citizens (CCC), the direct descendant of the White Citizens Council.[17] Bob Barr, fierce anti-Clinton advocate for impeachment, also had ties to the CCC.[18] Tom DeLay, then Republican majority whip, established a caucus known as the "Values Action Team." That "team's" Web page linked directly to James Dobson's Focus on the Family and Gary Bauer's Family Research Council, both hard-core conservative Christian groups.[19] And the list goes on.

The debacle known as the Clinton impeachment—and history, I'm sure, will show it to be just that—is a classic textbook example of why religion and government must not mix. Ever. The wasted millions of taxpayers dollars, the broken lives, the wasted months of our congressional representatives' time, were all the result of a "moral" witch-hunt, spearheaded by religious fanatics who felt it was their right to pry into the sex life of our president. *They had no right*. But we all paid the price for their zealousness. It was totally avoidable, and, if the wall of separation had been as strong as it should always be, it wouldn't have happened.

Clinton's "Happy Easter" message of 1996 has an ironically melancholy ring to it. It was almost a prophetic example of my main message here—gods and governments don't mix.

The Religious Right, in their determination to force *their* definition of sexual morality (at least their public definition—more on that later) onto the occupants of the White House, came close to undoing two hundred years of a successful democracy. To a certain extent, they actually did cause some irreparable damage. There is no way to undo an impeachment. There is no way to undo the actions of the 106th Congress, specifically the Senate, wherein there were *fifty votes* for removing the president from office—and all because of a sex scandal.

Their zealousness in their attempts was disturbing and a bit frightening. To a much smaller degree, of course, but under similar circumstances, I can now understand how German citizens might have said to themselves back in 1938–1939, "Well, nothing like that can happen in *this* country." I would have sworn the same thing about the witch-hunt that took place in *this* country in 1998–1999. And all of it was on national television and the Internet. Every sleazy detail.

The world is laughing at us, and we deserve it. While it's true that other countries have had their share of sex scandals, such tawdry affairs did not bring their governments to a grinding halt. Life went on. While he was married, Prince Charles absolutely *flaunted* his mistress, and the world yawned. Times have changed, but our collective puritanical sense of proper sexual conduct has not. Collectively, we are mired in the 1890s. Individually, we mate like jackrabbits. The word "hypocrisy" comes to mind.

On my Internet domain, *The Happy Heretic*, which has been active since 1997 and where I write monthly columns, I asked readers from around the world to give me their honest impressions of the Clinton impeachment. I received over thirty replies and I was surprised to find only *one* that was critical of Clinton. That person said that he didn't like Clinton, but felt his (Clinton's) conscience would be punishment enough, and that impeachment was a wild overreaction. The following are excerpts from the responses. All names have been used with permission.

Australia

I can't speak for everyone of course but generally most of us think you Americans have gone over the top. To make such a fuss about your president's sex life makes no sense. My roommate put it like this: "They've lost it. It's beyond the pale." I say he's spot on.

Brazil

It seems Brazilian people don't care about this stuff. TV news are brief and with no comments. People think this is a foolish internal stinky American affair. In our current opinion, high government representatives' sexual life is a personal matter, restricted to gossip areas.

Canada

Regarding the country's problems with the Office of the President, these problems belong to the Republican Party, and Kenneth Starr who saw a chance to become a part of history by misinterpreting what the Founding Fathers wrote, and turning a molehill into a mountain.

That Bill Clinton, married man and President, had a quasi affair with a girl in the Oval Office, is no-ones business but his own and his wife's, having no relevance to affairs of State. His devious answers and possible lies to questions he should never have been asked, reflect less upon the President's character than on the immorality of the Republican witch-hunt, and raise questions as to the legal scope of interrogation available to the Senate Committee under the law.

There is something wrong with the interpretation of the American Constitution when it allows the Public Prosecutor and the Senate to subject the President to disgrace, universal ridicule, and the bawdy humour of every nation on earth. The Constitution, in wake of this situation, may need refining word-by-word to prevent future fiascoes, since everything today revolves around a sharp legal axis.

While the U.S. Government raises not a few Canadian hackles over free-trade issues and such, on the whole we do like Billy and the American people, not the least because we arise from a common stock. As this Kangaroo Court continues its deliberations, we hope for the sake of the country and the world, the bad boys won't achieve a political lynching.

I think that the more-relaxed Canadians would be likely to separate sex from State in such a situation.

What a pity Billy didn't say "Your place, not mine."

Mary E. Garner

England

Personally, I think that the whole thing's a circus. By that I mean there has been a massive, hysterical over-reaction to what has happened. So he had an affair: did it affect his ability to do what appears to be a good job? No. From what I gather, crime is down and the economy is at its strongest in years. It seems to me also, that there's alot of hypocrisy: his critics say how immoral and seedy and pernicious he is for having an affair.

The general concensus in the UK, meanwhile, seems to be similar to that in the US: we're all bored with hearing about it by now, and we all want it to end as quickly as possible.

Matt Eccles

France

In general, I find the French view the OIC investigations and the impeachment proceedings against Clinton ("la destitution de Clinton") to be ill founded and inappropriate as well as a grave threat to democracy whose consequences extend far beyond the U.S. They also seem to have lost a lot of respect for America and remind themselves that they are glad to be French Citizens.

The Netherlands (Holland)

I live in The Netherlands (Holland) and the impeachment-affair is covered by our news. In general: I think that most people think its a farce, a cruel joke, very hypocritical. And, because the most of us think that this kind of 'misbehaviour' is a private matter. As we understand from our tv-news, the majority of Americans neither want Clinton to go, so its a political game: the democrats vs the republicans. There can only be losers.

Minze Wijma
Nijmegen, Netherlands

Singapore

I think we are getting a bit sick of all the intense U.S. media coverage (which gets reported in our press and TV too). Don't they have something better to do? Especially since the 'torrid' details read like a cheap dirty novel. Glad Our Government isn't like that.

Republicans—bloodhounds driven mad by the scent of 'dirty laundry.' Who says the American system is the right and only way? The global cop looks like a global mockery. No wonder Saddam Hussein dares to constantly taunt the U.S.

A grave concern is that the U.S. government and public is excessively self-absorbed in this epic 3rd rated soap-opera at the expense of the larger world community.

Li Zhixiang

Sweden

I must admit that I do not follow the debate over Clinton any more, I got sick and tired of it in about a weeks time. I do admit I downloaded the Starr report and read bits and pieces of it, but it was rather boring so I went back to something much more amusing, watching my newly painted wall dry . . . sorry :)

Anders "Ichi" Pettersson

South Africa

I'm not really familiar with American politics, but here on campus almost everyone agrees that President Clinton has done a good job. We can't understand why you want to throw him out of office because of sex. If we used those rules here we'd have no professors at all!

I certainly hope we've learned something from all this. They say adversity makes us wiser, but this trial by ordeal was too much for most of us. It would appear that we survived more or less intact, but in the back of my mind I keep thinking, Precedent. Precedent. Precedent.

However, chickens can come home to roost. When Larry Flynt, publisher of *Hustler* magazine, ran advertisements offering large cash sums for anyone who could prove they had had an illicit sexual affair with any major public officials, Washington went into a panic alert. Newly chosen Speaker of the House Bob Livingston not only abruptly resigned as Speaker, but announced his resignation altogether from the House of Representatives, effective immediately. Subsequently, more and more sexual liaisons came to light, and the airwaves were filled with more smut.

I am neither condemning nor condoning Flynt's actions. What I am saying, though, is that this is precisely what we should expect once we begin the game of slinging sex-scandal mud. There is probably no one in Washington who is not vulnerable to one degree or another. (Remember John Kennedy's bedroom antics?!) The unavoidable result of such mudslinging will be the loss of otherwise valuable public servants, and a never-ending, ongoing probe into our elected officials' sex lives. Is this what we want? Shall we create a sex police? Is this where we want to head? If so, we've made an excellent start. If not, we've made a ghastly mistake, the consequences of which, I believe, have not even begun to be felt.

Perhaps, though, we should let the government get back to the business of governing, and leave the morality speeches to homes and religions—where they belong.

Government's business is to provide its citizens with health and safety; defense against enemies; education; and the freedom to pursue life, liberty, and happiness. Among our cherished freedoms are the freedom of speech and the right to worship as we please. It is *not* government's business to promote one religion over another. Government must stay out of religion, and *religions must stay out of government.*

If history has taught us nothing else, it has taught us that gods and governments don't mix. From the thirteenth to the sixteenth century, Middle and Central America, whose nation-states were dominated by their religions, saw the ritual slaughter of hundreds of thousands of humans, many of them innocent children, to appease the gods. When the Roman Catholic Church dominated politics in Europe, from the thirteenth to the sixteenth century, the Holy Inquisition tortured and murdered countless "heretics," in numbers that can only be guessed at—some putting it at hundreds of thousands, some even higher.

After the Reformation, the various European monarchs warred with each other, and killed their own subjects, with a ferocious zeal based solely on—religion. In 1649, Charles I of England was executed by zealous Puritans, led by Oliver Cromwell. After Cromwell's death, there was a backlash and the Puritans were persecuted, and laws were passed outlawing their worship. When Puritans escaped to the United States, one of their first acts was to establish a religious police state—persecuting *other* religions. And, under their rule, the Salem Witch Trials of the 1690s took place.

How did Northern Ireland become such a seething cauldron of terrorism? In the sixteenth century, Henry VIII of England, secular *and* religious leader, attempted to push Protestantism on "his" Ireland, and the Catholics there rebelled. The rest, as they say, is pipe-bomb history.

Iran has long been a thoroughgoing theocracy, and in 1989 Iran's Ayatollah Khomeini offered a $3-million reward for the death of author Salman Rushdie because of a book, *The Satanic Verses*, which allegedly blasphemed Islam. A book. One book.

And yet, even with full knowledge of this sorry history of theocratic disasters, here, in the Land of the Free, Christian fundamentalists are *still* trying to force their brand of religion into our classrooms and courtrooms. We *are* slow learners, aren't we? The House of Representatives voting in favor of displaying the Ten Commandments in public buildings was bad enough (see chapter 7). But the state of Kansas was determined to outdo the House in challenging the Constitution.

KANSOZ

Close your eyes, click your heels together three times, and repeat, "There's no place like home . . . there's no place like home . . . there's no place . . ." and Presto! You're back home in Kansas! Home of the rugged farmer, the fields of corn, and one of the most outrageous school boards that ever existed in the civilized world. Welcome to Oz. KansOz.

On August 11, 1999, the line between the mythical Land of Oz and the real land of Kansas was officially blurred. Oz may have had talking scarecrows, wicked witches, and Munchkins; but Kansas decided it had no evolution, meaning nothing in its history is older than around six thousand years, meaning it must be . . . the Garden of Eden! So that means Kansas has a wicked Satan, talking snakes, and two adult human beings with no belly buttons. Take *that*, Dorothy!

The Kansas School Board voted six-to-four to remove the science of evolution from the teaching curricula of all public grammar, middle, and high schools.[20] What a powerful group of ten people *that* was! Just think: By a show of hands the board undid an entire century of science and discovery. That is *power*. Rumor has it they are entertaining the idea of repealing the law of gravity. Just for the hell of it.

Marching doggedly backward, apparently destined for the thirteenth century, the board demonstrated the very real dangers of allowing religious beliefs to force their way into public policy. The result is, as it always has been and always will be, chaos. A group called the "Creation Science Association for Mid-America" helped write Kansas's curriculum proposal. The sound that echoed throughout the nation when we read *that* bit of news was a battering ram punching a gaping hole in the wall of separation of church and state. The association's director, Tom Willis, said of evolution, "It's deception. You can't go into the laboratory or the field and make the first fish. When you tell students that science has determined [evolution to be true], you're deceiving them."[21] This is very true. You cannot make the "first fish" in a laboratory.

But there are a *lot* of things you can't make in a laboratory. A few examples would be stars, planets, Queen Elizabeth I, sharks, a giant sequoia, and a Christmas fruitcake that actually tastes good. But does that mean these are not real? Never existed? Weren't *true*? Except for the fruitcake, they are all quite real. Nor have I ever heard any reputable scientist even suggest that such an outlandish laboratory experiment should ever be possible. They would tell you that such a straw man is pure bunk. I would call it pure bull.

Many humanists believe that this Christian fundamentalist "push" of the last decade or so represents the death throes of fundamentalism. They're losing members, losing control, and are desperate to regain their former power. I don't know. Without a crystal ball there's really no way to see how this will all play out. But Christian fundamentalists are pushing for the combining of God (theirs, of course!) and government. They are longing for the day when their religion will rule the Western world. Perhaps they forget that such a time has already been and gone. It was called the Dark Ages.

NOTES

1. Plato, *Apology*, sct. 29.

2. Lisa Beyer, "The Price of Honor," *Time*, January 18, 1999, p. 55.

3. "Congress shall make no law respecting an establishment of religion, or prohibiting the free exercise thereof." Amendment I, United States Constitution.

4. "The Senators and Representatives before mentioned, and the Members of the several State Legislatures, and all executive and

judicial Officers, both of the United States and of the several States, shall be bound by Oath or Affirmation, to support this Constitution; *but no religious Test shall ever be required* as a Qualification to any Office or public Trust under the United States." Article VI, United States Constitution; emphasis mine.

5. References to our presidents' religions are taken from Franklin Steiner's *The Religious Beliefs of our Presidents: From Washington to F.D.R.* (1936; reprint, Amherst, N.Y.: Prometheus Books, 1995).

6. Rob Boston, "Joel Barlow and the Treaty with Tripoli," *Church & State*, June 1997, p. 11; emphasis mine.

7. Ibid., p. 13.

8. Joseph L. Conn, "Tear Down the Wall," *Church & State*, May 1997, p. 9.

9. Vashti Cromwell McCollum, *One Woman's Fight* (Madison: Freedom From Religion Foundation, 1993), p. 187.

10. Vincent Bugliosi, *No Island of Sanity* (New York: Ballantine, 1998), p. 116.

11. Rob Boston, "Paula's Pals," *Church & State*, March 1998, p. 5.

12. Bugliosi, *No Island of Sanity*.

13. Ibid.

14. Boston, "Paula's Pals," p. 7.

15. "At Work for the Moral Majority," *MSNBC On Air Today* [online], www.msnbc.com/news [April 1, 1999].

16. "Review of *Blinded by Might*," *MSNBC On Air Today*, [online], www.msnbc.com/news [April 1, 1999].

17. Joe Conason, "Why Lott and Barr Hate Clinton," *Salon* [online], www.salon.com [December 22, 1998].

18. Ibid.

19. Joe Conason, "Strong-arm and Hammer," *Salon* [online], www.salon.com [December 8, 1998].

20. "Kansas School Board Drops Evolution; New Curriculum Guidelines Exclude Scientific Theory," Reuters [online], www.msnbc. com/news [August 11, 1999].

21. Ibid.

6

DEAR JUDITH...

> *There is nothing you can say in answer to a compliment. I have*
> *been complimented myself a great many times, and they always*
> *embarrass me—I always feel that they have not said enough.*
> — Mark Twain, *Mark Twain's Speeches*

S INCE JANUARY 1994, I HAVE written for many secular publications, and several online sites. In 1997 I initiated my own
Internet domain and named it *The Happy Heretic*. As a result, I've
received hundreds of letters and e-mails from all over the world.
The following are excerpts from that correspondence. Any names
are used with permission. I've edited for space, but the gist of the
messages has been left intact. And, except for a few comments here
and there, I have not included my responses. But I do answer almost
all of my mail, and I answered the following as politely as possible.
Which wasn't always easy.

Dear Judith,

I really like your essays! Could you please send me the history
of Christianity, from its founding right up to today? I'm writing a
paper on it. Thanks.

Dear Judith,

I too grew up as a strict Christian, so I think I understand what you went through because I am now an atheist too. I agree about the god thing and how we made him up to make us important. You are also right about the human ego causing us to imagine flying saucers with space aliens coming to visit us and all the rest. There has only been one alien spacecraft to ever land on earth, and it came down in my backyard on July 29, 1986.

Dear Judith,

Our humanist group is planning a luncheon for next month. We would like you to speak at our meeting. We realize you're in California and we're in Texas, and that travel can be expensive. But there are only 17 members in our group so far, so we can't help with that. However, we all like your writing, so lunch is on us! We haven't decided on the exact date yet, but we'll give you two weeks notice. Looking forward to meeting you,

Dear Judith,

I enjoy your columns on the internet. I am an agnostic and unfortunately my wife is a fervent Jehovah's Witness. I have to have my freethought mail sent to my office so she won't see it. I really love my wife, but when she starts talking about Jehovah she just won't stop until I leave the room and sometimes I even leave the house. It's driving a wedge between us that gets worse every year. Our children are being raised as Jehovah's Witnesses. Her whole family is religious. I feel so isolated sometimes, being with the people I love but feeling shut out. I just can't find it in my heart to believe any more (I too used to be JW) and I can't force myself to believe what I don't believe. I often wish I could though. It's very hard when you love someone and have this wall between you.

Well, sorry to cry on your shoulder, keep writing, I'll read your columns as long as I can.—[Sad.]

Dear Judith Hayes,

You know nothing at all about Christanity [*sic*] and have no bussiness [*sic*] writing about it. Jesus died for your sins too and considring [*sic*] what you write He really had to. Yours in Christ,

Dear Judith,

Go for it girl!!!

Dear Ms. Hayes,

Your articles are a breath of fresh air! So much of the atheistic writing is juvenile ranting. It is wonderful the way you express your thoughts with such clarity and humor. I am a writer also; but I write with a felt-tipped pen while you write with a stick of dynamite. I hope you never stop!—[This letter is definitely in the front of my album.]

Dear Miss Hayes,

If birth control is such a good thing, like you say, then how come there are so many people in the world???!!!!

Dear Judith,

My son says the devil is going to torture me forever because I don't know how to memorize the Lord's Prayer but do you think that's true because someone sent me one of your articles and I don't think you do but I'm not sure if that is true anyway because why would the devil want to torture me? I don't believe in the holocaust.

Dear Judith,

Your writing is a waste of everybody's time. The World is Ending as Propheseid [*sic*] in God's Bible. It may be as soon as Thursday. The floods are there for a reason and if you can't read the Message you will be Doomed along with the rest of us!!!!!

Dear Mam,

I'm writing from prison in [edit] and just wanted to let you know how much the guys here on death row enjoy your articles.— [Not answered.]

Dear Happy "Heretic,"

You are not a heretic. You are an apostate.

a·pos·tate (e-pòs'tât', -tît) *noun*

One who practices apostasy.

[Middle English, from Old French, from Late Latin *apostata*, from Greek *apostatês*, from *aphistanai*, to revolt. See APOSTASY.]

— a·pos'tate' *adjective*

a·pos·ta·sy (e-pòs'te-sê) *noun*

plural a·pos·ta·sies

Abandonment of one's religious faith, a political party, one's principles, or a cause.

[Middle English *apostasie*, from Old French, from Late Latin *apostasia*, defection, from Late Greek, from Greek *apostasis*, revolt, from *aphistanai*, to revolt : *apo-*, apo- + *histanai*, to stand, place.]

her·e·tic
her·e·tic (hèr'ĭ-tĭk) *noun*

A person who holds controversial opinions, especially one who publicly dissents from the officially accepted dogma of the Roman Catholic Church.

adjective

Heretical.

[Middle English *heretik*, from Old French *heretique*, from Late Latin *haereticus*, from Greek *hairetikos*, able to choose, factious, from *hairetos*, chosen, from *hairêisthai*, to choose. See HERESY.]

Sincerely,—[Sheesh!]

Dear Ms. Hayes,

I will pray for your soul. Matthew tells us . . . [edit six hand-written pages] . . . and remember that we are all God's children and He loves even people like you.

Dear Judith Hayes,

All atheists are communists and all communists are assholes. So guess what that makes YOU???????—[This one not answered.]

Dear Judith,

Your article about the Pope was terrific but you didn't go far enough. Birth control is the most important issue in the world and the population explosion will destroy us all unless we do something about it NOW. The only solution is to separate the smart, techno-logically oriented people from the dumb ones and shoot all the dumb ones. It may sound cruel but it's the only way mankind can continue to exist. You should write about that.—[Don't think so.]

Dear Judith,

I just finished your first book and I had to write to tell you that I loved it. It was WONDERFUL. I was sorry when it ended. I'm going to read it again only a little slower. The first time I read it in one huge gulp. Your thoughts are so well expressed and so clear and your arguments are flawless. I hope another book is on its way soon! . . . Your newest fan,—[Definitely the front of the album.]

Dear Mrs. Hayes,

I just love your articles! You're witty, eloquent and obviously very smart. Your descriptions are so good you make the words come alive. Very few writers can say as much as you do with so few words. It's too bad you're going to burn in Hell.

Dear Judy,

I thought your book was great. Your ideas about sex are so true. I am a lonely, sexually frustrated man in my mid-forties. I am interested in meeting someone like you . . . [edit—not answered.]

Dear Ms. Hayes,

Your essays on the foolishness of religion are among the best I've ever seen. Robert Ingersoll and Mark Twain would be proud of you. Today there is no one who can come close to your imaginative prose. I live in [edit] and impatiently await the delivery of each *Freethought Today*. Please continue to write forever!—[This one is framed.]

Dear Judith,

You should open your heart to Jesus. He can take away your shame and bring light into your world. He died for our sins and His true love can give you a reason for living. I don't think you have one and it is obvious that Satan is the author of your articles.—[I use no ghostwriters of any kind.]

Dear Judith,

I am a closet atheist. I was thrilled when a friend sent me your articles (she knows about me) because I thought I was alone. Everyone I know is a Christian, and I had no idea there were groups anywhere that talk freely about atheism! I live in the Bible Belt and anyone who talked like that would be run out of town on a rail. Do you know of any other publications that have articles like yours? I've read what I have over and over and would appreciate anything new to read.—[A *very* long list of publications was sent.]

Dear Judith,

The enclosed 673 pages are the rough draft of a book I wrote. It is about atheism. I would appreciate it very much if you would critique it. Thanks in advance,

Dear Sister Judith,

I can tell by your writing that you are deeply troubled. But with the grace of Allah you can learn the way to true happiness. The Prophet learned the way and shared it with the rest of us. Paradise awaits those of us who heed the Truth, but Infidels will be fed to the dogs.

May Allah be with you,

Dear Judith Hayes,

I just found your site and I'm confused. I've seen your name many times. Are you the Judith Hayes who writes for "Focus on the Family" and the Christian Coalition?—[Hardly.]

Dear Judith,

I would like to know if you are a nudist. I don't see how anyone claiming to be a humanist cannot be a nudist. Our humanity includes our nudity. I'm assuming you are a nudist because of the way you write.—[Uh, well, no.]

Dear Judith,

I wish you would write more often! Monthly columns are not enough. I eagerly anticipate the first of the month to check out your site and I always want more. If you can be addicted to writing (!) then I am addicted to yours. I've made copies of all of your columns and sent them to everyone I know. You are the best thing going on the Internet and I thank you for your thoughtful, beautifully written work. Keep it up! (Only maybe more??) . . . Your admirer,—[This one is bronzed.]

Dear Judith,

This is the fourth time I have tried to email you. My messages keep coming back to me and I don't know why. I don't know what's wrong. I don't know if it's my computer or AOL or maybe your address isn't right. It's so frustrating! If you don't receive this, let me know and I'll try again.

Dear Judith,

Have enjoyed your articles. Have you thought of putting them together in a book? Also, are you the lady who wrote about President Eisenhower and how he only voted once and that was for himself? This darned typewriter skips spaces and doesn't spell right either.—[No, I'm not the lady, but my old typewriter made spelling errors too.]

Dear Judith,

Thank you for your column and related materials. You strike me as one of the more enlightened and relaxed among the scores of atheists, freethinkers, rationalists and their kin who for some incomprehensible reason choose to parade their ignorance, psychological reactivity, infantile thought, vindictiveness, poor grammar, lack of reading, comprehension and other winning traits on the Internet. You are a beacon of clarity and readability, casting about over a wasteland of quasi-enlightened neuromuscular droppings. I mean that as a sincere wry compliment. And may the farce be with you!

Hello Judith:

Just reading your Happy Heretic columns—excellent stuff. It's nice to come across a well-reasoned, intelligent atheist Website. So many atheist sites tend to consist of "Jesus is crap, and here are 200 links to other sites that say the same." Please keep up the good work.

Dear Judith,

Either come out of the closet or go back in and shut up. Your whining about missing music is just a way of disguising the fact that you are still a closet Christian. If you miss that church music so much why don't you go buy a CD?—[This person has never heard a pipe organ in a cathedral.]

Dear Judith,

Just finished your columns. So refreshing! I can identify with your love for the old hymns and choir music, as I sang in choir for years and it is a truly valued part of my youth. I was at church every time the doors were open—a lot of wasted time, but I did like the music.

If you want to be part of a really caring and altruistic group of people, become an alcoholic. [!!] Alcoholics Anonymous, although overpopulated with religious nuts, is really a great group of people, more so than most groups of Christians I have known.

Hi Judith:

I am a closet atheist. A few of my friends know my feelings about religion, but for the most part atheism is a rather solitary philosophical place in which to dwell. So thank you for your well written and "right on" articles. I wish I could be as articulate on behalf of atheism and illustrating how absolutely inane are the moronic antics of the evangelical dolts I must put up with every day.

The net is fine for reading your refreshing essays, but I'd like to have a book of your writings on my coffee table.—[I'd love to be on his coffee table.]

Dear Judith,

Your "Victual Virgins" was an extremely funny piece. [See chapter 1.] Embedded within was a nugget of truth: nothing like the Virgin Mary to get the turnstiles spinning and the cash registers over-flowing. It's dinner time here and I just made spaghetti for my wife and boys. The spaghetti sticking to the bottom of the pot looks suspiciously like the Virgin Mary. I am contemplating calling the Associated Press. Got to go . . . keep up the good work.

Dear Judith:

[Edit five handwritten pages] But what I really want to know is why is it that secular humanists are better in bed than Christians? I've always found that to be true and I want to know why. I've been a Christian all my life [!] and believe me it's true.

Judith:

Though we are all cells in the body of humanity, we are not all brain cells. Sympathy, not empathy, for those less able to comprehend our reality, is the more productive path. A life lived is a life lived, whatever the circumstance. A life not lived means as much. To be or not to be—what is the question?—[Is he selling what he's smoking?]

Hello!

Judith, I couldn't have said it better myself. In my own personal journey, I called myself an agnostic, back when my common sense was telling me there was no God, but my heart still wanted there to be one. Now that I've gotten over this childish desire for a great sky father to protect me, and care for me, I proudly call myself an atheist. Not weak or strong, nor freethinker or humanist or what ever euphemism you want to use, just atheist.—[Me too.]

Dear Judith,

I enjoy your columns and it sounds like you've had some experience with Mormonism. I'm amazed that as large as the Mormon Church is it doesn't get more critical review. It's history is damning, the historicity of the Book of the Mormon is hilarious not to mention the content, which, when read, has an effect only matched by nitrous oxide. Keep your columns coming!

Dear Judith:

Thank you so much for answering my questions for my friend. She and I have known each other since elementary school. Most of my other "friends" have told me to get lost when they found out I am an atheist.—[So much for Christian love, huh?]

Dear Judith,

When I saw a friend at a convention, who knows you, I asked him to tell you that I am in love with you—but he said he felt the same way about you and that he wasn't about to play John Alden to my Miles Standish. Before you began writing for the paper, I used to leave my copy of *Freethought Today* in conspicuously public places after I had read it, but I can't bear to part with one of your articles. I save them and re-read them, often.—[I think I'm in love too.]

Dear High Priestess Hayes,

Your prose is sour and your thought processes completely demented. You represent everything that is wrong with self-appointed, megalomaniacs spewing forth their insipid, fatuous excretions and passing them off as sagacity. Get off the Internet and go back to your crayons and coloring books where you belong.—[I don't think I'm in love with this one.]

Dear Judith,

I like your articles. The last one made me wonder: What would Christians have done if the story had been that Jesus hand been hanged, or burned at the stake? How could you hang a gallows from a necklace?!

Dear Judith,

I really had to chuckle when you mentioned in your article that your Lutheran minister grandfather had scribbled in the notes of one of his sermons, "Argument weak—holler like hell!" Ain't it the truth?

Dear Judith,

I like your articles. They're not just religion bashers (enough of those on the web) and they're often funny too. Now, if only so many of the cute girls that I know were not devout Christians, I'd be a much happier guy!

Dear Judith,

You said on your Internet site that you hoped we'd all forgive you for the "sin" of liking anchovies on your pizza. Well, so do I! Now if we could just get all of us anchoviphiles together. . . .

Dear Judith,

I bought your first book about a year ago. It literally started me on a path away from dogmatic Christianity. In the words of my lovely wife, "You've changed!" I'm now more caring and care-free. As I write this I'm listening to African drumming. I've also accumulated a wonderful variety of friends who are friends regardless of our religious and/or philosophical differences. I'm not bothered by those that tell me I'm going to hell. I respond to them, "If I don't believe in God, why would you think I'd be scared by hell?" Anyway life in general has taken a wonderful turn for the better ever since I shed the fear based religion.

Which brings me to my point. The accountant at work has two women working for her. The accounting office is across the hall from mine. I constantly hear one-way god-speak from her. (She tried to convert me once but she was embarrassed by her lack of thoughtfulness after I asked her some deep philosophical questions arising from the question of evil.) The accountant gave one of the clerks a book. It was one of those trashy "End of the world, we'll all get raptured pretty soon, and those that don't will get eaten by scorpions" dribble books. It literally scared her to the verge of converting. Over lunch she mentioned her dilemma, she was scared by the prospect of going to hell. I asked her the next time she read it to ask the question, "How does the author know this?" The next day I gave her my copy of your book. For the first time in a week I saw her do something remarkable: she laughed.

Christianity is really based on fear: fear of hell, fear of change, fear of any information that dis-confirms one's point of view. I would not be able to help the poor lady with Bertrand Russell or Smith. It took some pointed humor from your book to break her from fear.

Thanks for all the work you've done for freethought.

Mark Smothers

[This is the sort of message that warms my heart and makes me feel that I am not, as I sometimes think when I'm discouraged, a lone, unheard voice in the wilderness.]

Dear Judith:

I love your stuff! Every American should be forced to read your last column. You should be syndicated!—[Don't I wish!]

Judith,

Oh, how your book changed my whole out-look on life!

I was raised Catholic and found myself a teen-age fundie, lost and alone in the youth group crowd, suicidal and non-communicative, carrying my bible like a shield against the big bad world. I spent so much time looking for god that I ignored my family. I had so many questions about my religion and the god I thought I served. All the fundie-teen propaganda books said the same basic thing, Just Have Faith. So I did.

At 18, I finally admitted to myself that I was indeed gay. I had to find peace with myself, my sexuality, and my god. I discovered Bishop Spong's book, *Living in Sin?* and MacNeill's *Taking a Chance on God*. Something wasn't right. I was apologizing for something that was a part of me. I fought daily with the faith and the reality.

About age 20, I couldn't take the "faith" cop-out any longer. I started reading for myself, always looking over my shoulder, worrying about what god thought about what I was reading. The topics were innocent enough—history of the Church, world history . . .

Slowly the Christian in me was dying. Psychology. Sociology. History. Basic Science I denied myself as a fundie-teen. Straddling the religious fence, I decided agnostic was safe enough. I wasn't a heathen, nor was I a Christian. I could freely read and explore my world. Anthropology. Philosophy. World Religions.

Then I treated myself to your book *In God We Trust*. I read it cover to cover several times, hugging it in my sleep—glad to have "met" someone who understood and was able to answer my oldest questions! One morning it just all clicked. The sun was just rising outside my window. Birds were chirping. My cats were sleeping at the foot of my bed. My girlfriend slept quietly and gently at my side. The last traces of Christianity that remained in me turned to ashes and blew away in the gentle morning breezes. I rose from bed that day as an atheist.

So in this small way, I had to thank you for writing your book. Humorous and real, it gave me much to think about. It's the most worn book in my little personal library, and probably one of the most loved. It's the Velveteen Rabbit of books!

I look forward to your new book! I shall be on the lookout for it!

Much indebted to you,
Jennifer

[This eloquent, moving message took my breath away. All writers hope their words will have some impact on some people. But this message from Jennifer is the most poignant I've ever received. To think that a tormented, suicidal young woman (tormented and suicidal *only* because of religious intolerance) could find comfort and strength in my words, is both extremely rewarding and extremely humbling. The reward is self-evident; what makes it humbling is the knowledge that words have power and can hurt or heal, and we'd best be careful indeed when employing them. In this instance, I take heart in the fact that for Jennifer, at least, I had found the right words.]

As you can see, my mail call is certainly *interesting*. These few snippets are fairly representative of my mail overall—though the "oddball" messages are overrepresented. But they are so intriguing I just had to include them. It's fascinating to wonder about what sort of person would sit down and write letters like those. On the other hand, it's a bit depressing to think they are probably allowed to vote and drive cars.

By far the most common type of message, representing about one full third of my mail, concerns the feelings of isolation that atheists feel and surprise that there are others out there who doubt the validity of religion, especially Christianity. Over and over people express a truly poignant sense of gratitude just to be able to read *anything* other than the standard fundamentalist Christian tracts. And they all, from Oklahoma to Maine, refer to themselves as living in the Bible Belt. That must be one hell of a big belt! But the sense of a smothering pressure to conform comes through loud and clear in these messages.

Overall, though, my correspondence is one of the most appealing aspects of my writing. I never know what to expect after "Dear Judith."

7

TWENTY QUESTIONS

What is there that confers the noblest delight? What is that which swells a man's breast with pride above that which any other experience can bring to him? Discovery!
— Mark Twain, *The Innocents Abroad*

THERE ARE SO MANY UNANSWERED and/or unanswerable questions about religion generally and the Judeo-Christian tradition specifically, that's it's hard to know where to begin when searching for answers. But here are twenty questions worth thinking about.

1. WHY IS IT ALWAYS BIBLICAL CREATIONISM VERSUS EVOLUTION?

When we allow our opponents to frame a debate, we've already half lost it. I am constantly surprised at the number of debates that are labeled "creationism versus evolution." I am even more surprised at the number of evolutionists who are willing to take part in such a rigged debate. Scientists and philosophers alike, not to mention laypeople, fall into this trap. But look at the premise.

Before anyone even utters the first word in a debate like this, there is the tacit assumption that if evolution were somehow to be proven false, *then the story of creation in the Judeo-Christian Bible would automatically be proven correct*. This is the height of sophistry.

There is a plethora of fundamentalist Christian publications that deal solely with finding flaws in the sciences of evolution and natural selection. They pound away at it with righteous zeal. And if they find *any* tiny discrepancy or *any* two evolutionists disagreeing over *any* minutiae, they pounce on it and claim it a "victory" for biblical creation. This is pure poppycock. But far too often we take the bait and go on the defensive. We try to minimize any apparent inconsistencies, playing right into their hands, and looking like fools in the process. The burden of proof should be volleyed right back where it belongs—squarely on their shoulders.

A good way to do this is to take the position, for argument's sake, that the science of evolution is false. Evolution never happened. We have not found all those thousands of fossils; there is no archaeopteryx; *Lucy* has not been found; the fossil record of the horse is unknown; and so on. Assume we don't know *where* the hell we came from.

Now. How in the world does this validate the six-day creation story in the Bible?! How does this make Adam and Eve and talking snakes historical facts? Perhaps the Mayan version of creation is correct. The Mayas believed that the universe had been, and would continue to be, created and destroyed multiple times, and that each such cycle lasted somewhat longer than five thousand years. By their estimate, the current universe had begun in the equivalent of the year 3114 B.C.E. and would be destroyed in the equivalent of the year 2012 C.E. (Oops! We're due!) Evidently the Mayas believed that the cycle of creation and destruction would repeat itself forever, with each successive universe being an exact duplicate of the previous one.

Or how about Brahma, the Hindu God, who is said to be the creator of the universe? In the *Manu Smriti* or *Laws of Manu*, Brahma is described as self-existent and as evolving the world from an egg—the doctrine of the cosmic egg—and his existence endures for an eon that is practically eternal. Perhaps we came from an egg.

Then there's the Egyptian account of creation: Only the ocean existed at first. Then Ra, the sun, came out of an egg (a flower, in some versions) that appeared on the surface of the water. Ra brought forth four children, the gods Shu and Geb and the goddesses Tefnut and Nut. Shu and Tefnut became the atmosphere. They stood on Geb, who became the earth, and raised up Nut, who became the sky. Ra ruled over all.

There's so much more, but—point made. If the science of evolution were to crumble to dust tomorrow (and it surely won't—it gets stronger daily) that *still* would not establish the validity of the Judeo-Christian Bible. The debate is not biblical creationism versus evolution. It is biblical creationism versus every other creation story in the history of humanity. The Hebrew Bible has no more claim to fame than . . . the Cosmic Egg.

2. IF JESUS WAS A CARPENTER, DID HE EVER SMASH HIS THUMB WITH A HAMMER?

This is not a tongue-in-cheek question. It is quite serious. Did Jesus ever smash a thumb or accidentally wound himself in the course of his profession? Christians want us to believe that Jesus had a so-called dual nature—human *and* divine. Well, the human part would necessarily have had to deal with headaches, insect bites, cuts and scratches, and all other human maladies. If Jesus was subject to none of these human ailments then he was not human. Logic itself.

However, when we think of Jesus, whether we're believers or not, some images just don't work. So try it. Imagine Jesus as portrayed in our society. Close your eyes and picture whatever image your mind's eye brings forward. Then, imagine a rumbling, resonating belch emanating from that image. Does it work? No, it doesn't. From indigestion to bad breath to a sprained ankle, none of it works. Why? Because the idea of a clumsy or ill eternal, omnipotent God contradicts all logic. The Christian assertion of a dual nature fails utterly. No one can be both. You must choose. God or human—one or the other. If in doubt, close your eyes again and imagine Jesus slipping on a banana peel and falling on his rear end. It doesn't work.

3. WHY DOES THE POPE WEAR FANCY FROCKS AND SILLY HATS?

This is actually a very good question. Whenever popes wave to crowds, it must be a lot trickier than it looks. They must be weighted down with forty or fifty pounds of silk and brocade. Why must they dress like twelfth-century sultans and wear embarrassingly silly hats? Those hats make them look somewhat like the Grand Vizier of the KKK. Would a pope's words carry less meaning and authority if he was turned out in a Brooks Brothers suit? That must be the case or else popes wouldn't dress so flamboyantly. This is a most telling eccentricity. Words of truth and wisdom should need no window dressing.

So the next time you see pictures of the pope standing out on the balcony, waving to the throng in St. Peter's Square, imagine that he is wearing a sport shirt and sunglasses. If that makes you laugh, so should the insistence that his words are somehow divine and more than mortal. Brocade does not a Holy Man make.

4. WHAT IS A CULT?

A twelve-year-old boy is led by his male elders to a wide stream. Everyone clad in ceremonial robes, the group solemnly approaches the gently flowing water. Wading out to a three foot depth, two men slowly lower the boy, face up, into the water until he is completely submerged. While the youth struggles to hold his breath, the men mutter incantations. "Mucsibov xap," they murmur in unison. "Sibon anod, sutcnas sutirips," they intone. The boy wishes they would intone a little faster. This breath-holding is harder than they said it would be.

Finally, lungs ready to burst, the boy is pulled from the water, gasping for air, as his mother smiles, teary-eyed, from a distance. Women are not allowed to participate in these sacred ceremonies. Later, the entire tribe will celebrate this mystical, momentous occasion.

On the other side of the world, streams are not flowing at all, and the crops are not growing, as drought has gripped the land. Genuine terror fills the hearts of everyone in this small village, for a year of famine looms as a near certainty. Prayers have been offered. But no clouds grace the horizon. The worried leaders, all male, hold a secret meeting, desperately trying to understand how they have displeased the Great Spirit in the sky. Someone suggests that perhaps their prayers have not been sincere enough. Maybe they were merely reciting the words while their hearts were elsewhere. All eyes immediately lower, gazes fixed firmly on the ground, guilt fixed firmly in their hearts. Then just as quickly they all look up, each knowing with a certainty that just one individual offering the occasional insincere prayer could not have brought this disaster upon them.

Finally the High Priest holds up a hand for silence. He announces, gravely, "We all know why this has happened to our people." Uneasy glances are exchanged as he continues, "The Great Spirit is angered because the Evil One is among us, and we know where the Evil One resides." The sidelong looks are more anxious now, as several men clear their throats. "The girl is possessed, and she must die," pronounces the priest. "As long as she lives, we shall see no rain." Heads nod slowly in agreement. The deed must be done.

The thirteen-year-old girl in question is at this moment weaving together some strands of wild grasses. Humming a lilting melody as she works, her fingers fly as she deftly laces the strands into a lovely garland. She will wear it in the upcoming festival to celebrate the return of spring. There are many in the village who think she has too much talent, from her artistic abilities to her exceptionally sweet singing voice. Most agree that for one so young, she is suspiciously accomplished. And they wonder about the source of those many talents. In addition, she is exquisitely beautiful, in face and figure, arousing bitter envy in the women, and a burning lust in the men.

But this lovely girl will never wear her garland. It lies on the ground now, unnoticed, as the girl's first screams echo in the stillness of dawn. She has been tied to a small tree, and as the first flames reach her feet, she struggles desperately, but futilely, to pull away from the heat—a heat she never knew existed. As the flames grow higher around her, her screams become deafening, causing many to comment later on the unearthly, almost inhuman, ear-splitting noises emanating from such a fragile creature. The chanting of the group is almost drowned out by the agonized screams. Finally, though, the screams end abruptly as the girl's throat can no longer produce sound. Gleaming eyes watch her disappear in the flames; all are transfixed by the sight; a few back away as a slight breeze carries with it the stench of death.

Then, at last, it is done. The Evil One is no longer among them, and the Great Spirit is appeased. Now, surely, the rains will come.

A man lies facedown, prostrate on the ground, bare to the waist. Arms and legs spread-eagled, he feels the first sting of the whip as it rips into his back. A red stripe appears just as the next lash makes his body jerk. A group is gathered around to watch. For his impiety and offenses against the gods, this man is being publicly beaten by the shaman. The elders of the clan have decided that this is a just punishment for his blasphemy. He will not be beaten to death; however, he will not recover for several weeks to come.

A young warrior, brave and strong, is selected as the victim. Religious ceremonies are performed that imbue him with all of the powers of their god. After that has been accomplished, he is respectfully and ritually killed. Careful attention is paid to every religious nuance and detail. Then, with great reverence, his body is dismembered and eaten. Every member of the community will eat a small piece of the body and drink a small amount of the blood, thereby making them at one with their god. They all feel stronger, more protected, and at peace with themselves.

The above activities sound like the barbaric rituals of uncivilized cults. Yet they are all part of a religion known as "Christianity." The only place I fudged a bit was in the ritualistic, sacrificial death of the warrior; although the sacrificial death of Jesus is uncannily similar. And the symbolic drinking of human blood and eating of human flesh, known as Christian "communion," is only slightly less barbaric than the real thing. Pretending to eat human flesh? Pretending to drink human blood? What the heck is that all about? To think that people are still doing this, today, is truly remarkable, in a depressing sort of way.

To those who would cry, "Foul!" at some of my depictions, I would point out that all you have to do is insert "God" for Great Spirit, throw in the name Jesus, and you've got Christianity. Baptism, witch-burning, flogging (along with many other bizarre forms of punishment), and communion are all part of the Christian saga. But when they are described as I have just (accurately) described them, their primitive nature simply cries out for recognition. The incantations were simply Latin words spelled backward. But as they say, "It's all Greek to me!"

When mainstream religions condescendingly refer to "cults," they fail to see the irony in their position. Anything is a cult from someone's perspective. Worship of a Mother Goddess, or Earth Goddess, was widespread, enduring for centuries, thousands of years ago. But today's (male chauvinistic) historians summarily dismiss this religion as a "fertility cult." They do so, however, at the risk of their own credibility.

Likewise, modern Christians patronizingly chuckle at cults like

Jim Jones's, David Koresh's, and Heaven's Gate. But they would do well to remember that in its infancy, Christianity itself was viewed with that same condescension by the worshippers of Mithra. Mithraism was the big-time religion in the Mediterranean at that point in history, and its adherents viewed Christianity as nothing more than yet another obscure cult. These humble, cultish origins must be pondered and reckoned with by Christians. Such contemplations will provide some much needed perspective as we search for the exact meaning of "cult."

Defining "cult" is no easy task. Some have suggested that if a religious group is really small, meaning it has not been embraced by any respectable percentage of the population, then it is a cult. But since Christianity began as a mere handful of people, was it therefore a cult? Did it then "grow" into a religion? The same could be asked about Islam and any other religion ever known.

What, then, does define a cult? Someone once offered, "An IRS ruling." That may be close to the truth. We humans are so egocentric that we have trouble being objective about anything, and religion is certainly no exception. Our attitude is generally, "What I believe is religion; what you believe is superstition." I think that sums it up nicely, and so the bottom line seems to be this: A cult is anything you believe that I don't.

Can I get an "Amen!" on that?

5. IF ONE TRAIN LEAVES ST. LOUIS AT 3:45 P.M. CST, TRAVELING EAST AT 45 M.P.H., AND ANOTHER LEAVES PHILADELPHIA AT 4:15 A.M. EST, TRAVELING NORTH AT 64 M.P.H., WHAT TIME IS IT IN CLEVELAND?

I always *hated* those questions, didn't you? In my mind's eye I invariably pictured a head-on train crash—no people injured, just those two damn trains destroying each other. It helped. (I never said the questions were all about religion. I just said they were worth thinking about. Which they are.)

6. WHATEVER HAPPENED TO THE SHEP-HERDS AND THE THREE WISE MEN?

This is a serious puzzle. If you take the Bible seriously, the birth of Jesus as recorded in the Gospels is inexplicable. The most popular version of the nativity, Luke's, is asking us to believe that an honest-to-goodness angel came "down" from heaven to announce the birth of the Savior of the world to a small group of shepherds.

Put yourself in the shepherds' place. The angel's visit alone should have been the experience of a lifetime. How many people are visited by angels, for any reason? Not too many of us, as a show of hands will confirm. But if the purpose of the visit was to announce the birth of the Savior of the world, surely you would be giddy with excitement and would think you had moved into your actual Twilight Zone. This is earth-shattering stuff here. An *angel* would have bestowed upon *you* the honor of witnessing *this*.

Supposedly the shepherds "made known abroad" the existence of this newborn Savior. ". . . all they that heard it [all thirty or forty of them, I guess] wondered at those things which were told them by the shepherds" (Luke 2:17–18). Then the shepherds returned to their fields, glorifying God, never to be heard from again. So it's tend your flocks, be visited by an angel, go witness the newborn Savior of the world, tell some people about it, and then back to your sheep. All in a night's work.

Once the shepherds had "told abroad" their story, would they have just gone back to their sheep-tending? Or, like normal human beings, would they have raced back to the stable, never again to leave the side of this newborn Savior? After all, he could prove someday to be a most powerful friend indeed.

The abrupt and permanent disappearance of the shepherds is one of the most mystifying, unbelievable segments of the nativity story, yet it is rarely discussed. The part the shepherds play in the story is so highly suspect it rivals the virgin birth itself.

The Three Wise Men who suddenly appear, present their gifts, and then just as suddenly disappear forever are as mysterious as the unconcerned shepherds. Do you suppose they met each other on their trek to the stable? You can almost imagine them, shaking hands and introducing themselves:

"Hello there, we're Wise Men from the east, come to worship the Savior, and offer him gold, frankincense and myrrh. And you?"
"Oh, we're shepherds, come to worship also. But we didn't think to bring gifts."
"And where are you headed after you finish worshipping?"
"Well, we're just going to go back and tend our sheep. You?"
"We'll be going back to our own country. In the east."

If this exchange seems implausible, then the entire nativity story is implausible. People are people. To regard miraculous appearances of angels as mundane, everyday occurrences would have been as bizarre then as it would be now. Such odd behavior was no more likely to happen two thousand years ago than today. So, today, if you were to be visited by an angel who then escorted you on a visit with the world's Savior, could you then just casually go your way, back to your old haunts and digs? If such an adventure could qualify as a mere footnote to your life, then you are having one hell of a spectacular life. Apparently, though, no more spectacular than that of a simple shepherd.

7. WHY DID GOD CHOOSE SUCH AN IMPRACTICAL MEANS OF ANNOUNCING THE BIRTH OF JESUS?

Who were the recipients of the most important message ever delivered to any humans in the entire history of the world? A handful of shepherds. A lousy handful of shepherds. Now, I mean no disrespect toward shepherds in general, as theirs is certainly an honest and useful occupation, especially if you like wool sweaters. However, if you were the Almighty Creator of All Things, and you were preparing to inform all of humanity of the birth of your son (a Savior who would make eternal bliss possible for those same humans) would you have done it like that? Would you have entrusted this amazing news to only a few shepherds who all lived in the same small village in ancient Judea? What were the shepherds supposed to *do* with this extraordinary news?

Put yourself in God's place. Let's say you had an urgent message for all of humankind. How would you try to convey it? Would you go up on the Internet and do your best on the World Wide Web? Or would you scribble your message on a piece of paper, put it in a corked bottle, toss it into the ocean, and then hope someone finds it? Amazingly, this latter option was the one exercised by God in deciding how to announce the birth of his son, Jesus.

To be sure, there was no Internet in Jesus' day. But God had something far more powerful than any computer network ever designed. He had *supernatural* powers at his beck and call, and there is no limit to the number of possible means he could have employed in getting his message to humans. He could have sent legions of angels to every corner of the earth. Instead, though, he sent his message to a couple of shepherds.

Luke says that after seeing the Blessed Babe in Bethlehem, the shepherds "made known abroad the saying which was told them concerning this child." One may assume "abroad" did not refer to a grand tour of Europe. On foot, the shepherds could not have notified more than a score or two of people. (On race horses, not many more.) This meant that almost the entire population of the world at that time did not hear this all-important news. God must surely have known that the probability of this message actually reaching all of humankind was nil.

And that's more or less how the word spread about this Savior. It took a millennium and a half for the Word to reach South America. It never really took hold in Asia or India or, ironically, most of the Middle East, where it all supposedly began. In that part of the world, Islam and Judaism reign supreme.

But how were people in, say Europe, supposed to hear about this miraculous birth? It could not have been from our little band of shepherds. So why were no angels dispatched *there*? Or to the Kushan kingdom in India? Or the Han government in China? Or

Japan and Africa and the Americas? Did God think the Mayas wouldn't be interested? The simplistic narrative of the angels and the shepherds belies the narrowly focused, primitive nature of its authors. There is no avoiding this glaring problem. The story of Jesus' nativity was written by men who knew nothing of the world outside their own little area. The account is replete with ignorance and naiveté. An omnipotent God would most certainly have done a better job of spreading the Word.

8. IF GOD DIDN'T WANT HUMANS TO BE SINNERS, WHY DID HE CREATE THEM THAT WAY?

This is another way of phrasing the Question of Evil, which has plagued theologians of all faiths for centuries. They have yet to provide an answer. The reason for this is that their own definitions of God have backed them into an impossible corner. They have created their own conundrum by insisting that God is simultaneously omniscient, omnibenevolent, and omnipotent.

Therefore, theologians must agree that, by definition, an omniscient (all-knowing) God would have known that ultimately evil would stalk the world he was creating. There can be no doubt that evil is here; so God must have foreseen it.

Theologians must likewise agree that an omnibenevolent (all-merciful) God would never inflict pain and suffering on his own purportedly beloved human creations. And finally, they must agree that an omnipotent (all-powerful) God would have had the option of creating a world with no evil in it. Nothing in the entire universe could have prevented him from doing whatever he wanted, since he is omnipotent. So, how did evil arrive on the scene?

Blaming Satan won't work, since an omnipotent God could have created a universe with no Satan in it. Blaming humanity's "free will" won't work either. An all-knowing God would know exactly where that "free will" would lead—to evil. So if he didn't want evil to exist, he shouldn't have created free will.

There's no getting around it. If God did not know evil would be in the world, he could not be all-knowing. If he knew there would be evil and chose to allow it, he could not be all-merciful. If he knew there would be evil but could not do anything to prevent it, he could not be all-powerful. If you insist on insisting that God is omniscient, omnipotent, and omnibenevolent, you must then also insist that there is no evil in this world—which of course is nonsense.

True Believers are stuck with this insolvable problem. The Question of Evil single-handedly destroys the argument that posits an all-powerful, all-merciful, all-knowing god.

9. WHAT IS PASCAL'S WAGER?

Pascal's wager is a most overrated and overly discussed proposition. Seventeenth-century French philosopher Blaise Pascal held that belief in God is a better wager than nonbelief because there are infinite rewards to gain and little to lose by believing, versus infinite rewards to lose and little to gain by not believing.

Pascal's wager has three major flaws. First, which God are we supposed to believe in? Jehovah? Vishnu? Allah? Ra? One of the hundreds of other gods humans have worshiped over the centuries? These different gods all come with mutually exclusive characteristics, histories, and belief requirements. So according to Pascal, which one should we believe in? The many critics who have argued that God might reserve a special place in hell for people who believe in him on the basis of Pascal's wager (since belief should be sincere and not the result of a bet) are guilty of the same simplistic oversight that Pascal himself was; namely, *name your God first* before proceeding to discuss whether or not to worship her/him/it/them.

The second refutation is the one heard most often. It states that prostrating ourselves before a judgmental God, and thinking of ourselves as unworthy and deserving of eternal hellfire, is not conducive to mental health or an appreciation of human worth. It is a stifling, degrading view of humanity that closes off so many aspects of the human potential. So yes, there is much to be lost by believing.

But the biggest problem, in my opinion, which I have never read about anywhere (though of course that doesn't mean it hasn't been written somewhere) is that you cannot turn belief on and off like a faucet. To say, "Well, go ahead and believe! What have you got to lose?" is silly. I can't toss a coin and, based on its landing, suddenly decide, "Well, I now believe in Christ crucified." People cannot force themselves to believe in something they just don't believe in. I do not, for example, believe in the Tooth Fairy. And no amount of argumentation, high-stakes wagers, or anything else can make me believe. So Pascal's wager is really moot.

10. WHAT IS THE FIRST CAUSE ARGUMENT?

The "nothing comes of nothing" argument, usually known as the First Cause argument, is the easiest to refute. It asserts that since nothing can come from nothing, something must have created the Earth. That something is known as God.

Hmmm. Nothing comes from nothing. Well, that means that God cannot have come from nothing. Therefore, something must have created God. To say that God always existed is to beg the question. You could as easily say that the universe always existed. If you continue looking back for a cause, you must ultimately explain what caused God. Which leaves you going backward, inexorably, forever. The First Cause argument *demands* an explanation of who or what caused God to come into existence.

11. WHAT IS THE ARGUMENT FROM DESIGN, SOMETIMES KNOWN AS PALEY'S WATCHMAKER ARGUMENT?

What eighteen-century theologian William Paley said, in essence, was that just as an elaborately complex watch demands a watchmaker, so too does our complex world demand a designer. Sounds like a good argument. But there are two problems with it. First, it suffers from a shortcoming similar to the First Cause argument. If the world requires a designer because of its complexity, then the assuredly more complex God also requires a designer.

Second, it fails for the simple reason that anyone using it does not understand evolution. Mutation is almost always random. Cumulative natural selection, of which we are but one of the products, is the quintessential *opposite* of randomness. Richard Dawkins's excellent book *The Blind Watchmaker*[1] addresses this issue in exquisite and convincing detail.

12. DOES GOD REVEAL HIMSELF TO US TODAY?

Indeed he does, according to many believers. There are weeping statues and stigmata episodes and angel apparitions and faith "healings." And the Virgin Mary showed up on a tortilla somewhere, and on a waffle, while Mother Teresa's visage appeared on a sesame seed bun. Or was it a cinnamon roll?

As bizarre as all that may be, it's hard to beat the stories that hit the wires a few years ago. They included hungry hippos in Jerusalem's Biblical Zoo on Passover, a holy heifer born in the Holy Land, and a sacred tiger fish in Lodi, California—all wonders courtesy of Judaism and Islam. Welcome to Oz.

It seems that the zookeepers in the Jerusalem zoo were worried that during Passover week they, or possibly some visitors, might accidentally touch some of the leavened bread that is usually fed to the animals. Observant Jews aren't supposed to eat or even touch leavened bread during this holiday because they are celebrating the escape of the Jews, led by Moses, from Egypt. You see, Moses and company were in a hurry when they were escaping from the pharaoh. So they didn't have time to wait for their bread to rise. So they had to eat unleavened bread. So today they celebrate the Great Escape by eating only unleavened bread during Passover. And over the years they tightened up the rules, so now they're not even allowed to *touch* leavened bread. Are you following all this?

Well then, to avert the looming catastrophe (the possible inadvertent touching of the wrong kind of bread) the zookeepers withheld the animals' regular feed and replaced it with a "special kosher-for-Passover mixture approved by Israel's rabbinical establishment."[2] We're talking kosher elephants and hippos. I am not making this up. This AP story ran on April 10, 1998. Really.

And on May 29, 1997, there was quite a stir about a red heifer that was born in the Holy Land. The AP photo showed Rabbi Shmaria Shore deep in thought as he stroked the animal's nose.[3] This red heifer, "Melody," was believed to be the first red heifer born in the Holy Land in two thousand years. Obviously someone must have been keeping track of such things. Else how would they know? There must be a rabbinical representative with the title "Official Heifer Color Checker." I wonder if the job pays well. With all the traveling involved you'd think it would.

But the point is that there was speculation that Melody might be the "harbinger of the Messiah." What a stunning thought! What a cunning, spectacular, godly manner in which to announce the coming of the Savior of the Chosen People—the birth of a cow. Such a heavenly announcement may be a little oblique, to be sure, requiring extraordinary powers of interpretation of the Divine Will.

On the other hand, there were those who believed that Melody should be destroyed because she was an evil omen. Once again this interpretation was based on an exquisitely fine-tuned understanding of the Divine. It was diametrically opposed to the *other* exquisitely fine-tuned understanding, but let's not quibble. For centuries soothsayers have been predicting future events by reading goat entrails, for example. It is an ancient and honorable art. Let those who have never read goat entrails cast the first stone.

Not to be outdone by Judaism's carrot-topped cows, Hyatullah Ahmadi of Lodi, California, proudly offered, for the world's admiration, one of Islam's sacred signs from Allah. It was swimming. In a saltwater aquarium. It was a fish.

According to Ahmadi, the albino tiger oscar fish had the word "Allah" clearly emblazoned on its right flank. Red letters on white fish flesh. Just imagine. God on a cichlid fish. "Allah" was in

Arabic, so evidently the fish was Arabic. I'm guessing it was also Muslim. (This animal husbandry is a tricky science.) Validating this holy manifestation was none other than the president of the Lodi Muslim Mosque, Taj Khan. "It's very, very distinctly written," said Khan. Hard to argue with that, then. Ahmadi had been offered $1,000 for the fish, but would not part with it because it was "a symbol of God's power and omnipresence."

And you thought the heifer was silly.

Expanding on some of the lesser-known tenets of the Muslim faith, Ahmadi continued. "Each person has two angels on each shoulder. Each time you mention Allah's name, it's written in your book for Judgment Day." Well then, I say "Allah." Thinking this principle through most cleverly, Ahmadi named the fish "Ayat-ullah" which means "sign of God." That way he'll mention the Almighty often. Good thinking, Ahmadi.

Allah.

Not as distinct, but still written on this same amazing fish, on its left flank, is a portion of Islam's most fundamental teaching: "There is no God but one God." (I think the Jews would agree with this one. So would the Catholics. And the Baptists. And the Christian Scientists. But I digress. Allah.) Taj Khan assures us that as interesting as this aquatic vertebrate may be, it is not unique. No, says Khan, there have been several similar miracles which included some fruits and vegetables and, possibly, a cow. (A bit of copycat here?) "In England," agreed Ahmadi, "there was a tomato that said Allah three weeks ago." (The date on this *Lodi News Sentinel* article was June 28, 1997. Allah.) Now "said" is the past tense form of the transitive verb, "say." It's probably safe to assume that Ahmadi didn't mean to imply that the tomato actually uttered an audible sound, but rather had the word etched on its skin or something. But the article isn't clear on that point. And with miracles, who knows? A talking tomato would be an attention grabber, wouldn't it?

At this point I have a confession to make. It is a little known fact, but I actually do acknowledge a deity. His name is Bob. Bob the Rain-god. For years Bob has manifested himself to me in the form of various animals—though I've never seen him on a tomato.

But I have seen the name "Bob," clearly and unambiguously, adorning many different species. I naturally saved and nurtured them for as long as I could. Holy animals don't just drop out of the sky you know! Allah. And, naturally, I named them all. So, at various times, my own Miracle Menagerie consisted of a silverfish named Silver, a spider named Spy, a caterpillar named Cat, and a cockroach named Herbert.

Each of these holy messengers spoke volumes to me, and convinced me more than ever that there really is a god out there—in my case, Bob. I also learned the meaning of true humility and how to humble myself before a silverfish. Whether it is a redheaded heifer, an autographed tiger fish, or a holy caterpillar, such creatures can be the key to understanding eternal truths. Now if only we could *talk* to these animals . . . say, is Dr. Doolittle still around?

Allah.

13. WHAT IS THE NAME OF THOSE LITTLE PLASTIC THINGS ON THE ENDS OF YOUR SHOELACES?

I think I knew the answer to that once, but I've since forgotten it, and I don't know how to look it up. Things like that drive me crazy. I also wonder what moths ate before we created sweaters.

14. HOW CAN WE RID OURSELVES OF THE PAST YEAR'S SINS?

One way is to sacrifice a live chicken. Ultra-orthodox Jews observe the ancient rite of *kapparot*, which means sacrificing a live chicken to atone for your sins. Here's what you do. You take a live chicken, and swing it over your head in circles while chanting a prayer asking for forgiveness of your sins. The ritual prayer is designed to transfer all of your previous year's sins onto the chicken. I am not making this up. You do this in preparation for the holiest of holy days in the Jewish calendar—Yom Kippur, the Day of Atonement.

After you finish swinging the chicken over your head and saying your prayers, you kill the chicken and give the remains to charity.

And you thought the heifer was silly.

The newspaper story that carried a photo of a man dressed in black suit and hat, swinging a live chicken over his head, also featured several quotes from swinging/atoning Jews in Jerusalem. One fellow said, "I don't really believe this chicken can expiate my sins—it's symbolic, a way of preparing for what's to come."[4] But he said this after swinging a squawking bird over his small sons' heads and reciting the traditional prayer.

For some reason I have an unaccountable craving for chicken soup.

15. SHOULD WE DEBATE THE EXISTENCE OF GOD?

There are many atheists who believe, ardently, that theists should not be debated. Period. It's a waste of time, they argue. You'll never change theistic minds anyway, and simply by discussing theism you grant it a credence it does not deserve. And in any case, the only people who believe all that rubbish are loonies who cannot distinguish between fantasy and reality.

This is the gist of the argument that says we should ignore theism and instead promote humanism. It sounds like a pretty good argument. But there are two major problems with it. First, it requires us to ignore something like 70 to 80 percent of the population. We must pretend that these people do not hold public office, frame public policy, rule on church/state issues, influence public school textbook decisions, and so on. This is your definite ostrich position—ignore them and maybe they'll go away. The problem is, they won't.

Second, the argument implies that all theists are idiots. Aside from the obvious fact that labeling an overwhelming majority of the population "fools" is a foolish thing to do, since it just can't be true; there is a personal element involved in this painting with such a broad brush. Many of us have loved ones who are theists, and it is impossible to look at all of them as nutcases.

I am the first to attack most theistic arguments, believing they are silly or cruel or incomprehensible—and sometimes all three at once. But this is a far cry from saying that all theists are dimwits. My own father was one of the brightest individuals I have ever known. He was well-read, knowledgeable in many areas, he liked to recite Poe and Dickinson, and he was witty. He held an important multistate executive position with the Sherwin-Williams Company, and he was also an accomplished pipe organist. Oh, and he was an ardent Lutheran. Strictly a fundamentalist. But does he sound like an idiot?

Likewise, my grandfather Dr. John Meyer, a Lutheran minister, was quite comfortable in *seven* languages—English, German, Spanish, Portuguese, Latin, Hebrew, and Greek. How many of us can make such a claim? My uncle, also a Lutheran fundie, was a senior engineer for RCA before being recruited to work on the early warning systems for the Department of Defense. I could go on, but enough said.

It is jolting and insulting, not to mention arrogant and condescending, when humanists refer to all believers as "nuts." It is as silly and self-defeating as when True Believers refer to all atheists as "evil." Some of us are, and some of us aren't. Some believers are loons and some of them aren't. But so far, in my own experience, when it comes to intellectual capacity, my theistic friends and my nonbelieving friends are in a dead heat. It's too close to call. But then, why should we have to? Why do we feel the need to denigrate believers simply because they *believe*?

Evil popes and torturers for the Inquisition, on the other hand, deserve any bad names that come to mind. But simply *believing* should not make people fair game for name-calling. If it does, it is the same as the name-calling that accompanies all forms of bigotry. Condemn the evil, and the evildoers, but not the well-intentioned, misled believers.

I have said before, and will say again, that as soon as Christians (and/or any other religionists) stop trying to force their religious beliefs into our public classrooms, courtrooms, and public policies, then I will shut up and go away. There will be no need for theistic criticisms because religion will remain where it belongs—in homes and churches. However, we should all live so long.

In the meantime, if Christians want to push their beliefs into public forums, then those beliefs should be examined—as publicly as possible. We cannot pretend that Christians are not all around us, exerting considerable influence. The fact that legislators in the state of Tennessee even *considered* firing teachers who taught evolution as fact should give us all pause. I take no comfort whatever in the fact that such legislation was not adopted. That it was even discussed is frighteningly mind-boggling.

Closer to home, in my own right-next-door San Joaquin County, the Board of Supervisors adopted the policy of reinstating prayer at all of their official functions. So it's "Our Father" and then down to business. There was only *one* dissenting vote. One of the supervisors unabashedly claimed that when *he* offered *his* prayers, spoken aloud, he would naturally mention "Our Lord and Savior, Jesus Christ," because he knew no other way to pray. So Jews and Buddhists be damned, I guess.

So, we're surrounded and might as well deal with it. I did my own part for a while by writing a few essays, which were published in the religion section (!) of our local newspaper. This was followed by many letters to the editor. When I stated in one of my letters that there was *no such thing* as a "Christian" viewpoint, since all the sects disagreed wildly with each other, the Christian responses made that point better than I did. They were hopping mad, but it was not because I had called them all morons, as many of my fellow humanists often do. They were utterly frustrated by their own inability to define "Christian." My letters remained calm and inoffensive, but were apparently dead on the mark. I refused to be drawn into discussions of how this nation must return to its Christian values. I simply asked them to define "Christian" and all hell broke loose. Because they couldn't do it.

This sort of debate is very valuable, in my opinion. If name-calling is avoided, it can be very productive. Fence-sitters, especially, will benefit from such exchanges. Christian fundamentalism is on the rise and *we* are fools if we don't recognize it and deal with it. If I feel qualified, I will rip an argument to shreds. But I will not sink to ad hominem nonsense. And nonsense it is.

A little sarcasm goes a long way; but even knowing that, I catch myself now and again condescending and preening rather smugly. We must avoid these tendencies, although it *is* difficult when we see people stampeding to catch a glimpse of a statue crying tears of blood or some such thing. Or swinging those chickens. But we should not avoid theological debates. If we have learned nothing from the frightening convergence of the Religious Right and our Congress, which led to an unbelievable presidential impeachment, then we are just not paying attention.

Debates about theology need not get bogged down in the tiresome, tedious business of examining precise Greek translations of specific biblical phrases. Such discussions sometimes have their place, but unless you are very knowledgeable in this area, this can backfire. Christians love to pounce on minuscule, insignificant translation errors and then gleefully claim some kind of victory. But looking at the larger picture, who really cares about such things? Unfortunately, though, it seems that almost all nontheist debaters *do* get mired in such trivia, while nontheist "purists," if you will, keep a disdainful distance from debate altogether. There seems to be no middle ground.

In my first book, although I do engage in a bit of that wordplay, my main thrust, and the entire opening, focuses on defining "God." It is not an easy task. True Believers usually don't realize this until they try to do it, out loud, in front of a nonbeliever. Without being nasty or condescending, a nontheist can quietly ask if their definition means the God who inspires the pope. Or is it the one who inspired Muhammad? Or Joseph Smith? The pope question alone usually sends Christians running for cover because, obviously, they cannot answer that question without splitting Christendom right down the middle. And this by itself takes some of the wind out of the "Christian Nation" sails.

When high-profile, professional Christians begin to beat their drums and take control of school boards, *someone* has to take them on. And we're it. If we dismiss them as lunatics, unworthy of our attention, we do so at our own peril. All it takes for America to become a theocracy is for nonbelievers to do nothing.

16. EVEN IF THE BIBLICAL STORY OF JESUS' CRUCIFIXION WERE TRUE, WHAT DID HE ACTUALLY SACRIFICE?

Surprisingly, there is very little discussion about this, in religious or secular circles. The historical accuracy of the event is discussed endlessly, but not the actual *nature* of the supposed event. According to the Bible, God sacrificed his only son, Jesus, for the salvation of humankind. Imagine. Sacrificing your only child, a beloved son, for the good of someone else. What compassion! Assuming your son feels a similar altruistic fervor about the whole thing, what a magnanimous act by both of you! John 3:16, one of the most frequently quoted Bible verses of all time, describes this benevolence. "For God so loved the world, that he gave his only begotten Son, that whosoever believeth in him should not perish, but have everlasting life." It's a hard act to follow.

We can only view this gesture of supreme love in human terms. We try to imagine what it would be like to sacrifice a much loved son. (Interestingly, the idea of sacrificing a virginal *daughter* sounds offensively pagan. Doesn't it?) But we have trouble coming to terms with child sacrifice. It is just too painful.

Of course we have sent our sons off to war for as long as there have been wars, and a great percentage of them never come back. But there is always that flicker of hope. Perhaps our son will return to us. A straightforward sacrifice, however, leaves no room for hope. If a death is required, a death it shall be. And in the case of Jesus' death, there was the added grim horror of torture. Crucifixion is not a pretty thing.

We'll set aside for the moment the fact that there is no cross, *anywhere*, in the Bible. The Greek word that has been mistranslated over the centuries as "cross" is really "stake," with no cross beam even implied. However, since most Christians *believe* in a cross, we'll stay with that imagery. Besides, if you're going to affix someone to a piece of wood to await an agonizing death, does it really matter whether you nail him to it or impale him on it?

So, now we are faced with the harrowing specter of a loving God offering up his only son for prolonged torture in addition to certain death. And why? Because we are all worthless sinners in need of "redemption." It is all for us. Tears well up at the thought. This is emotional dynamite.

Let's take a deep breath, though, and look at this scenario more closely. As I have noted on many other occasions, with the reminder that it always bears repeating (because it does), there is a need to justify Jesus' sacrificial death in the first place. An all-powerful God would have had the option of creating any kind of creature he wanted. So for him to have created wicked sinners who would need some sort of redemption seems arbitrarily cruel. Why not create perfect people and avoid all this grief? There could have been nothing to prevent an omnipotent God from doing this. However, no one has ever solved this puzzle, so let's move on.

The love of this God for his human creations was supposedly so strong that he sacrificed his own son on their behalf. But what does the word "sacrifice" mean, literally? Well, it means the ritual slaughter of an animal or a person; the forfeiture of something highly valued for the sake of something considered to have a greater value. Almost everyone will claim to know what the word means. Yet Christians, as well as most of the rest of us, fail to recognize the serious difficulty in the Jesus-as-sacrifice scenario. That is, if Jesus was actually sacrificed, why isn't he still dead?

Consider again the forlorn parents sending their son off to war. If their son is killed during battle, that's the end of it. They have truly sacrificed their son. *They will not be receiving a message in a couple of days telling them that their son is now just fine.* Jesus, however, was not only "just fine" on the third day after his crucifixion, but he was also allowed to ascend into Heaven, there to reign with God the Father for all eternity. How can this possibly be considered a sacrifice?

There is a world of difference, for example, between putting your child in an abusive environment for three days, and shooting him in the forehead with a sawed-off shotgun. The two events are not even remotely related. But they demonstrate, in a grisly way to be sure, the enormous difference between the "sacrifice" of Jesus, and the sacrifice of a normal human child. Actually, the differences are greater still.

A normal child, one may assume, would have no supernatural powers, and would therefore not know in advance if or when the abuse was going to end. Jesus, on the other hand, would have known to the nanosecond how long his ordeal would be. Moreover, an ordinary child would have no way of mitigating his suffering. He would simply have to grit his teeth and endure. Jesus, once again with his supernatural powers, need not have suffered at all. He could have placed himself in a state of euphoria if he chose. Or, for that matter, slept through it all. Nothing would have been beyond his powers. If he *chose* to suffer, it was his own doing. Most assuredly, then, Jesus cannot be regarded as some sort of passive, sacrificial lamb, as he is so often described. He controlled his own destiny.

In the same way, God the Father cannot be considered to be an average, grieving parent. He, along with Jesus, would know that the suffering, if they chose to accept it, would end when they chose to end it. They would know that the so-called death state would be of very brief duration indeed. And, when viewed this way, the whole crucifixion is a pointless sham. It is playacting. It includes voluntary (or only simulated) pain, a temporary death, and a glorious ascension into heaven. Where exactly does the word "sacrifice" fit in here? Real death and pretend death are not the same thing, and any ten-year-old can tell you that. And even if there had been a real Jesus who went through a real crucifixion, there are, sadly, thousands of World War II, Korean War, and Vietnam vets whose suffering could make Jesus' problems look like a day at the beach.

Why would anyone be sad, or even feign sadness, on Good Friday, if they know Easter is right around the corner? As a comparison, suppose you were to tell a group of friends that a mutual friend had just died. Then, you end this dreadful announcement with a cry of, "April Fool!" Aside from the probably justified fear that someone may go for your throat because of this stunt, would there be any other reason for you to feel dismayed? Since you knew all along that there was no problem with your "dead" friend, how in the world could you feel sad about him? Similarly, how could God feel sad about the pretend death of his son, Jesus? It bears all the earmarks of an April Fool joke.

So the next time some proselytizing Christian launches into a teary-eyed account of Jesus' sacrificial death, just ask, in all seriousness, "*What* sacrifice?!"

17. WHY DO PEOPLE ALWAYS THANK GOD AFTER A TRAGEDY?

A four-year-old victim of a car accident is rushed into the emergency room and a code is called. Immediately people fly into action, their movements urgent but amazingly coordinated. The tiny, seemingly lifeless body is surrounded by medical professionals who will challenge their own skills and race the clock. The paramedics have already performed their magic by delivering a critically injured but *alive* patient. Now it is up to the doctors and nurses to try to put this young life back together. While the little girl is being stabilized, a surgical team is being organized. Of the many injuries, one will require exquisitely delicate spinal surgery, which is always tricky, but so much more so when the patient is so small. Permanent paralysis is a very real possibility.

After five hours of grueling, intense concentration and effort, the surgery ends. The surgical team heads back to the changing room, saying little as their brains begin the slow process of de-tuning, of letting go of the intense concentration. They will not feel the full extent of their exhaustion until long after they are back at their homes, allowing themselves the luxury of an effortless thought.

Things look good for the girl, who will probably walk again.

But now begins the round the clock vigil in the ICU. After all the shock and trauma, this frail four-year-old could go sour very quickly. The little body is trying to heal itself, but it needs one hell of a lot of help. Thirty years ago the girl would have been dead shortly after the accident. Today she is alive.

Ten days and much nursing care later, the little girl is smiling at her parents. She is going to live and she is going to walk again. And what is the community response to this symphony of dedicated medical labors? Why, family and friends go to church to thank God for the "miraculous" recovery! No! No! NO! You thank the tireless medical staff. You thank the research and development people who made all of this possible. You do *not* thank God. Besides, if there was a God who had anything at all to do with this girl's life, *why didn't he just prevent the accident to begin with?*

The devastating fires that raged in Florida in the summer of 1998 were disastrous and my heart went out to the victims. But I knew if I heard one more prayer of thanks because no one died in the fires, I would have spit up. The *reason* no one had lost their lives at that point was because firefighters risked *their* lives fighting the incredibly destructive forces of a raging wildfire. Thank God? No. Thank the firefighters.

Every year tragedies are averted because someone is willing to risk life and limb to save someone else. People jump into icy rivers, risking their own death from hypothermia in the process, to try to rescue victims of an airplane crash. Firefighters rush into burning buildings and save victims from an otherwise certain death. Cops risk their lives every time they answer an "in progress" or chase a recklessly speeding car. At no small risk to themselves, ski patrols race to the still-dangerous sites of avalanches and "miraculously" manage to rescue people buried beneath the snow. After the grisly business of removing the bodies of the unfortunates who did not survive, the rescue workers finally end up huddled back at the lodge, sipping coffee or brandy, utterly exhausted and chilled. And what cheers of praise do you hear? "It's a miracle! Thank God there were any survivors at all!" No. Thank the ski patrol.

People can be terribly cruel to each other. But we can also be marvelously compassionate and helpful well above and beyond the call of duty. When that happens, as it often does, those people should be *thanked*. Thanking some invisible God for the hard work and self-sacrifice of other humans is callously insensitive. And stupid. And it always sends me through the roof, as you can probably tell.

Similarly, there was a front-page story in our local newspaper after the horrible July 1998 shooting in the Capitol building in Washington, D.C. It was simply tragic and awful. The paper naturally had its front page filled with the story. It was continued on page 8, and used most of that page as well. But guess what was emblazoned across the entire top of page 8, spanning all six columns, in something like 40 points? *"I got down on my knees and prayed and thanked God my daughter wasn't hit."*

These effusively earnest and totally insensitive words were uttered by a woman who was visiting the Capitol with her six-year-old daughter, Hannah. They heard the shots. Well, I certainly understand the woman's relief about her daughter. But while her wonderful God was protecting little Hannah, that same God allowed two men, Officers John Gibson and Jacob J. Chestnut, to be shot dead in that same violent episode.

How can anyone, anytime, anywhere, be so callously indifferent to the suffering of others? How can anyone be so egotistically smug about their own supposed importance in the eyes of their supposedly munificent God, without seeing the cruel arrogance implicit in such an assertion? Anyone offering such a prayer of thanks is *also* saying, "Thank you, God, for killing *those* people instead of me and mine." What a ghastly, self-centered, cold-hearted way to look at the world. If there really were a merciful God, *no one* would ever be murdered.

I intend no disrespect whatever toward the unfortunate victims or the survivors of tragedies like the U.S. Embassy bombings in 1998 or the Oklahoma City bombing in 1995. But having witnessed real tragedies myself, the constant thanking of God for *not* killing the rest of us always astounds and offends me. If you believe there is a God watching over all of us, then bombing victims are not the result of senseless killing. No. It is senseless mercy.

The following prayer might have been appropriate for the governor at the commemoration ceremonies that took place one year after the Oklahoma City bombing:

> Our Heavenly Father,
>
> We are gathered here today to commemorate the tragic loss, one year ago today, of our dearly beloved family and friends. The terrible explosion that wrought destruction and terror on the lives of hundreds of citizens of Oklahoma City is difficult for the human mind to comprehend. But we are thankful for your mercy in sparing the lives of the hundreds of people here with us today. We humbly offer our thanks for their lives, even as we grieve for those who for some reason weren't worth saving.
>
> Of course Jennifer Washington, the little fourth-grader, was only reading at the second-grade level, so there wasn't much of a future for her anyway, when you get right down to it. And that Jason Clark was a troublemaker from the day he was born, so whose loss is that? No one ever liked the Grady twins and the less said about them the better. May they rest in peace. You might have cut us some slack on that two-year-old, Erica Garcia, because as far as anyone knows, she was a heck of a neat little toddler. But we won't nitpick.
>
> As we bow our heads in prayer on this day of remembrance, we are reminded of the thousands of acts of mercy you show us every day. We thank you for the clothes we wear, the homes we live in, the food on our table, and our really terrific computer games. And thanks again for killing all those other people instead of us.
>
> Amen.

Too callous? Maybe. Then again maybe not. In any event, on behalf of all the well-intentioned but seriously misguided individuals who light candles and thank the empty skies, I want to extend a heartfelt *thank you!* to all rescue, police, fire, and medical people out there. I hope I never have cause again to thank you in person, but if I do, you can be certain that thanks will go where thanks are due. To you.

18. WHY ARE SO MANY CHRISTIAN HYMNS DEGRADING AND DEPRESSING?

It's because Christianity is degrading and depressing. To be sure, there are hymns of praise and thankfulness. But the most common theme running through Christianity is how unworthy we all are, and how we all deserve to burn in hell. One of the most famous hymns in the world begins like this:

"Amazing Grace, how sweet the sound, that saved a wretch like me. . . ." See? We're all wretches. Another well-known hymn, "Rock of Ages," contains: "Let the water and the blood, from Thy riven side which flowed. . . ."

Less well known, except maybe to Lutherans, are the following, which were literally chosen at random. They are all taken from the Evangelical Lutheran Hymn-Book, edition of 1931, the pages of which are drenched with blood and misery:

- "Arise, my soul, arise, shake off thy guilty fears, The bleeding Sacrifice in my behalf appears; Five bleeding wounds He bears, Received on Calvary, His spirit answers to the blood, and tells me I am born of God . . ."
- "He sprinkled with His blood, the mercy-seat above . . ."
- "Foolish, and impotent, and blind, Lead me a way I have not known . . ."
- "Destitute, despised, forsaken, Thou from hence my all shall be . . ."
- "Go, then, earthly fame and treasure! Come, disaster, scorn and pain! . . ."
- "They crown Thy head with thorns, they smite, they scourge Thee, With cruel mockings to the cross they urge Thee . . ."
- "There is a fountain filled with blood, Drawn from Immanuel's veins . . ."
- "Just as I am, without one plea, But that thy blood was shed for me. . . . Just as I am, poor, wretched, blind . . ."
- "Jesus, Thy blood and righteousness, My beauty are, my glorious dress . . ."

- "Lord Jesus Christ, true man and God, Who bore the anguish, scorn, the rod, And died at last upon the tree, To gain Thy Father's grace for me . . ."
- "Not all the blood of beasts, On Jewish altars slain, Could give the guilty conscience peace, Or wash away the stain . . ."
- "Therefore, when my God doth choose it, Willingly I'll yield my life, Nor will grieve that I should lose it, For with sorrows it was rife . . ."
- "I would not live always; no, welcome the tomb; Since Jesus hath lain there, I dread not its gloom . . ."
- "Whether to live or die, I know not which is best: To live in Thee is bliss to me, To die is endless rest . . ."

And, of course, there's Bach's famous, "Come soothing death; come sweet repose. . . ."

Yuck. This is all quite depressing. And I was surprised, after all these years, at the emotions that stirred while I was leafing through that old hymnal. The themes are just as I remembered them. We are wretched, miserable creatures; copious amounts of blood must be shed to atone for that; and death is much better than life. What a terrible message! I seriously doubt that any adult Christians ever give this a passing thought as they sit with their children, singing those dreadful words. I remember as a child I would feel real fear when singing some of those hymns, and I adored Easter and Christmas as a result. On those holidays we sang nothing but happy, uplifting hymns and carols. I still enjoy Christmas carols, and after my refresher course in hymns, I can see why. In fact, right now a couple verses of Jingle Bells sound pretty good.

19. IF WATER SWIRLS DOWN THE DRAIN CLOCKWISE IN ONE HEMISPHERE, AND COUNTERCLOCKWISE IN THE OTHER HEMISPHERE, HOW DOES IT GO DOWN THE DRAIN IF YOU'RE SMACK ON THE MIDDLE OF THE EQUATOR?

Maybe it doesn't go down at all. Maybe it just sits there. Hmmm. I always wonder about stuff like this. I have this insatiable desire to *know* things. Maybe someday I'll find out for myself. Maybe I'll go to Ecuador and take a bath.

20. WHAT IS AN AGNOSTIC?

A nonexistent person. I should know. I used to be one. I don't mean I was a nonexistent person, but I called myself an agnostic. Why? The same reason people do it today—to avoid using that awful "A" word. Atheist. What ought to be a fairly simple, straightforward task—defining the word "atheist"—has turned into a philosophical nightmare requiring postgraduate courses and a thesis adviser. And it isn't just the religionists who have screwed things up so royally by heaping undeserved, malicious baggage onto that little word. (Atheist = immoral, communist scumbag.) No, we nonbelievers are wrangling over it ourselves, and the whole thing is just plain silly.

The word "agnostic" means literally "without knowledge" or, more simply, "I don't know." But it is really just a cop-out word for atheist. It is a word that society has not yet blackened with foul adjectives. It's safer to utter in mixed company. However, it's impossible not to "know" whether or not you acknowledge a deity. If you do, you know it. If you don't, you know that too. And if you don't, you are an atheist—a person without theistic beliefs.

To say, "I am an agnostic" is to say, "I don't know whether I believe in God or not." Which is nonsense.

Even my hero, the late Carl Sagan, spoke of atheism as a position that couldn't be justified because no one can provide any "compelling evidence," as he put it, that a God does not exist. His full statement: "An atheist is someone who is certain that God does not exist, someone who has compelling evidence against the existence of God."[5] This is simply not true. This is *not* the definition of an atheist. Neither I nor any atheists I know make the claim of having "compelling evidence against the existence of God." Nor are we required to have such evidence! The burden of proof lies squarely with those who claim knowledge of the existence of God. If you so claim, you must prove. I do not believe in a God. That position requires no demonstration or "proof." If you claim there *is* a God, you are making a claim that absolutely requires demonstration. As Sagan himself used to say, extraordinary claims require extraordinary evidence.

No one can provide any "compelling evidence" that leprechauns do not exist. So what? Does that mean then that we have a-leprechaunists and agnosti-leprechaunists, with the former claiming leprechauns don't exist and the latter withholding judgment until all the evidence is in? No. You either do or you do not believe in leprechauns. So it is with gods.

But the problem lies in the hairsplitting that goes on about whether or not someone simply does not acknowledge a god, or goes further and actually claims there *is* no god. Atheists do not make this claim. When we atheists emphatically state that we do not believe in a god we will sometimes say, "Oh, bull! There *is* no god!" But what we're talking about are the human creations such as Jupiter, Thor, Jehovah, Krishna, Jesus, Allah, and so on—the gods we've been spoon-fed since childhood but still find thoroughly unconvincing. So we lump them all together and pronounce them all nonexistent, and here is where the confusion comes in. When we claim nonexistence for a god we mean *of those so far offered as candidates.*

No one can claim a god absolutely does not exist unless he can claim infinite knowledge of the universe. I have never heard any atheist make this claim either. In fact, if any atheist reading this can make the certain claim that no god does or could exist, and can back it up, I would like to hear about it. It would be fun to meet someone who possesses infinite knowledge of the universe.

To the extent that none of us can claim infinite knowledge, all atheists are "agnostics." But when you say "I don't know if there's a god or not," you obviously do not acknowledge one, which makes you an atheist. On the other hand, if an authentic winged creature suddenly filled the sky from horizon to horizon; and everyone in the whole world saw it at the same time; and it announced that it was "God"; and we all heard it in our own languages—I'm in. I'm buying it. And so would every diehard atheist I know.

If you acknowledge a deity, you are a theist. If you do not acknowledge a deity, you are an atheist. It is really so simple that all the fuss made about it is not only astonishing, but tiresome.

21. WHAT ARE THE TEN COMMANDMENTS?

[I know I said there were going to be twenty questions; but there are exactly twenty questions here just like there are exactly ten commandments in the Bible.]

On June 17, 1999, the House of Representatives voted in favor of displaying the so-called Ten Commandments in public buildings, including, of course, schools. The vote was 248–180.[6] There are two *major* problems with this. First, the unconstitutional nature of such a proposal should have been so obvious as to preclude any discussion of such a thing, let alone a vote on it. The enormity of the implications of the House's actions was lost on many of us. But this 1990s full-court press by the Religious Right made some of us quite nervous. Unless we're going to amend our Constitution and adopt a state religion, such discussions have no place in Congress or any other governmental body.

Second, there *are* no "Ten Commandments" anywhere in the Bible. While it is true that in book of Exodus, chapter 20, there is a list of things to do and not to do, it is *not* true that the list has ten rules. The only way to wring the magic number ten out of it is if you ignore some of the directives and lump several others together and call them one. It is totally arbitrary, totally misleading and just plain wrong.

For example, the so-called Ten Commandments begin in

Exodus 20, verse 2 or 3, and end with verse 17. Yes, it takes fifteen or sixteen verses to name ten directives—if you accept that there *are* ten directives. The Jewish version of the first of these commandments is "I am the LORD thy God" (Exod. 20:2); but Christians consider that a preamble, and claim that "Thou shalt have no other gods before me" (Exod. 20:3) is the first commandment. So who is correct? They can't both be right, can they?

In addition, in Exod. 20:24, just seven verses after the misnamed Decalogue, there is *another* definite commandment. It is clearly an imperative: "An altar of earth thou shalt make unto me, and shalt sacrifice thereon thy burnt offerings, and thy peace offerings, thy sheep, and thine oxen: in all places where I record my name I will come unto thee, and I will bless thee." So why is this commandment simply ignored? How is it any different from the others?

Those 248 House members should be sacrificing sheep and oxen in their backyards. They were clearly told to do so. There is no ambiguity in that commandment. It should be oxen-and-sheep time everywhere in the Bible Belt.

But even worse than the oxen-and-sheep thing is what happens in Exodus chapters 13, 23, 34, and 35—in fact, the entire Old Testament. It is literally *packed* with commandments just as forceful and just as clear (or unclear, depending on your point of view) as those in Exodus 20 (however many there are). But somehow they didn't make the Top Ten list.

Confusing things further, in Exodus 34, the commandments given there are actually described as "replacements." Why? Because Moses dropped and broke the first set of tablets, the ones he got in Exodus 20. What a klutz! "And the LORD said unto Moses, Hew thee two tables of stone like unto the first: and *I will write upon these tables the words that were in the first tables*, which thou brakest" (Exod. 34:1) [emphasis mine]. With these words, along with slamming Moses, God is saying that the words from the first tablets will be the same as those on the second set. Again, no ambiguity.

But the two lists aren't even close. Compare the two lists, supposedly identical, keeping in mind that I, like everyone else, have to arbitrarily number the commandments:

Exod. 20:2–17

1. Thou shalt have no other gods before me.
2. Thou shalt not make unto thee any graven image.
3. Thou shalt not take the name of the LORD thy God in vain.
4. Remember the sabbath day, to keep it holy.
5. Honor thy father and thy mother: that thy days may be long upon the land which the LORD thy God giveth thee.
6. Thou shalt not kill.
7. Thou shalt not commit adultery.
8. Thou shalt not steal.
9. Thou shalt not bear false witness against thy neighbor.
10. Thou shalt not covet.

And here's the "replacement" set:

Exod. 34:12–27

1. Take heed to thyself, lest thou make a covenant with the inhabitants of the land whither thou goest, lest it be for a snare in the midst of thee: But ye shall destroy their altars, break their images, and cut down their groves:
2. For thou shalt worship no other god: for the LORD, whose name is Jealous, is a jealous God:
3. Thou shalt make thee no molten gods.
4. The feast of unleavened bread shalt thou keep. Seven days thou shalt eat unleavened bread, as I commanded thee, in the time of the month Abib.
5. All that openeth the matrix is mine; and every firstling among thy cattle, whether ox or sheep, that is male.
6. But the firstling of an ass thou shalt redeem with a lamb: and if thou redeem him not, then shalt thou break his neck.
7. Six days thou shalt work, but on the seventh day thou shalt rest.
8. And thou shalt observe the feast of weeks, of the firstfruits of wheat harvest.
9. Thou shalt not offer the blood of my sacrifice with leaven; nei-

ther shall the sacrifice of the feast of the passover be left unto the morning.

10. Thou shalt not seethe a kid in his mother's milk.

How can those two lists be so utterly different? The second set was supposed to be a duplicate, remember? So who decided which were to be *the* Ten Commandments? And how did they decide? Did someone take a vote? Toss a coin? Arm wrestle for their favorites?

Furthermore, why are the multitudinous *other* commandments never talked about? Here's a random sampling: Sons that are gluttons and drunkards shall be stoned to death. (Deut. 21:21) Nonvirginal brides *shall* be stoned to death. (Deut. 22:21) Homosexuals *shall surely* be put to death (Lev. 20:13). Beat your children with rods (Prov. 23:14). Women must keep their mouths shut and learn only from their husbands (1 Cor. 14:34,35).

The exclusion of these clear commandments, among scores of others, highlights the arbitrary nature of the so-called Ten Commandments. But even if you look at only that list of "ten," consider what is *not* mentioned. Nowhere are there any words forbidding: sexual or physical abuse of a child, rape, slavery, torture, kidnapping, or spousal abuse. But almost as bad is that there is no mention of *love* and *compassion* for others. What kind of grand moral code would not mention those things? A very bad one, that's what kind. Almost *anyone* could come up with a better list of moral values than that touted as the Ten Commandments.

Such selective editing and culling of the biblical commandments (actually it's slash-and-burn editing and culling since it eliminates 99 percent of the Bible's commandments) is the result of the embarrassingly *primitive* nature of so many of the excluded commandments. Sacrificing animals to gods, for example, reflects a Neanderthal mentality.

However, if fundamentalists are going to insist on their right to force *their* primitive commandments into public places, then any of the rest of us should be able to post *our* primitive suggestions for moral behavior, such as the Code of Hammurabi; or the biblical parts about seething kids in their mothers' milk; or the *Aranyakas* from the Hindu Veda. Those courtroom and classroom walls are going to be plastered, aren't they?

Our separation of church and state has stood the test of time and must be left alone. But if someone is going to challenge it, at the very least they ought to be able to come up with something better than the so-called Ten Commandments.

NOTES

1. Richard Dawkins, *The Blind Watchmaker* (New York: W. W. Norton, 1996).

2. "Stomachs Grumble at Zoo Passover Diet," *Lodi News-Sentinel*, April 10, 1998, p. 19.

3. "Holy Cow," *Lodi News-Sentinel*, May 29, 1997, p. 22.

4. "Soul-Searching in Israel on Yom Kippur," *Lodi News-Sentinel*, October 3, 1998, p. 20.

5. Carl Sagan, *Broca's Brain* (New York: Ballantine, 1980), p. 365.

6. Joanne Kenen, "House Gun Debate Focuses On Religion, Hollywood," Reuters [online], www.excite.com/news [June 17, 1999].

CONCLUSION

W HILE I WAS WRITING THE segment about Christian hymns, my powerful sense of déjà vu was accompanied by a profound sadness. Once again I was struck by the almost universally *depressing* nature of most religions. It is exceedingly difficult to reconcile the inherent doom-and-gloom messages of these religions with the purported rapturous bliss that is supposedly being celebrated. They are oil and water. Or oil and blood, I guess. If you take the messages seriously, as I did and many others still do, life is nothing but a place to wait for death. And it's an ugly, destitute, contemptible place at that. We're all wretches and the world sucks.

Even the yoga of Hinduism affirms the doctrine that through the practice of certain disciplines one may achieve liberation from the limitations of flesh, the delusions of sense, and the pitfalls of thought and thus attain union with the object of knowledge. Such union, according to the doctrine, is the only true way of knowing. And most Buddhists are on a lifelong quest to achieve a state of "enlightenment" which, though possessing many noble ideas, is still a means of defeating and/or escaping our humanity.

There may of course be another side to the death = paradise maxim. It may possibly ease the suffering of someone who is looking death square in the face. That appears to have been the case with a dear friend of mine, Dorothy. Though she had moved away several years earlier, we remained close and corresponded frequently. Then there was a long silence, and finally a brief letter from her saying that cancer had "invaded" her body and she was "joyously looking forward" to meeting her Lord. Meaning no disrespect to Dorothy's memory, I found that difficult to believe.

As I mentioned earlier, if Christians really, sincerely believed that death meant a glorious joining with Jesus in heaven, there should be no tears at any Christian funeral. There should be nothing but gala celebrations. We all know this is not the case, so something is wrong with the death = paradise scenario.

But more than that, Dorothy's life represented so much that is bad about Christianity. Personally she was a lovely, kind person. But at an early age she had wrapped herself in the cocoon of her religion and closed off all avenues of learning and discovery. She was remarkably ignorant about so many aspects of human life that I often stared, mouth agape, at some of the things she said. She was not a stupid woman—far from it. But she was so naive and unfamiliar with worldly events, that I sometimes wondered how she managed to produce children. Her husband, though, was more worldly, so maybe that explains it.

I loved and miss Dorothy. But to see such human potential smothered and unexplored is sad. It is also the antithesis of the goals of secular humanism. The very name, "humanism," implies the importance of human beings and all that we can aspire to. We have brains as well as bodies, and to leave our minds shrouded in a superstitious veil of ignorance is simply wrong—wasteful and wrong.

Dorothy reminded me of a couple of Mormon missionaries who rang my doorbell back during the Gulf War of 1991. I was very surprised to see that they were female (I guess the Mormons had taken too much heat about their historically misogynistic position on women) but they were very nice young ladies. They were extremely polite, seemed quite bright, and we chatted for a few minutes on the porch. As they were getting into their spiel, I quietly interrupted to ask what their church's position was on the ongoing Gulf War. They looked at each other as if I had just asked a technical question about DNA sequencing. Then one of them said quietly, as the other one nodded in agreement, "We don't read newspapers. We don't want to confuse ourselves." I will never forget those words. There it was. Bottled and marketed indoctrination. Don't use your minds; just do what we say. Simplified: shut up and listen.

Many religions possess this don't-think-just-do attitude, and it's a shame. Human potential should never be squandered. The world can be an astounding teacher, if given the chance. There is so much beauty and excitement in this world, waiting only to be explored. And there is so much latent human love, compassion, and talent, if only we will encourage it!

This is where humanism shines. Unfettered by superstition or religious hatred, we seek only to improve the human condition—for *everyone*. We feel no need to pretend that the world is something it is not. It's lovely enough as it is. We accept our humanity and try to make life the best that it can be. Obviously there are many unpleasant aspects to life, but ironically, many of those unpleasant aspects are the direct result of the religions that seek to escape them! If all the energy and money that have ever been put into religions (and religious wars!) had instead been directed toward the betterment of all humanity, what a world this might be today! We have the skills, and most of us have the compassion, to eliminate most of humanity's suffering. We can never eliminate it all, of course, but we most assuredly could be doing so very much better than we are now.

The smugness with which some religionists view their brand of morality can often be heard on the airwaves, whether TV or radio. One representative example is a popular advice giver, a psychologist. She exudes such religious pomposity and self-congratulations that her opinions are presented as if from On High. Perhaps she thinks they are. Her repeated theme is that we "pagans," a word apparently coming back into vogue, have no moral underpinning, in the form of religious values, and therefore cannot have morals. We do what *feels* right, not what *is* right. And how does one learn what *is* right? From one's religion—by Divine Commandment. Pagans, so says the psychologist, have no solid foundation, no consistent set of rules, no *absolutes*; therefore, our actions are totally arbitrary, meaning totally amoral.

Such simplistic assertions ignore the fact that different religions have completely different "Divine Commandments." In considering just three Biggies—Judaism, Christianity, and Islam—you will find *no* consistency. Their teachings are so different that if you follow one, you are absolutely violating the tenets of the other two. Therefore, in choosing one over the others, you are being *precisely as arbitrary as any pagan*. And this doesn't even include the world's other major religions, each with its own set of *contradictory* "Divine Commandments."

True Believers come equipped with blinders, blocking out all logical thought about this inescapable but insolvable problem. Somehow they don't *see* any other religion but their own. Their obtuseness, however, does not eliminate the problem. Bearing in mind the wildly differing world religions, where is this "solid foundation" Ms. Psychologist acclaims and glorifies? Where is this "consistent set of rules?" What *absolutes*? If religionists are blessed with moral absolutes, then where does the eating of pork chops fit in? Is it an absolute no or an absolute yes? Come on, now, let's not be *arbitrary*!

Obviously the list of questions is practically endless. Are cows sacred? Is Jesus the Savior of humankind? Did God speak to the Prophet Muhammad? Is there reincarnation? With just these four straightforward questions, let's try to find that much-vaunted consistency we've heard so much about—that which is so sorely lacking in pagans. Well, you're welcome to try, but it can't be done because it doesn't exist. There *is* no consistency among religions. Religions are as *arbitrary* as the absence of religion. Might as well throw darts at a board in determining what is "right" and what is "wrong."

So, when theists ask atheists *the* inevitable question: "How can you lead a moral life with no religious values to base your morals on?" they do so at their own peril. They haven't a leg to stand on. So it is truly ironic that when they ask *the* question, they do so with a piercing gleam in their eyes. As if they had just presented you with an irrefutable, powerful conundrum, painting you into an impossible corner, you can sense their rapid heartbeat as they prepare to close in for the kill. But the question itself is wholly invalid.

Unfortunately, too many atheists (or pagans) squirm when they hear this supposedly razor-sharp challenge. The question itself, in addition to suffering from the lethal pitfall—*which* religion/God are you basing your morals on—has an even simpler but profound defect. Most human beings have learned approximately 90 percent of their moral values by the age of seven, even though at seven most of us still believe in Santa Claus. Religion or lack of it has no effect whatever on how children learn to behave. They of course mimic their parents in religious ceremonies, but they haven't a clue what any of it means.

We are all taught at a very early age not to do certain things and not to say certain things. Everyone goes through it. "Stop that! Can't you see you're hurting her? Tell her you're sorry. Now!" "Put that back! That doesn't belong to you. That's stealing!" And so on. We learn the code from our elders, and form the basis for future moral decisions depending, in large part, on how strict our parents are, and how determined they are to see us "behave."

The Jesuit priest who said, "Give me a child until he's seven and he's mine for life," may have had it right. But at seven, children have no intelligible concept of God—let alone an understanding of covenants, theories of blood atonement, or any other theological concepts. They still believe in flying reindeer. *However*, depending on the teachings of their parents, they can easily have a solid moral foundation by that age. And anyone, theist or atheist, can teach their children kindness. And those lessons do not have to be accompanied by threats of hellfire or bogeymen.

So, if you're an atheist and someone asks you *the* question, just answer, "My parents taught me kindness and I'm teaching my children the same." If they ask what your kindness is based on, you can easily reverse the question, and ask your questioner which God he's basing *his* morals on. This usually stumps anyone asking *the* question. Blinders, you know. A simpler response might be to say that through parental guidance, and the experience of living itself, you have discovered that life is so much more pleasant and rewarding, for all concerned, when people are kind to each other.

It is simplicity itself. And it beats the hell out of frightening little children with unimaginable pain and misery in some eternal fiery inferno if they misbehave. There is also no denying that children are influenced most by *example*. If parents behave with kindness and compassion toward others, children will observe and usually follow suit—theologies notwithstanding. Sad proof of this lies in the fact that children raised in violent homes tend to copy *that* sort of behavior as well—theologies notwithstanding. And neither we nor our children need supernatural coercion or extortion to behave decently toward each other and reap the rewards of a life well led. Loving is far more pleasurable than hating.

As a Christian, I used to be told what to think. Now I think for myself.

I used to be afraid of God, hell, and Satan. Now I love people, daffodils, sunsets, puppies, the sound of the ocean, piano concertos, humor . . .

I used to be afraid of dying. Now I enjoy living.

From *The Affirmations of Humanism: A Statement of Principles*, published by the Council for Secular Humanism: "We believe in optimism rather than pessimism, hope rather than despair, learning in the place of dogma, truth instead of ignorance, joy rather than guilt or sin, tolerance in the place of fear, love instead of hatred, compassion over selfishness, beauty instead of ugliness, and reason rather than blind faith or irrationality."

Amen.

BIBLIOGRAPHY

Asimov, Isaac. *Asimov's Guide to the Bible*. New York: Avenel Books, 1981.

Basil, Robert, Mary Beth Gehrman, and Tim Madigan, ed. *On the Barricades: Religion and Free Inquiry in Conflict*. Amherst, N.Y.: Prometheus Books, 1989.

Berra, Tim M. *Evolution and the Myth of Creationism*. Stanford: Stanford University Press, 1990.

Bugliosi, Vincent. *No Island of Sanity: Paula Jones v. Bill Clinton*. New York: Random House, 1998.

Burr, William Henry. *Self-Contradictions of the Bible*. 1860. Reprint, Amherst, N.Y.: Prometheus Books, 1987.

Cloulas, Ivan. *The Borgias*. New York: Barnes & Noble, 1993.

Dawkins, Richard. *The Blind Watchmaker*. New York: W. W. Norton, 1996.

de Rosa, Peter. *Vicars of Christ*. London: Corgi Books, 1988.

Dershowitz, Alan M. *Sexual McCarthyism*. New York: Basic Books, 1998.

Dossey, Larry. *Healing Words*. New York: HarperCollins, 1993.

Eisenman, Robert, and Michael Wise. *The Dead Sea Scrolls Uncovered*. New York: Barnes & Noble, 1994.

257

Gimbutas, Marija. *The Language of the Goddess*. New York: HarperCollins, 1989.

Hammer, Richard. *The Vatican Connection*. New York: Holt, Rinehart and Winston, 1982.

Hayes, Judith. *In God We Trust: But Which One?* Madison: Freedom From Religion Foundation, 1996.

Hitchens, Christopher. *The Missionary Position: Mother Teresa in Theory and Practice*. London: Verso, 1995.

Humphrey, Derek. *Final Exit: The Practicalities of Self-deliverance/Assisted Suicide for the Dying*. New York: Dell, 1991.

———. *Dying with Dignity*. New York: Birch Lane Press, 1992.

Incognito, Magus. *The Secret Doctrine of the Rosicrucians*. New York: Barnes & Noble, 1993.

International Inductive Study New Testament. Precept Ministries. Chattanooga: Harvest House Publishers, 1993.

Kennedy, Sheila Rauch. *Shattered Faith*. New York: Henry Holt, 1997.

Laake, Deborah. *Secret Ceremonies*. New York: William Morrow, 1993.

Light of El Rante, The. Tokyo: Light of El Rante Publishing, 1991.

Manhattan, Avro. *The Dollar and the Vatican*. Springfield: Ozark Books, 1988.

McCollum, Vashti Cromwell. *One Woman's Fight*. Madison: Freedom From Religion Foundation, 1993.

Nickell, Joe. *Looking for a Miracle*. Amherst, N.Y.: Prometheus Books, 1993.

Paine, Thomas. *The Age of Resason*. 1794. Reprint, Cutchogue, N.Y.: Buccaneer Books, 1976.

Ranke-Heinemann, Uta. *Eunuchs for the Kingdom of Heaven*. New York: Penguin Books, 1991.

Rappoport, Angelo S. *The Love Affairs of the Vatican*. 1912. Reprint, New York: Barnes & Noble, 1995.

Rice, David. *Shattered Vows: Priests Who Leave*. New York: William Morrow, 1990.

Sagan, Carl. *The Demon-Haunted World*. New York: Random House, 1995.

———. *Billions & Billions.* New York: Random House, 1997.

Smith, Huston. *The Religions of Man.* New York: Harper & Row, 1958.

Smith, Morton, and R. Joseph Hoffman, ed. *What the Bible Really Says.* Amherst, N.Y.: Prometheus Books, 1989.

Stanton, Elizabeth Cady. *The Woman's Bible.* Seattle: Coalition Task Force on Women and Religion, 1974.

Steiner, Franklin. *The Religious Beliefs of Our Presidents.* Amherst, N.Y.: Prometheus Books, 1995.

Stone, Merlin. *When God Was a Woman.* New York: Dorset Press, 1976.

Tanaka, Kenneth K. *Ocean: An Introduction to Jodo-Shinshu Buddhism in America.* Berkeley: WisdomOcean Publications, 1997.

Taylor, Gordon Rattray. *The Great Evolution Mystery.* New York: Harper & Row, 1983.

Thompson, Edward K., ed. *World's Great Religions.* New York: Simon & Schuster, 1957.

Walters, Kerry S. *The American Deists.* Lawrence: University Press of Kansas, 1992.

Wells, G. A. *Did Jesus Exist?* London: Pemberton, 1986.

———. *The Historical Evidence for Jesus.* Amherst, N.Y.: Prometheus Books, 1988.

King James Version Bible

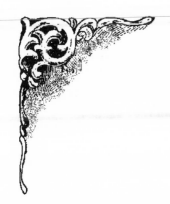

INDEX

Abel. *See* Bible condensed
abortion, 64, 74, 100
  selective reduction, 71–74
Adam
  penis control, 83
Adam and Eve, 82, 158, 214
Adams, John, 170
agnosticism, 205, 209
  definition of, 244–46
AIDS, 17, 78, 114. *See also*
  Roman Catholic Church
Albert the Great
  on women and sex, 81
Allah, 30, 201
  sacred signs of, 228–29
Allen, Ethan, 171
angels
  announcing Jesus' birth, 36
  God not using them at

nativity, 223
  guardian, 23
  Muslim angels on shoulders,
  229
  shepherds' reaction to at
  nativity, 221
Aquinas, St. Thomas
  on women and sex, 81
atheism
  Carl Sagan on, 244
  definition of, 244–46
  my own, 178
  why I became one, 36
Augustine, St.
  on women and sex, 80

Bakker, Jim and Tammy, 42, 69
Barbara*, 31
Barr, Bob, 184

---

*Fictitious names

261